# Figures of Simplicity

SUNY series, Intersections: Philosophy and Critical Theory

Rodolphe Gasché

# Figures of Simplicity

Sensation and Thinking
in Kleist and Melville

Birgit Mara Kaiser

Published by State University of New York Press, Albany

© 2011 State University of New York

Cover illustration, photograph of "The Match" (2003, fabric and Styrofoam) by Frances Bagley. Reproduced with permission of the artist.

All rights reserved

Printed in the United States of America

No part of this book may be used or reproduced in any manner whatsoever without written permission. No part of this book may be stored in a retrieval system or transmitted in any form or by any means including electronic, electrostatic, magnetic tape, mechanical, photocopying, recording, or otherwise without the prior permission in writing of the publisher.

For information, contact State University of New York Press, Albany, NY
www.sunypress.edu

Production by Kelli W. LeRoux
Marketing by Michael Campochiaro

**Library of Congress Cataloging-in-Publication Data**

Kaiser, Birgit Mara.
    Figures of simplicity : sensation and thinking in Kleist and Melville / Birgit Mara Kaiser.
       p.    cm. — (Suny series, intersections: philosophy and critical theory)
Includes bibliographical references and index.
    ISBN 978-1-4384-3229-8 (hardcover : alk. paper) 978-1-4384-3230-4 (pbk : alk. paper)
    1. Melville, Herman, 1819–1891—Criticism and interpretation.   2. Kleist, Heinrich von, 1777–1811—Criticism and interpretation.   3. Thought and thinking in literature.
4. Senses and sensation in literature.   5. Literature, Comparative—American and German.
6. Literature, Comparative—German and American.   I. Title.
PS2388.T53K35   2010
813'.3–dc22

2009054369

10 9 8 7 6 5 4 3 2 1

*Il y a deux manières de dépasser la figuration (c'est-à-dire à la fois l'illustratif et le narratif): ou bien vers la forme abstraite, ou bien vers la Figure. Cette voie de la Figure, Cézanne lui donne un nom simple: la sensation. La Figure, c'est la forme sensible rapportée à la sensation.*

*La sensation, c'est le contraire du facile et du tout fait, du cliché, mais aussi du « sensationnel », du spontané, etc. La sensation a une face tournée vers le sujet [...] et une face tournée vers l'objet [...]. Ou plutôt elle n'a pas de faces du tout, elle est les deux choses indissolublement [...].*

Gilles Deleuze, *Francis Bacon.*<br>
*Logique de la Sensation*

# Contents

| | |
|---|---|
| Acknowledgments | ix |
| Abbreviations | xi |
| Introduction: On Subterranean Connections | xiii |
| 1. Aesthetics: Sensation and Thinking Reconsidered | 1 |
|     The Copernican Turn | 7 |
|     The Folds of Small Perceptions | 11 |
|     Sensate Thinking | 19 |
|     Figures of Simplicity | 22 |
| 2. Sentimentalities | 27 |
|     Befuddling the Senses *(The Betrothal in St. Domingo)* | 31 |
|     Spectacularly Simple: Well-Willingly Seeing Nothing *(Benito Cereno)* | 41 |
|     Sentimentalizing Resentment | 53 |
| 3. Affectivity | 56 |
|     Resolute Simplicity *(Billy Budd, Sailor. An inside narrative)* | 62 |
|     Calculating Mindlessness *(Michael Kohlhaas)* | 76 |
|     Baroque Heroes | 85 |
| 4. Insistence | 88 |
|     On Passive Resistance *(Bartleby, the Scrivener. A story of Wall-Street)* | 90 |

Lingering before Consciousness
*(Das Käthchen von Heilbronn oder Die Feuerprobe)*   96
Supersensible Figures of the Fold   109

5. Conclusion   113
   Notes   120
   Bibliography   139
   Index   146

# Acknowledgments

As it is the case with any work, this book could not have been written without the support, help, and positive energy of many people. First and foremost, I would like to thank Anselm Haverkamp, who accompanied this project from the start. Without his confidence in its first outlines, and his encouragement throughout, which always came at the right moments, this book would not have been possible. He taught me a perspective on literature that continues to be an inspiration far beyond the narrow scopes of this project, and for which I am deeply grateful. I am also indebted to the members of my dissertation committee Cyrus R. K. Patell, Mikhail Iampolski, Nancy Ruttenberg, and Paul Fleming for their criticisms on a first draft of this book, as well as for the inspiring courses I took with them at NYU and the stimulating discussions, both personal and intellectual, that resulted from them. I would especially like to thank Nancy Ruttenberg for her enthusiasm for my project and for her professional support when it was most needed. I am also grateful to Avital Ronell for the inspiration of her teaching, which was one of the most energizing parts of my graduate studies at NYU.

I would like to thank the DFG Graduate Program "Representation—Rhetoric—Knowledge" at the European University Viadrina in Frankfurt (Oder), Germany for granting me the opportunity to finish my dissertation on a DFG-scholarship. The lively intellectual context of this remarkable circle of scholars was perfectly suited to my writing, and provided the right mixture of critique, correction, and inspiration.

It is an incredible honor to be part of a publication series that has established such long-standing and high standards in theoretical debates as "Intersections: Philosophy and Critical Theory," and I am thus very grateful to its editor, Rodolphe Gasché, for his interest in my project and the opportunity to be included in his series. In this context, I would also like to thank James Peltz, Kelli Williams–LeRoux and Andrew Kenyon at SUNY Press for their professional support, openness, and patience throughout the process of publication.

This book could not have come to fruition without the help of many friends who were, and continue to be, an intellectual and personal inspiration. They offered balanced, insightful, thought-provoking input for this book, and among them, I would especially like to thank Thomas Khurana, Dirk Setton, and Katrin Trüstedt for their careful readings of early versions of the chapters, Leonard Lawlor for his critique and encouragement, Monika Lanz for her incredible effort to "polish" what is not my mother-tongue, and Barbara Thiele and Cornelia Thiele for their meticulous and joyful way of going again and again through the written manuscript in search for yet another tidbit to correct. I would also like to thank Emy Koopman for her help with the index.

And last but not least, I would like to thank my parents and my brother for their loving support, and for their confidence in what I was doing, without which it would have been much harder to finish this project in good spirit. My most heartfelt gratitude, however, goes to Kathrin Thiele, for her love, the sharpness of her mind and her challenges to my thinking. Without her, work and life would not by far be as rich. I am grateful that she shares both with me.

# Abbreviations

Ä    Alexander Gottlieb Baumgarten, *Ästhetik*, vol. 1, ed. and trans. Dagmar Mirbach. Hamburg: Felix Meiner, 2007

ADE    Heinrich von Kleist, *An Abyss Deep Enough: The Life of Heinrich von Kleist in his Parables, Essays and Letters*, ed. and trans. Philip B. Miller. Boston: Dutton Books, 1982

BB    Herman Melville, "Bartleby, the Scrivener," in Herman Melville, *The Piazza Tales and Other Prose Pieces 1839-1860*, ed. Harrison Hayford, Alma A. MacDougall, G. Thomas Tanselle et al. Evanston/Chicago: Northwestern University Press, 1987

BBS    Herman Melville, *Billy Budd, Sailor (An inside narrative)*, ed. Harrison Hayford and Merton M. Sealts Jr. Chicago: University of Chicago Press, 1962

BC    Herman Melville, "Benito Cereno," in Herman Melville, *The Piazza Tales and Other Prose Pieces 1839-1860*, ed. Harrison Hayford, Alma MacDougall, G. Thomas Tanselle et al. Evanston/Chicago: Northwestern University Press, 1987

BF    Gilles Deleuze, "Bartleby; or, The Formula," in *Essays Critical and Clinical*. Minneapolis: University of Minnesota Press, 1997

BSD    Heinrich von Kleist, "The Betrothal in Santo Domingo," in *The Marquise of O—and Other Stories*, trans. David Luke and Nigel Reeves. London: Penguin, 2004

CPR    Immanuel Kant, *Critique of Pure Reason*. Amherst: Prometheus Books, 1990

F    Gilles Deleuze, *The Fold: Leibniz and the Baroque*. Minneapolis: University of Minnesota Press, 1988.

J    Herman Melville, *The Writings of Herman Melville. Journals*, ed. Howard C. Horsford with Lynn Horth. Evanston/Chicago: Northwestern University Press, 1989

| | |
|---|---|
| MK | Heinrich von Kleist, "Michael Kohlhaas," in *The Marquise of O— and Other Stories*, trans. David Luke and Nigel Reeves. London: Penguin, 2004 |
| OF | Heinrich von Kleist, "Ordeal by Fire," in *Three Plays. Prince Friedrich von Homberg, The Broken Pitcher, Ordeal by Fire*, trans. Noel Clark. London: Oberon Books, 2000 |
| P | Herman Melville, *Pierre; or, The Ambiguities*, ed. Harrison Hayford, Hershel Parker, and G. Thomas Tanselle. Evanston/Chicago: Northwestern University Press, 1971 |
| PB | Alexander Gottlieb Baumgarten, *Philosophische Briefe von Aletheophilus*. Frankfurt/Leipzig: Universität zu Halle, 1741 |
| SW I/6 | Heinrich von Kleist, *Sämtliche Werke*, Vol. I/6 ("Das Käthchen von Heilbronn oder die Feuerprobe. Ein großes historisches Ritterschauspiel"), ed. Roland Reuß in cooperation with Peter Staengle. Basel/Frankfurt/M: Stroemfeld/Roter Stern, 2004 |
| SW IV/1 | Heinrich von Kleist, *Sämtliche Werke*, Vol. IV/1, Briefe I (März 1793-April 1801), ed. Peter Staengle in cooperation with Roland Reuß. Basel/Frankfurt/M: Stroemfeld/Roter Stern, 1996. |
| SW II/1 | Heinrich von Kleist, *Sämtliche Werke*, Vol. II/1 ("Michael Kohlhaas" [1810]), ed. Roland Reuß in cooperation with Peter Staengle. Basel/Frankfurt/M: Stroemfeld/Roter Stern 1990 |
| SW II/4 | Heinrich von Kleist, *Sämtliche Werke*, Vol. II/4 ("Die Verlobung von St. Domingo"), ed. Roland Reuß in cooperation with Peter Staengle. Basel/Frankfurt/M: Stoemfeld/Roter Stern, 1988 |
| SW II/7 | Heinrich von Kleist, *Sämtliche Werke*, Band II/7 (Berliner Abendblätter 1), ed. Roland Reuß and Peter Staengle. Basel/Frankfurt/M: Stroemfeld/Roter Stern, 1997 |
| SWB | Heinrich von Kleist, *Sämtliche Werke und Briefe*, ed. Helmut Sembner. Munich: Deutscher Taschenbuch Verlag, 2001 |

## Introduction

# On Subterranean Connections

We start here from a hunch, at a venture, so to speak. We start from the impression of a curious connection between Heinrich von Kleist's and Herman Melville's texts. It is definitely a curious connection, because at first both writers seem to have very little in common, and it has been scholarly impossible to establish their awareness of each other. We cannot assume that Kleist was influential for Melville—Melville never stated anything like it, nor do we find implicit or explicit references to Kleist's writings in his texts. The American writer moved in a different intellectual and creative universe, years after the German writer had died. Nevertheless, there is a quality to their work, that renders them incredibly close, it seems. Their texts are populated by strange figures, which all in one way or another defy our common registers of calculation, deliberation, or reasoning. Upon a second look, thus, as this book would like to show, their bizarre figures interlock their works. But what is it exactly that these figures share and that allows us to speak of a connection between Kleist and Melville?

The readings that follow try to respond to this question, and in the course of the book I hope to show that what links Kleist and Melville is less an influence of one writer upon another than a subterranean connection: a connection in the sense that they share the same problem when it comes to the relation of literature and thinking. The strange figures that populate their writings seem to correspond to each other in that they circle around questions of thinking in a similar fashion and make similar propositions in regard to the forms thinking can take. In view of these strange figures, I will suggest that what these two writers ask us to consider, to reconsider perhaps, is the relation of affectivity and thinking. Commonly, these two terms are not seen as related. Affectivity is considered as linked to the body, as being the bodily reaction to external stimulation, and a perhaps more corporeal form of feeling, while thinking is understood as the internal operations of the mind, as occurring in reflective, cerebral, cognitive processes that fabricate ideas and generate understanding. The two are usually kept strictly apart in two different realms, where one does not disturb the other. What the writings of Kleist and Melville ask in this respect is whether such a strict separation between the two is really valid or if there are perhaps ways of thinking that are by intimation connected to affectivity; or, asked the other way around, if affectivity has perhaps the potential to also contribute in its own manner to the cognitive processes from which we would usually exclude it. Kleist and Melville try to think this connection and they do so in such a thought-provoking way that we might find it productive for broader considerations of what we call thinking as such. And—to add this straight away—we might also find their propositions productive for broader considerations of the role that we concede to literature when it comes to the question of thinking.

But before we can discuss their exposition of the relation of thinking and affectivity, we perhaps first need to motivate the relation between Kleist and Melville themselves, which is not immediately apparent either. In fact, we cannot explain their relation by the influence one writer might have had on the other. We even have to rule out any secret influences that could be brought to light in hindsight, for example by revealing unknown facts such as formerly unknown letters that were exchanged between them, and from which a relationship could be reconstructed. No such letters between Heinrich von Kleist and Herman Melville exist, nor does any secret acquaintance. Kleist died close to Berlin in 1811, and Melville was not born until 1819 in New York City, which means that they never could have met. And since Melville did not read German, he could not have read Kleist's texts either, since they were not translated into English until much later—some, such as *The Battle of Herrmann*, even only as recently as 2008. Melville might have read *about* Kleist, perhaps when he read Goethe in translation, or later, when he intensely read Schopenhauer, but that would hardly have been more than the encounter of a name. And the work that most encompassingly familiarized Melville with German literature, philosophy, and culture—Madame de Staël's *On Germany*—does not mention Kleist, which is surprising, since Madame de Staël valued Kleist's work highly and even knew him personally. We must thus conclude—and the lack of comparative studies on the two implicitly proves this—that Melville missed Kleist, and it needs no mention that the reverse is also the case. Hence, we are impelled to proceed differently when testing their connection. One alternative would certainly be to pursue their common sources. But with the exception of Shakespeare, whose importance has been demonstrated for both,[1] these sources are either so extensive or so difficult to ascertain that such an approach does not seem very productive either. Kleist drew—besides being familiar with much of late-eighteenth-century French and German literature and most contemporary philosophy—most significantly on Montaigne, was interested in Rousseau, in conflict with Goethe, and suffered from Kant, to name some of his main intellectual interlocutors. Melville was also well read in much of English romanticism and in English and American literature of the late eighteenth and the early nineteenth century. He had a particular

Introduction

interest in Coleridge and Carlyle, and great appreciation for his contemporary and friend Nathaniel Hawthorne. Despite this vast spectrum, however, there is not a single source that might explain Kleist's and Melville's shared concern with how to conceive of the thinking subject in the most appropriate way.[2] Both of them are too eclectic in their adaptations of material, and too idiosyncratic in their processing of what they adopt so that, in view of this, an intuited connection cannot be made plausible by a search for shared sources. A second—and more viable—alternative would be to search out the problem they are posing and to see to what extent it is a shared or linked problem. This is why I propose to consider Kleist and Melville in regard to their shared problem of the relation of affectivity and thinking.

Despite the general lack of comparative studies on these two authors, they have very recently and selectively begun to come up as a remarkable match. To give two examples—and to my knowledge the only literary studies that address them as an informative couple—there is, on the one hand, Martin Greenberg's comparison of Melville's *Billy Budd, Sailor* and Kleist's *Michael Kohlhaas*, which considers the exposition of justice and law in these texts. With this focus, Greenberg's reading stands in the tradition of the prominence that both writers individually have in the debates on law and its relation to literature. And on the other hand, there is Niels Werber's recent study on the geopolitics of literature, which considers Kleist and Melville as two prominent figures in the geopolitical reimagination of territory and space in the past two centuries.[3] Werber's study looks at their contribution to the medial imagination of social collectives, both in their potential to produce and to contest such a production of spatial and social entities. Werber makes explicit reference to Gilles Deleuze's and Félix Guattari's concepts of nomadic spaces and of deterritorialization, and elaborates a line of reading of Kleist and Melville that we find in Deleuze and Guattari's *A Thousand Plateaus*. Werber thereby points us to Deleuze's and Guattari's work as a third instance where our two writers are brought in conjunction. In fact, in many of Deleuze's and Guattari's texts, Kleist and Melville—certainly among other writers, but often in a more prominent position than these—appear as an informative couple. And much like Deleuze and Guattari in *A Thousand Plateaus*, Werber's readings put particular stress on Kleist's *The Battle of Herrmann* with its topos of the partisan battle and its reflection of incipient German nationalism during the Napoleonic Wars, and Melville's *Moby-Dick* with its exposition of oceanic space as both a contestation of state territories and a facilitator of imperial expansion in the nineteenth century. What he foregrounds are the geopolitical contributions of their writings to national and biopolitical reorganizations of the world. *A Thousand Plateaus* likewise engages prominently with Kleist's *The Battle of Herrmann* and Melville's *Moby-Dick* and suggests on that basis their interest in (geo)political struggles. From that perspective, Kleist is said to struggle with the state and to strive to counteract the sedimentation of state apparatuses, and Melville is seen to expose—in a different setting, and with a fascination for maritime spaces—the dynamics of rhizomatic space. From this perspective, Deleuze and Guattari call Kleist's literary writings a "literature of war," a term that is not to be misunderstood as patriotic literature—one of the predominant and reductive receptions of Kleist—but as a literature of partisan struggle with literary means. It struggles against and contests the sedimentation of power into state apparatuses and engages in finding ways to get away from, or get out of them, and to unsettle them. The chapter of *A Thousand Plateaus* that develops this idea for Kleist is fittingly entitled "Treatise on Nomadology—The War Machine" in order to make its alliance with nomadic space, and not with organized state space (as a reading of Kleist as patriotic literature would have it) obvious. And *A Thousand Plateaus* identifies a similar striving for the reopening of increasingly organized and ordered state structures in Melville—and other American writers—when it asserts D. H. Lawrence's affirmation that Melville attempted to write in a way to "get away. To get away, out!...To cross a horizon."[4]

The readings that follow in this book take inspiration from Deleuze and Guattari's proposition of an alliance between Kleist and Melville and affirm the connection they see between the two writers. I propose, however, to substantiate their connection slightly differently than Werber does in view of their contribution to geopolitical struggles. Without in the least contesting the value and merit of such an emphasis, my readings would like to foreground another perspective that emerges when putting Kleist and Melville in conjunction. While I do join Werber in finding in Kleist and Melville literary processes of knowledge production, I see these not so much in the medial, goepolitical, or spatial sense he takes from Deleuze and Guattari, but rather in regard to the cognitive processes of a subject. What is central to their texts, as I would like to argue, are the characters they deploy, and what these expose about the intricacies of thinking. These characters—figures of simplicity, as they are called in this book—are immersed in opaque situations and struggle to make sense of them, even if their efforts are not always met with the desired success. We follow the processes of understanding that these characters undergo, the difficulties they run into, and the pitfalls of their attempts to understand what is going on. We can think here of Melville's Captain Delano in *Benito Cereno*, for instance, who endeavors to figure out what he sees on board the *San Dominick*, and who, in endless perceptive efforts, tries to get a clear picture of what is going on. And although, as we will see, Melville has his "blunt-thinking eyes" fail in this endeavor, we are made to follow these efforts at understanding over the course of the text. Delano's particularly simple, chauvinistic ways cause him to misconstrue the plot, and the simplicity he displays is one—in this case unfortunate—way in which affectivity and thinking cross each other. Delano's misfiring efforts and Melville's experimentation with them are suggested here to be read as echoing Gustav von der Ried, who undergoes a similar experiment in Kleist's *The Betrothal in Santo Domingo*. We will look at their connection

Introduction

in chapter 2. In contrast to the unfortunate interferences between affectivity and thinking in these two characters, we can, however, also think of characters in Kleist and Melville who maneuver unintelligible situations with remarkable precision, and who seem to do so precisely by affectively assessing their surroundings. Melville's Billy Budd or Kleist's Michael Kohlhaas, for example, are thrown into situations, in which they find themselves antagonized by something or someone without being sure what exactly they are up against. They respond to this challenge not by trying to get a clear picture, but by operating with a blurred one, and do so by continuously adjusting to the moves of their opponents. They assess these moves and the evolving situation, remain susceptible to every twitch and turn of their opponents, and respond to these rather affectively. Their abstention from what we would usually call rational reflection and calculation might point to a more fortunate connection between affectivity and thinking, and we will consider this in chapter 3. And as another example, we can think of Melville's *Bartleby, the Scrivener* and Kleist's *Das Käthchen von Heilbronn*. In both texts, we are presented with characters who seem to be at first beyond any concern for either affectivity (both seem almost untouchable) or thinking (neither seems interested in cognition or understanding). Yet, if we look closely at how they operate in and with their surroundings—and the texts dwell on their operations, on their linguistic and corporeal maneuvers—we might find them to perform most perfectly of all what it looks like to think in a nonrational way. In chapter 4 we will consider what it might look like if affectivity is mobilized to assess and think, and what we are to make of these figures who defy all claims made on them in the name of reason, but who nevertheless prove to have quite accurate estimations of what is the case.

In their concern for processes of understanding, Kleist and Melville are of course not unique. Much of modern literature has made it its tasks to pursue and perform epistemological uncertainties, mainly, as we have learned from deconstructive and psychoanalytic literary analyses in the past decades, by exposing the intricacies and slippages of language. Yet very few writers show the same fascination as Kleist and Melville for the *affective* dimensions of these processes of understanding. The two are exemplary, I would like to suggest, in the way they present this dimension of thinking in their literary figures. They have their figures *operate with* such an affective dimension, rather than merely demonstrate the shortcoming and failures of rational thinking. In these operations, their strange characters act and "reason" in peculiarly "irrational" ways—if we think, to give another example, of Kleist's Marquise of O, who acts on her strange sensations, without knowing what has happened to her. What makes it difficult to speak about these ways of "reasoning" is to find the right terms for it. "Irrational" is not adequate since the characters are, as we will see, too strategic or too composed to be called irrational. And, particularly in view of the precision and effectiveness with which the characters "reason," it would be also inadequate to call them stupid in our common understanding of it as dumb, ignorant, or clueless. They seem to have a good idea of what is going on and what is to be done. But their ways of attaining this idea, of maintaining and claiming it, escape our normal registers of calculation and of conscious, rational reflection, and we certainly hesitate to call them rational. They are, rather, as this study suggests for lack of a better term, "simple": neither stupid in the sense of ignorant, nor irrational in the sense of foreign to reasoning or erupting with uncontrollable emotion, but reasoning with recourse to affective assessments, reasoning in a nonreflective, simple way. The minimal difference between such a simplicity and our common notions of stupidity and irrationality becomes evident precisely when we link Kleist's and Melville's characters. Billy Budd's simple ways unexpectedly correspond to the ragings of Michael Kohlhaas and help to see the distinct features of such a simplicity. The same is true for Melville's Bartleby, whose formula sheds light on Kleist's Käthchen, and allows us to see how both neither proceed by calculation or rationality, nor can be said to be ignorant. The conjunction and comparison of these at first sight disparate characters permits us to see *how* all of these figures are "simple"— seemingly dim-witted, yet capable of surprisingly apt responses to the situations they are confronted with. Their simplicity thus demonstrates, as this study suggests, a way of relating affectivity and thinking. Rather than separating them into two strictly opposed realms, they embody a claim that the two can inform each other, cross each other, and, if connected, permit a different consideration of what it means to think. In this regard, these *figures of simplicity* vouch for a folded relation between the two dimensions of affectivity and thinking that are commonly opposed, for their connection, yet without conflating the two into one. And their simplicity is thus also a marker of this fold—the "pli" of their sim*pli*city. Therein lies the subterranean connection between Kleist and Melville.

What these two writers, therefore, ask us to think are two things: Are there other forms of thinking than rational thinking, particularly in view of complex situations, in which the stability and clarity of a reflective distance is illusory or detrimental? And what are the stakes of literature in exposing or elaborating such nonrational thinking? To assert that this is what the two writers ask us to think means—first of all, independent of what it is they exactly ask us to consider—to affirm the fact that literature, and art more generally, thinks, exposes problems, and addresses questions. In this affirmation, I follow Deleuze and Guattari's claim that art thinks and that it does so in its own manner. In their book *Kafka. Toward a Minor Literature* they, for example, engage Kafka's writings from this perspective and find that Kafka pursues a problem that is specific to his writings, namely to perform and think through the conditions of a minor use of German in the Jewish German-speaking community of prewar Prague. Kafka's question, which Deleuze and Guattari derive from this, is, as they put it: "What is a minor literature?" The concept of minor literature has since become one of the predominant concepts in a reception of Deleuze in

## Introduction

literary and cultural studies. We must note, however, that the concept of the minor is quite specific to Kafka and cannot necessarily be transposed onto all literature. It is not the same for Kleist, for example, as Deleuze and Guattari stress in the same book: "Kleist is a different matter even in the deep influence that he had on Kafka." The questions, or the problems around which Kleist's and Kafka's works circle, are different: "Kleist's question isn't, 'What is a minor literature and, further, a political and collective literature?' but rather 'What is a literature of war?' This is not completely alien to Kafka, but it is not exactly his question."[5] The crucial point here, which is affirmed and wholeheartedly taken on board in the present study, is most importantly the principle of approaching literature by way of the problems it addresses, the thinking it produces, and the food for thought it provides. That is, inspired by Deleuze and Guattari, the principal conviction with which the present study works. In view of what has been said so far, my study suggests, however, a departure from the concrete question identified by them for Kleist—"What is a literature of war?"—and a reorientation of the question for the constellation of Kleist-and-Melville into the different directions that were proposed above. Less emphasis is thus put on the ultimately political struggle of literary writings for a different political collective—"another possible community ... another consciousness and another sensibility"[6]—that the concept of "minor literature as a political, collective deterritorialization of language"[7] suggests and that has been foregrounded by much of the reception of Deleuze and Guattari in literary studies. As we saw in the brief passage from *Kafka. Toward a Minor Literature*, different problems are central to different literary works, and Deleuze's and Guattari's many texts on literature differentiate these problems from each other with great precision.[8] In accordance with these differentiations I propose to move to a slightly altered perspective when engaging with Kleist and Melville *in conjunction*—and implicitly to make more aspects of Deleuze and Guattari's philosophy fruitful for literary studies than merely the concept of minor literature. This second point can only be touched upon in passing and would need to be elaborated in more depth and detail elsewhere. But what will be elaborated here, and what emerges from this specific assemblage of Kleist and Melville at hand is the question of nonrational forms of thinking. This is the direction into which we will take these two writers. But these slight shifts in emphasis notwithstanding, the present study is inspired by Deleuze and Guattari's incentive in *What is Philosophy?* that "[a]rt and philosophy crosscut the chaos and confront it, but it is not the same sectional plane; it is not populated in the same way. In the one there is a constellation of a universe or affects and percepts; and in the other, constellations of immanence or concepts. Art thinks no less than philosophy, but it thinks through affects and percepts."[9] How it does it, and what forms such a thinking could take, what results it could produce, and if and where it can go wrong—all of these are central aspects to the narratives of Kleist and Melville that will be read closely in this book. And by way of reading them—with their help—I hope to find a way to sketch the preliminary outlines of how literature might think, and what might come to pass if we link affectivity and thinking—how sensation[10] might perhaps be regarded as a nonrational form of thinking that emerges from this link.

If we consider Kleist's and Melville's writings in light of their concern for the conditions and operations of thinking, they emerge as distant and unexpected echoes of the debates of reason and thinking that have been constitutive for modern philosophy. By addressing the problems they address, they enter into a debate with philosophy and continue philosophical debates from a somewhat altered perspective, in a literary manner. As we will see, these debates were not necessarily contemporaneous with their writing. Rather, Kleist and Melville reacted to a philosophical *Gemengelage*—a palimpsest of hegemonic, canonized positions on thinking and sensation and oppositional, sometimes conflicting challenges to these—that has been in place at least since the Cartesian debates on the clarity of ideas and rational thinking. These debates have certainly undergone many shifts and are by no means monolithic, but with their figures of simplicity, Kleist and Melville respond to some of the main lines of argument in these debates. In order to be able to see the quality and the stakes of such a response, we have to begin by tracing the relevant components of this *Gemengelage*, and will do so in the first chapter of this book. One of the main shifts within this philosophical constellation that is relevant to our context is the shift in aesthetic debates around Kant. In the aesthetic debates of the eighteenth century before Kant, the relation between affectivity and thinking had been an important question. In the mid-eighteenth century, Alexander Gottlieb Baumgarten, Kant's immediate precursor, and, before Baumgarten, Gottfried Wilhelm Leibniz, on whom Baumgarten drew for some of his main philosophical concepts, had taken this relation into account and described it as a folded relation between sensibility and reason. To understand these two as enfolded vouched for the constitutive relation of one for the other, and consequently saw them not as two severed realms, but as connected. On this basis, Baumgarten made the concept of the fold—a concept that accounts for the seeming paradox of *both* differentiation *and* continuation between these two realms, as Deleuze explains for Leibniz, and as we will see in more detail in chapter 1—fruitful for his aesthetics,[11] which was to elaborate an understanding of "thinking" that relied on the enfolded rather than the severed relation between reason and sensibility. From their relatedness, Baumgarten argued, we can also deduct two types of cognition: rational and sensate thinking; and he moved on to claim that these two operate analogously as two different, but connected types of cognition. Aesthetics was envisioned by Baumgarten as the field of inquiry that preoccupied itself with the second type, that is, with sensate thinking. Aesthetics was, in Baumgarten's view, a field of philosophical inquiry with epistemological significance. This epistemological concern of aesthetics—or

Introduction

more appropriately *aisthetics* as it inquires into the epistemological challenges of *aistheta*, phenomena that are given to the senses—has been resurfacing recently, and the present study of literary articulations of *aisthetic* problematics hopes to contribute to them.[12] However, Baumgarten's understanding of aesthetics was largely overturned by Kantian transcendental philosophy and aesthetics. What became known as aesthetics with and after Kant significantly rephrased the relation between sensibility and thinking, dismissed Baumgarten's option of sensate thinking, and foreclosed the option of viewing affectivity as having any part in processes of understanding. Kant's intervention into the debates requires specific attention in our context, because Kleist and Melville reacted most immediately to the Kantian shifts in the relation of sensibility and reason. As we will see, Kleist was dissatisfied with Kant's transcendental resolution of the relation of sensation and thinking and explored alternative forms of such a relation in his literary writings. And much like Kleist, Melville was critical of Kant and, in distinction to the enthusiastic reception of transcendental philosophy among the homonymous transcendentalists around Emerson, his writings also began to explore dimensions of affectivity and their impact upon thinking. The results—their literary figures—reaffirm a relation between thinking and affectivity and assert a mode of thinking that occurs "in-between" the alleged oppositions of rational and irrational, or conscious and unconscious. Their figures of simplicity acquire a state of mind that blurs the strict division between either clear-rational-conscious thinking, or confused-irrational-unconscious mere sensation. To the extent that such a state of mind is not altogether foreign to thinking and an acquisition of knowledge, yet not accountable in terms of intelligibility and understanding either, it seems reminiscent of what Baumgarten called sensate thinking. And it is in this regard that Leibnizian and Baumgartian aesthetics resurface in slightly difracted ways in Kleist and Melville. We will begin by looking at the stakes of the aesthetic debates before Kleist and Melville, in order to better gauge the debates' effects in their writings.

Before we proceed to look into these debates, it is important to recall the danger that lies, as Brian Massumi rightly notes, in the attempt to sketch such a thinking, the danger, namely, that since there is not yet a vocabulary specific to affect "it is all too easy for received psychological categories to slip back in, undoing the considerable deconstructive work that has been effectively carried out by poststructuralism. Affect is most often used loosely as a synonym for emotion. But one of the clearest lessons ... is that emotion and affect ... follow different logics and pertain to different orders."[13] In view of this danger, we must note that the texts under consideration here make every effort to avoid such a conflation of affectivity with feeling or emotion. This difference between Kleist's and Melville's notions of affectivity and feeling or emotion requires specific mention here, since both have been viewed frequently in their histories of reception as precisely advocating emotion and feeling. They have been seen as idealizing feeling as a salvation from epistemological uncertainties, and as propagating the power of the heart over the head as a promise to return to certainty and innocence, and to restore a lost unity of the self.[14] As the consideration of their figures of simplicity hopes to demonstrate, however, the assumption of such a retreat to feeling as a warranty of authenticity and innocence misses the complexity of both oeuvres. The narratives do not present affectivity as a quest for epistemological certainty, but affirm the irremediable conditions of contingency and epistemological uncertainty, and within those conditions, gauge the potential of affectivity to contribute to thinking. In our readings of exemplary texts by Kleist and Melville we will see how both writers work with a renegotiated relation between affectivity and thinking, and how they present the effects of such a relation. Both present us with disconcerting figures—disconcerting precisely because they account for the fold of sensibility and reason, which comes across as simplicity, yet whereby they expose, some to a greater, some to a lesser extent, an affective thinking that strikes them "with a constitutive weakness, but also with a strange beauty."[15]

## Chapter 1

# Aesthetics

## Sensation and Thinking Reconsidered

On March 22, 1801, Heinrich von Kleist wrote a famous letter to his fiancée Wilhelmine von Zenge, telling her of his shocking encounter with Kantian philosophy: "I recently became familiar with the more recent so-called Kantian philosophy, and I may impart one of its leading ideas to you without fear of its shattering you as deeply, as painfully as it has me."[1] Kleist-criticism has read these and the ensuing lines to Wilhelmine—together with the letter written to his sister Ulrike the following day (*ADE*, 97–98/*SW IV/1*, 512)—as markers of an intellectual crisis, provoked by the encounter with Kant: an encounter that crushed Kleist, the young officer, and out of which Kleist, the writer, emerged in 1802 with his first literary work, *Die Familie Schroffenstein*. Much has been written about this crisis and the potential texts by Kant to which Kleist reacted so strongly. Despite differing suggestions to which of Kant's texts the "crisis-letters" of March 1801 refer,[2] the often held conviction is that the letters give evidence of the experience of a tremendous loss due to reading Kant. Kleist is seen to have lost his formerly held naïve Enlightenment belief in progress and transparency, in the possibility to perfect one's life and mind through education, and to acquire objective truth and lasting knowledge. With this ideal gone, Kleist-criticism largely saw Kleist emerging as the melancholic poet of the Fall.[3] Friedrich Cramer articulates this in his preface to Christian-Paul Berger's study on Kleist's *On the Puppet Theater*. Seeing Kleist's oeuvre as articulating this experience of loss, Cramer notes that Kleist's essay *On the Puppet Theater* symptomatically marks a decisive turn in the larger European history of thought: from the static, closed-off Leibnizian system that described nature as a continuum—*natura non facit saltus*—of the material and spiritual world, hierarchically organized by monads, in view of perfection, to a Kantian limitation of reason and a system of critique. "At the turn from the Enlightenment to modernity stands Kleist."[4] This epochal turn from an ideal and enclosed Enlightenment world labeled as Leibnizian to a modern world—from Leibniz's continuous and hierarchical world of monads, in which increasing perfectibility was possible and desired, to Kant's contention that we cannot know anything beyond our senses (except for the reflective knowledge of this finitude of our knowledge and our incapacity to conceive of the things in and of themselves)—Cramer sees exemplarily marked by Kleist's work. Although Kant argues that we nonetheless have to strive—within those limits—to purify philosophical thinking from all empirical residues in order to attain transcendental a priori knowledge, Kleist is generally thought to have lost his "highest goal" (*ADE*, 95/*SW IV/1*, 505), as he himself declared at one point. And in fact, as his letter of March 22, 1801, to Wilhelmine von Zenge confirms, he was familiar with Leibniz before becoming acquainted with Kantian philosophy. The letter notes that he "already as a lad (I think by the Rhine, while reading Wieland) adopted the idea that Perfection is the goal of creation" (*ADE*, 95), probably referring to Wieland's poem *Die Natur der Dinge oder Die vollkommenste Welt*, which considers the concepts of perfection and truth as presented in Leibniz's *Theodicy*. It encouraged him to believe, Kleist notes, "that after death we should progress from the level of perfection achieved on this planet to a higher one beyond, and that we should be able there to make use of the trove of truths collected here" (*ADE*, 95).[5] Familiar with Leibniz's philosophy, as can be expected at the end of the eighteenth century, which still stood under its influence, Kleist then also read Kant. He tries to convey the new insights to Wilhelmine—hoping that an account of Kant's central positions will not shock her as much as they had shocked him—in said letter of March 22, 1801.

> If everyone saw the world through green glasses, they would be forced to judge that everything they saw *was* green, and could never be sure whether their eye saw things as they really are, or did not add something of their own to what they saw. And so it is with our intellect. We can never be certain that what we call Truth is really Truth, or whether it does not merely appear so to us. If the latter, the Truth that we acquire here is *not* Truth after our death, and it is all a vain striving for a possession that may never follow us into the grave. Ah, Wilhelmine ... my one, my highest goal has sunk from sight, and I have no other. (*ADE*, 95)[6]

These letters have been read as indicators that—due to gaining from Kant the devastating insight that reason cannot penetrate beyond what our senses give us and that truth is therefore only finite, preliminary, and not to outlast death—Kleist's Leibnizian, rationalist worldview collapsed. But was it Kant's limitation of reason that Kleist was so shaken by? Was he disturbed by the screen of sensibility that Kant slid between the world and our reasonable assessment of it? Did he, in other words, accept Kant's philosophical assumptions and work out the dismay they caused him in his literary writings? This book pursues these questions and argues that if we consider the unusual twist that Kleist's work gives to one of Kant's main assumptions, namely to the relation between reason and sensibility, the thesis of an acceptance of and suffering from Kantian philosophy might need to be revised. Kleist's characters opt neither for rational, conceptual thinking, nor for its romanticized flip side of sensitivity and irrationality. They instead display a peculiar steadfastness in what they do, a steadfastness that does not rest upon rational choices or articulable convictions, and we can, thus, not say that its reasons are "known" to them. But simultaneously, they operate with a "knowledge" that is surprisingly apt to the situations they are in, and that grants them more adequate assessments of these situation than mere feeling could. This makes one wonder if the strong reaction to Kant was really due to a disillusionment with the scope of rationality and rationally acquired knowledge. Reading Kleist's texts, it seems that they struggle less with the finitude of knowledge, but rather with another moment of Kant's philosophy, related to the former. As this book suggests, what Kleist cannot agree to and what his own work works out differently than Kant, is the strict separation of sensibility and understanding, by which Kant discarded the idea of a complex continuity between sensibility and thinking present in Leibniz and thinkers indebted to him. Not the question of perfectibility but rather the question of continuity is decisive, as I would like to suggest, in understanding not only Kleist's encounter with Kant, but also the aesthetic claims Kleist made on that basis. The effects of Kant in Kleist's oeuvre are underestimated, if they are read as the disillusionment of a formerly naïve (Enlightenment) belief in reason, and I agree with Carol Jacobs that one "is tempted ... to call this confrontation Kant's Kleist crisis—at the risk of disrupting our conventional concept of time-order."[7] Instead of a assuming a unidirectional reaction, Jacobs continues that "Kleist's text is not that which necessarily follows from Kant's, although, it might be heard as a kind of repetition, an echo of the voice of philosophy, with results that are incalculable."[8] What is at stake here is the incalculability of these results, the observation that Kleist's texts echo the voice of philosophy and throw it back in a productively distorted—that is, in this case: literary—form. Kantian philosophy did not so much devastate Heinrich von Kleist's worldview—at least that is of lesser interest—but it triggered Kleist's literary texts, which echo the voice of philosophy, and by repeating philosophical concerns in a different voice these texts produce something unforeseen, something that is missed, if we assume a straightforward causal relation to Kant. A predominant concern that Kleist's texts—much like Melville's, as we will see momentarily—take up from Kant is the question of thinking and its relation to sensation and sensibility. The responses given to it, however, are different from Kant's. Throughout the preceding century, this question of the relation of thinking and sensibility had driven a field of inquiry that became known shortly before Kant as aesthetics, a field forming in the wake of Baumgarten and Kant as a branch of philosophy that investigates the relation of the senses, sensibility, pleasure, and desire to thinking. By taking up this concern in his texts, Kleist along with many others firmly asserts a position within this field—however, as we heard from Jacobs, with incalculable results. Howard Caygill phrases these various incalculable effects in his *Kant Dictionary*—significantly in the section entitled "Aesthetics"—and notes that the dissatisfaction by Kant's critics "was almost immediately apparent in the emergence of new forms of philosophical and para-philosophical writing in the field of aesthetics. These ranged from Schiller's edifying letters on aesthetic education, to Novalis and Friedrich Schlegel's fragments, to Kleist's short stories, Jean Paul's ironic manual for beginners in aesthetics and to Schelling's and Hegel's historical narratives."[9] Although Caygill lists Kleist's short stories among a whole list of responses to a dissatisfaction with Kant's answer for the "aesthetic problem," my aim here is to carve out one specific aesthetic response: one that answers in the form of short stories (as opposed to responding, for example, by ironic manuals, historical accounts, or the logic of the fragment), and that answers specifically to Kant's separation of sensation and thinking by experimenting with the continuity between them and sketching a type of thinking we could call sensate, or affective thinking. In order to better carve out this specific response, this book couples two writers, whose responses are strikingly similar and whose conjunction helps to contour the affective thinking their texts engage with. As the following chapters will show, both Kleist and Melville expose a similar discontent with the transcendental settlement of the question of thinking as reason and conceptual thought, and devise figures of simplicity, which offer a more complex approach to the relation of sensation and thinking and claim their continuity. On this account, their figures have also allowed contemporary thinkers—prominent among them Gilles Deleuze with his philosophical concern for this question and his frequent recourse to both Kleist and Melville—to approach affectivity as a mode of thinking. In tracing these figures, this book wishes therefore not only to engage with affective thinking, its operations, its dilemmas, and its potentials, but also to challenge the disciplinary demarcations of the field of aesthetics.

While Kleist read of Leibniz's philosophy in a poem on the banks of the river Rhine, Melville learned of Kant's philosophy crossing the Atlantic in October 1849. Exhausted by the many books he has written, but also by their waning success over the course of their publication, Melville took this first literary "business trip" to England—after he had sailed for years as a common sailor on whalers and navy vessels.[10] On October 12, 1849, he notes in his travel journal: "Have tried to read, but found it hard work. However, there are some very plasant [sic] passengers on board, with whom to converse. Chief among these is a Mr Adler, a German scholar, to whom Duyckinck introduced me."[11] George J. Adler, professor of German at New York University, was to remain Melville's friend and interlocutor on philosophy until Adler's death in 1868. The journal introduces Adler as being "full of the German metaphysics, & discourses of Kant, Swedenborg &c" (*J*, 4) and tells of Melville's increasing acquaintance with him, and with what he calls "metaphysics" during the four weeks of his sea journey. On October 22, he notes: "Clear & cold; wind not favorable.... [L]ast night about 9½ P.M. Adler &

## Aesthetics

Taylor came into my room, & it was proposed to have whiskey punches, which we did have, accordingly" (J, 8). They had an "extraordinary time" and "talked metaphysics continually, & Hegel, Schlegel, Kant &c were discussed under the influence of the whiskey" (J, 8). We have to note that "talking metaphysics" with Adler and Taylor was no more a first encounter with it for Melville than had been the case for Kleist, as we saw in his "crisis-letters." In Melville's case, Kant has already appeared in *Mardi* (1849). Neither, of course, are his conversations with Adler Melville's only known encounter with philosophy, and Melville-criticism has meticulously traced his extensive readings and intellectual stimulations.[12] But what the entry shows—also, when we hear that five days later, they were "riding on the German horse again" (J, 9)—is that Melville's encounter with philosophy was from the start more humorous than Kleist's. Melville was not shaken by it, but rather seems somewhat stoically amused, much the way his characters are a little more stoic than Kleist's stouthearted and rash ones. The appearances of Kant in Melville's texts are not dramatized by Melville—nor by Melville-criticism—as effecting a crisis, or an enlightenment. Familiar with idealist and Kantian philosophical positions, as much as with the American transcendentalist philosophy associated with Ralph Waldo Emerson, Melville distances himself from these by satirizing them: Emerson most notably in *The Confidence-Man* of 1857,[13] and Kant most pointedly in *Moby-Dick; or, The Whale* and *Pierre; or, The Ambiguities*, which were both written after returning from his journey to England in 1849, and immediately preceded his turn to tales. When we come to Melville's tales in chapter 2, we will see that the tales move away from the explicit satire of philosophical positions in these earlier novels and transform their critique into the presentation of an alternative to the problem: the tales no longer express the dissatisfaction with Kantian, idealist, and transcendentalist parameters by way of satire, but their form, language, and characters perform a relation of sensibility and thinking that significantly differs from Kantian, idealist, and transcendentalist convictions. Thereby, they truly become "para-philosophical writings" in Caygill's sense: next to philosophy, their echo distortedly repeats and produces something new in the repetition, something the "simpletons" that predominate the tales under scrutiny in this book allow to emerge. But we must not rush ahead of things. Let us briefly stay with *Moby-Dick*, where Kant makes his most frequent and most commonly known appearance. Here, Kant figures alongside Locke, when both philosophers are likened to the heads of different whale-types. During Ahab's chase of the white whale, halfway through the novel, a sperm whale is killed and hoisted alongside the *Pequod*. The order is given, "if opportunity offered,"[14] to also hunt a right whale, and when opportunity indeed offers, a right whale is killed.

> The boats were here hailed, to tow the whale on the larboard side, where fluke chains and other necessaries were already prepared for securing him. "Didn't I tell you so?" said Flask; "yes, you'll soon see

this Right Whale's head hoisted up opposite that parmaceti's." In good time, Flask's saying proved true. As before, the Pequod steeply leaned over towards the Sperm Whale's head, now, by the counterpoise of both heads, she regained her even keel; though sorely strained, you may well believe. So, when on one side you hoist in Locke's head, you go over that way; but now, on the other side, hoist in Kant's and you come back again; but in poor plight. Thus, some minds for ever keep trimming boat. Oh, ye foolish! throw all these thunderheads overboard, and then you will float light and right.[15]

Humorously fitted into the cetological section of the novel, which gives meticulous details of the art of whaling, Kant appears as the counterpoise to Locke, both equally weighing down on the vessel. This is no unusual pairing, as Ralph Waldo Emerson for example had suggested the same in his essay *The Transcendentalist* in 1842.[16] Conceiving the difference between materialists and idealists, into which thinkers have generally divided themselves, along the lines of Locke on the one side, and Kant on the other, Emerson in his essay clearly leans toward Kantian positions. Melville's suggestion, on the other hand, is to throw both overboard; or, to be more precise and in line with the text: to just keep them hoisted alongside, as they are bound go down anyway: "Look your last, now, on these venerable hooded heads, while they yet lie together; for one will soon sink, unrecorded, in the sea; the other will not be very long in following."[17] Both Lockean and Kantian philosophy, the passage suggests, unduly and one-sidedly tilt the vessel, either toward sensuality (Locke) or toward rationality (Kant). It would be too precipitous—given Melville's pronounced interest in philosophical questions—to conclude that the passage suggests throwing philosophical concerns at large overboard. Rather, it seems to recommend refraining from a too one-sided valorization of one of the two sides and perhaps consider the problem from a different angle.

In order to see what Melville's and Kleist's "para-philosophical" writings propose, we nevertheless need to first look at what they reacted to, and when we consider the recurring confrontation of Kant as a philosophical persona in their writings, we can suspect—with Anselm Haverkamp—that it was the "precariously limited construction of Kant's transcendental aesthetics."[18] In this chapter, we will therefore first look at the scenario of Kant's construction: at what it turned away from itself, at what it buried in this turn, and at the mortgage it carried, upon which the dissatisfied reactions were in turn able to build. Considering this scenario will allow us to appreciate the figures of simplicity in Kleist's and Melville's tales as genuine interventions into an aesthetic debate, as the re-turn (under modern conditions) to an aesthetics that was not so much concerned with the nature of beauty and the assessment of art, but rather with questions of perception, thinking, and their relation to sensation. It is by way of this re-turn that Kleist and Melville have become two of the most prominent writers for Deleuze, as their writings allow him—and others thinking about a revised relation of thinking to sensation[19]—to reassess aesthetic debates and revive—in a still largely post-Kantian setting[20]—their untapped *aisthetic* potentials.

## The Copernican Turn

In his *Critique of Pure Reason* (1781), Kant's project of transcendental philosophy had demarcated the lines along which aesthetics was to be thought, and his *Critique of Judgment* (1790) developed aesthetics—within these limits—along the notions of the beautiful and the sublime as "subjective" aesthetics.[21] In order to follow the scenario of its—however precariously limited—construction, we must take note of the fact that Kant's aesthetics, both of the first and the third Critique, resulted from a dissatisfaction that Kant himself felt with his precursor Alexander Gottlieb Baumgarten in regard to the field of aesthetics. The first footnote in the *Critique of Pure Reason*—setting off Kant's own transcendental aesthetics—values Baumgarten as a superb analyst, but dismisses his aesthetic project as a disappointed hope.

> At the foundation of this term [aesthetics] lies the disappointed hope, which the eminent analyst, Baumgarten, conceived, of subjecting the criticism of the beautiful to principles of reason, and so of elevating its rules into a science. But his endeavors were vain. For the said rules or criteria are, in respect to their chief sources, merely empirical, consequently never can serve as determinate laws à priori, by which our judgment in matters of taste is to be directed. (*CPR*, 22)

Dismissing Baumgarten's aesthetics as a vain attempt amounts, as Caygill has argued in his reassessment of the Baumgarten-Kant relationship, to nothing less than a reinvention of aesthetics under transcendental parameters that were never Baumgarten's: "Kant's aesthetics, which determined the later [aesthetic] debates, were themselves a re-invention of the Baumgartian original and in many respects reduced the latter's complexity."[22] Before we turn to these complexities—complexities that echo in the "para-philosophical" reactions under scrutiny in this book—let us stay for the moment with the reversal, or reinvention, which Kant's disappointment provoked him to conduct.

Since philosophy for Kant had to be transcendental philosophy, and the rules for the judgment of the beautiful specified by Baumgarten remain only empirical, they cannot provide the a priori that Kant's philosophy was after. According to Kant, Baumgarten tried to subsume the empirical realm of sensibility under the rules of reason—a judgment that was to dominate most of the reception of Baumgarten until recently.[23] The *Critique of Pure Reason* outlines what Kant instead envisioned as transcendental aesthetics. The introduction demands that

> [t]he principal thing we must attend to, in the division of the parts of a science like this, is that no conceptions must enter it which contain aught empirical; in other words, that the knowledge a priori must be completely pure.... Transcendental philosophy is consequently a philosophy of the pure and merely speculative reason. For all that is practical, so far as it contains motives, relates to feelings, and these belong to empirical sources of cognition. (*CPR*, 17–18)

Although we can hear Kant attribute feelings to empirical sources of cognition, and thus suggest a cognitive aspect of feeling, the introduction ends on a summary remark that clearly distinguishes them from each other as receptivity on the one hand (sensibility) and thinking on the other (understanding). "Only so much seems necessary, by way of introduction or premonition, that there are two sources of human knowledge (which probably spring from a common, but to us unknown root), namely, sense and understanding. By the former, objects are given to us; by the latter, thought" (*CPR*, 18).[24] Thinking is only conducted by the faculty of the understanding, while sensibility is the reception of impressions and representations of objects. Consequentially, in order to achieve the desired transcendental purity, the first part of the first Critique begins by announcing that

> [i]n the science of transcendental aesthetic accordingly, we shall first isolate sensibility or the sensuous faculty, by separating from it all that is annexed to its perceptions by the conceptions of understanding, so that nothing be left but empirical intuition. In the next place we shall take away from this intuition all that belongs to sensation, so that nothing may remain but pure intuition, and the mere form of phenomena, which is all that the sensibility can afford à priori. (*CPR* 22)

And the mere form of phenomena—"mere" in the sense that they contain nothing of what pertains to the empirical or sensibility[25]—comes in but two dimensions: space and time, which the transcendental aesthetics of the first Critique establishes. By a clear separation, transcendental aesthetics hopes to evade the philosophical ambiguity or imprecision that Kant saw in the eighteenth-century tradition of a critique of taste, which had hoped in vain to subject the critique of the beautiful to principles of reason. Far from providing rules for taste or judgment, transcendental aesthetics was merely to purify or isolate sensibility in a way that nothing remained but what can be thought of it a priori. It thereby, as Jacques Derrida remarks, excludes all "that is not theoretical knowledge: the affect (*Gefühl*) in its two principal values (pleasure/unpleasure) and the power to desire (*Begehrungsvermögen*). It cuts out its field only by cutting itself off from the interest in desire, by losing interest in desire."[26] After the founding act of positing a separation of sensibility and understanding, after the faculties of reason, understanding, and imagination had been clearly separated and a transcendental difference had been proclaimed between intuition and concept, Kant's third—and more commonly considered aesthetic—*Critique of Judgment* responds to this separation. While the different faculties had been subjected in the *Critique of Pure Reason* under the rule of the understanding, and in the *Critique of Practical Reason* under the rule of reason, the *Critique of Judgment* tests the possibility of a free play of the faculties, intending to reconcile the separation between the spheres of the sensible and the intelligible, which the project of transcendental philosophy itself had postulated, by providing reflective judgment as their intermediary member. As Caygill notes, this offers a version of aesthetics "that posits a transcendental difference between sensibility and understanding in the first Critique, only to bridge it in the third Critique under the guise of a harmony amongst intuition and understanding."[27]

In exemplary circumstances, Kant knew, there were modes of experience that could neither be accounted for by reason, nor by the understanding: the experience of beauty, for example. Thus, the *Critique of Judgment* inquires after the conditions and processes of a subjective judgment of taste, which can be conducted neither by reason nor by the understanding—as that would unduly subject sentiments or sensations, which do not belong to reason, under its rule, something that Kant held against Baumgarten's aesthetic project. The cases that Kant's third Critique focuses on are a "disinterested pleasure" in the beautiful, on the one hand, and the experience of collapsing synthetical powers of the mind vis-à-vis the sublime, on the other.[28] In both cases the exercise of judgment as an a priori faculty is at stake, and its critique is written with the transcendental subject in mind. What is experienced in the sublime, according to Kant, is the collapse of the mind's power to synthesize, its failure of cognition and understanding. Such moments of a loss of power of the mind incite the free play of the faculties, and test the limits of the mind without contributing anything to the understanding. Although Kant confronted these challenges and provided—as Derrida shows—the paradox of both a separable part and a "nondetachable part, since it forms the articulation between two other"[29] faculties—a "*Mittelglied* [that ...] forms the articulation of the theoretical and the practical (in the Kantian sense)"[30]—he tried to defuse the explosiveness this intermediary member could have implied. Faithful to the transcendental separation between intuition (*Anschauung*) and concept (*Begriff*), reflective judgment could not but be subjectively aesthetic—that is: of no contribution to the understanding, and laying the basis for what we have called subjective aesthetics, which has defined the realm of aesthetics for the next two centuries, although the paradoxical complexities and potentials of Kant's aesthetics have been noted from early discontents to recent deconstructions, by "Kant's critics from Schiller (1793) and Hegel (1835) to Derrida (1978) and Lyotard (1988)."[31]

Nevertheless, the decisive cuts that his philosophy made for the conception of thinking by severing sensibility from the understanding largely remain determinant for the territorial limits between philosophy and literature, and continue to inform the definition of aesthetics as being of no epistemological import. Caygill is certainly very right to remind us that Kant's take on sensibility and understanding cannot be reduced to a simply oppositional or hierarchical relation, and that Kant was precisely trying to avoid "the idealist Scylla of reducing sense to the 'confused perceptions of reason'" (which Kant criticized Leibniz for), and "the empiricist Charybdis of abstracting reason from sense"[32] (which were his discontents with the sensualists and Locke). Accordingly,

> Kant argued that both tendencies elided the distinction between sensibility and the understanding, the one by subordinating sensibility to understanding, the other understanding to sensibility. [For Kant, s]ensibility must be distinguished from the understanding, but nevertheless possesses a formal element; the formal element, however, does not subsume the objects of sensibility in the same way as a concept. Similarly, sensibility is receptive, as opposed to the spontaneity of the understanding, but this does not mean that it is a passive *tabula rasa* merely registering impressions.... Thus sensibility is neither the confused perception of a rational perfection maintained by the Leibnizian school, nor the immediate receptivity to impressions of Locke, but seems to partake of aspects of both positions, while being fully committed to neither.[33]

Given the aspirations of transcendental philosophy, Kant maintained the a priori of the transcendental aesthetic of the first Critique, and tried to combine or balance the rational character of idealist accounts of sensibility with the receptive character of empiricist accounts. The crucial point, which these rough outlines of Kantian aesthetics were meant to lay out, is that albeit designing transcendental philosophy as neither idealist nor empiricist, it proclaims a separation between sensibility and the understanding, which deprived the former of epistemological import and cognitive value. Against this background, we can again take up our question after what it was that in turn sparked the dissatisfactions with Kant, and called forth the "para-philosophical" writings Caygill had listed before. The bone of contention was the same Kant had struggled with: the relation of sensibility and reason and the exigencies of thinking. This not only incited the later reactions to Kant, but it had already provoked Kant's disappointment with Baumgarten, and his reinvention of the precursor's aesthetics. Nearly every introductory text on the history of aesthetics cites

Baumgarten as the founder of the discipline.[34] As the disciplinary narration of aesthetics goes, Baumgarten's aesthetics attempted to recuperate sensibility to its due status in philosophical thinking, but remained—in the formation of the discipline—a mere precursor of Kant. Presuming that Baumgarten's aesthetics unduly mixed the realms of sensibility and reason, Kant severed the two in accordance with his own transcendental project, as we saw, and rejected the continuity between them, upon which Baumgarten's whole notion of aesthetics had, as Kant judged, erroneously, rested. Most of nineteenth- and twentieth-century aesthetic debates subscribed to the separation Kant had posited, and aesthetics became the philosophy of art, approaching art as the realm of subjective experience, and the test site of processes of cognition, of the play of the faculties, but of no cognitive value itself. Recently, a far greater complexity to the history of aesthetics—and with this, the potentials of aesthetics—has come into view, and it becomes increasingly evident that Baumgarten cannot seamlessly be discarded as a Kantian antecedent, and that his work "instead of being history, continued to break ground and take effects that by-passed Kant."[35] The transition from Baumgarten to Kant did not correct certain conceptual shortcomings, but it was a break that set a new course for subsequent aesthetic debates. And as a break, as Haverkamp remarked, this transition entailed an excess that bypassed Kant and continued to resurface in the incalculable results of the "para-philosophical" writings, which expressed a discontent with the Kantian framework. With its specific approach to aesthetics, and its specific historical position immediately before Kant, Baumgarten's work harbored a potential that in philosophy "has been blocked for the longest time by Kant's Copernican revolution,"[36] but which had nevertheless incalculable literary, "para-philosophical" effects.

## The Folds of Small Perceptions

Alexander Gottlieb Baumgarten is generally considered the founder of aesthetics. He taught philosophy, ethics, and law at Viadrina University in Frankfurt an der Oder at the Prussian border with Poland, and lectured on a *disciplina aesthetica* for the first time in 1742. The notes of these lectures formed the basis for his 1750–58 publication of the two-volume *Aesthetica*. Baumgarten's project, which culminated in the *Aesthetica*, was to develop aesthetics as a *scientia cognitionis sensitivae*, and to make it the sibling of rational thinking and philosophy—or more precisely its younger sister, "like her elder sister logic."[37] Although the main goal of his aesthetics was and is generally seen as the attempt to emancipate sensibility from its "expulsion" from thinking by a too narrowly framed logic, the precise manner of this emancipation has always been under contention. Baumgarten's claim of a *cognitio sensitiva*, translated perhaps best as *sensate thinking*, stresses the epistemological dimension of the sensate and aesthetics as the field of inquiry into such a widened concept of thinking. Rather than seeing aesthetics as a philosophizing on art as subjective experience, and on the mind's limits demarcated in this experience, Baumgarten's aesthetics inquired into the relation of sensate to strictly logical thinking, and proposed a modality of their relation different from the one Kantian aesthetics later very effectively solidified. The opening of the *Aesthetica* asserts: "§ 1 Aesthetics (as a theory of the liberal arts, as doctrine of lower cognition, as the art of beautiful thinking, and as the art of thinking analogous to rational thinking [*ars analogi rationis*]) is the science of sensate thinking" (Ä, 2). Such a program for the discipline implies—and this was one of Baumgarten's main contentions—that sensate thinking is analy*zable*, that is does not merely function as an indefinable *je ne sais quoi* that marks the outside of understanding (as Descartes had posited it),[38] and of which we can only know that we cannot know, that is, define, it. Baumgarten's aesthetics instead proclaimed that we can analyze it— just like its older sister logic, but according to its own terms. In view of this more general epistemological relevance of the "lower faculties," the *Aesthetica* proclaims aesthetics, among other things, "as doctrine of lower cognition" (Ä, 2), something that Baumgarten takes, as we will see momentarily, from Leibniz's theory of perception. The exemplary field to study the epistemological processes specific to the "lower faculties" is art, because the cognitive processes set off by art do not operate according to demonstration and analyses, as logical thinking would, but in a sudden grasping of the vivid impression of the whole. In view of this, art is exemplary for the cognitive process that can be linked to sensate thinking in the wider sense, and to that extent Baumgarten proclaims aesthetics to be equally "a theory of the liberal arts" (Ä, 2); to that extent, Baumgarten's aesthetics expresses "an interest in the thinking [*Erkenntnis*] of art—a thinking in and about art (genitivus subjectivus and objectivus)."[39]

Throughout the history of reception of Baumgarten, however, his labeling of sensate thinking as an *analogon rationis* has provoked confusion. Proclaiming it as *analogous* to rational thinking led to its dismissal as being modeled *according to* rational thinking, and thus as an eventually rationalist subsumption of the sensate under principles of reason, which was judged to be in line with the Wolffian-Leibnizian tradition, under which Baumgarten was largely subsumed. Reading his *analogon* in this vein is misleading, as it continues to model sensate thinking according to rationality, without considering that a completely different conception of rationality itself is required, if the analogy is supposed to gain plausibility. In other words, such readings misconstrue the process of analogy as a unidirectional assimilation, and not as a reciprocal relation that is in itself not a logic but an analogic relation, that is, a relation that is not predetermined by or subsumable under the rule of reason. Baumgarten's aesthetic propositions run counter to this very model.

In the weekly philosophical letters *Philosophische Briefe von Aletheophilus*, which Baumgarten published in 1741 in German, their fictive author Aletheophilus laments—most markedly in the second letter—the reductive equation of philosophy with logic. He notes that if philosophy is the science of the enhancement of thinking (*Erkenntnis*), and logic "has as its subject only understanding in the narrow sense and reason..., but we possess far more faculties of the soul that serve understanding than those attributed to understanding or reason,"[40] then one has to conclude that "logic, when claiming to improve our thinking as such, and in the end attending only to distinct insight and its rectification, appears to promise more than it keeps" (*PB*, 6). The reproach that philosophy promises too much, if it restricts its attention to distinct ideas, echoes the debate of the categories of ideas, which Descartes had established in his *Discourse on Method*. Lamenting its narrow scope and wanting to account for a wider approach to the faculties, the friend of truth Aletheophilus directs the reader's attention to the work of an allegedly unknown author (Baumgarten himself), whose undertaking is said to stand in line with that of the "baron Leibniz, whose expanse of thorough insight has consistently been most admired" (*PB*, 6). Both Leibniz and Baumgarten, the letter suggests, welcome the revision of a too narrowly conceived philosophy, and wish to broaden it by considering forms of thinking that are other than purely "distinct." Baumgarten, "thus, envisages it [logic in the narrow sense] as a science of the cognition of the understanding or of distinct insight, and reserves the laws of sensate and vivid thinking, even if it should not rise to distinctness in its most precise sense, for a separate science" (*PB*, 7). This latter has been named "aesthetics... [dividing] the science for the enhancement of sensate thinking into the arts that attend to thinking itself and into those that attend mainly to vivid representation" (*PB*, 7). We find here already the two dimensions of aesthetic concern that Baumgarten will later include in his first paragraph of the *Aesthetica*, making aesthetics a doctrine of lower cognition and a theory of the liberal arts. In pointing to the name of this separate science, the letter refers to an even earlier coining of the term *aesthetics*, which had already appeared in Baumgarten's dissertation *Meditationes Philosophicae de Nonnullis ad Poema Pertinentibus* (1735). The dissertation was the first moment of envisioning a science that should guide the "lower" faculties to think in a sensate manner, making it "the task of logic *in its broader sense* to guide this faculty in the sensate cognition of things."[41] Such logic in a broader sense encompasses more than what the narrowly outlined field of logic—according to Baumgarten and Leibniz too strictly demarcated by both Descartes and Wolff—permits,[42] and since logic in the narrow sense concerned itself with ideas (*noeta*) or all things thought, it had to be assisted by a logic that concerned itself with phenomena (*aistheta*) or all things perceived. And this logic of the *aistheta* is coined in the penultimate paragraph of the *Meditationes* (§116) as aesthetics:

> The Greek philosophers and the Church fathers have already carefully distinguished between *things perceived* [αἰσθητά] and *things known* [νοητά].... Therefore, *things known* are to be known by the

superior faculty as the object of logic; *things perceived* [are to be known by the inferior faculty, as the object] of the science of perception, or **aesthetic.**[43]

While this early prospect of 1735 still envisioned the new science as supplement to conceptual logic, Baumgarten gradually transformed it over the course of his writings into a logic in its own right: a logic of sensate thinking.[44] But from the start, aesthetics was for Baumgarten *aisthetics*, a reconsideration of the perceptive and sensate dimensions of thinking and cognition, of the cognitive dimensions of perception and sensation. He drew not only the support, but also the philosophical tools for such a revision of philosophy from Leibniz, in particular from the latter's work on perception. In distinction to Wolff, who based his own hierarchical conception of the lower faculties—and their disavowal as unruly, unenlightened, and of no epistemological import—on his influential rationalist reading of Leibniz, Baumgarten read Leibniz different than Wolff and argued for the careful consideration of the complex relation of the lower faculties to the understanding and of their contribution to thinking. Asserting a logic of sensate thinking that operates differently from conceptualization, Baumgarten called such *cognitio sensitiva* "confused" thinking in line with Descartes' fourfold categories of ideas. In his *Discourse on Method*, Descartes had introduced a fourfold categorization of ideas comprising obscure, clear, confused, and distinct ideas, categories that were taken up and significantly modified by Leibniz and later by Wolff. According to Descartes, only clear and distinct ideas are true, for as long as there is "something confused and obscure about them," ideas contain some falsity, "because in this they participate in nothing."[45] This momentous identification of conceptual, rational thinking with truth, of thinking with clarity and distinctness, and of sensation with confusion and nothingness, provoked Leibniz to revise Descartes' categorization, and to claim not only a positive status for confusion, but also a continuity between the different kinds of ideas. Leibniz's *Meditations on Knowledge, Truth, and Ideas* note that an idea is obscure if it "does not suffice for recognizing the thing represented" and it is clear "when it makes it possible for me to recognize the thing represented."[46] Obscure ideas do not allow the recollection of an object, or its recognition as something that one has seen or known before, nor to relate the object to anything else. Clear ideas, on the other hand, allow the recognition of an object. Such clarity, however, and this is Leibniz's crucial point, is a feature of both confused and distinct ideas. Our ideas are clear-confused (or short: confused), if we (re)cognize or know something, but are unable to enumerate the marks of this object in respect to others. "Thus we know colors, odors, flavors, and other particular objects of the senses clearly enough and discern them from each other but only by the simple evidence of the senses and not by marks that can be expressed."[47] Ideas are, on the contrary, clear-distinct (or short: distinct), if we recognize something, *and* are able to enumerate its marks.

## Aesthetics

The decisive point is that these kinds of ideas are not attributed to realms that are severed from each other, but are part of a continual transformation from the perception of confused wholes to the apperception of more distinct, but less marks. As Leibniz notes in *The Principles of Nature and of Grace*,

> It does not cease to be true that at bottom confused thoughts are nothing else than a multitude of thoughts which are in themselves like the distinct, but which are so small that each separately does not excite our attention and cause itself to be distinguished. We can even say that there is all at once a virtually infinite number of them contained in our sensations. It is in this that the great difference between confused and distinct thought really consists.[48]

Every concept or clear-distinct idea is the conscious enumeration of the distinct marks of an object. These marks, Leibniz confirms, can be differentiated again into an infinite number of confused ideas, so that "no concept is ever wholly free of a residual confusion from its sensuous origin."[49] Contrary to Leibniz, Descartes had not only argued that to the extent to which they contain anything confused, ideas "participate in nothingness," but Descartes also—as Deleuze observes, and he marks a crucial difference between Descartes and Leibniz here, crucial for our reading of Baumgarten's reception of Leibniz in opposition to Wolff—"believed that the real distinction between parts entailed separability" (*F*, 5). From this followed not only the Cartesian separation of two realms—that of reason, the understanding, and thinking from that of sensation, the senses, and the passions—but also the establishment of their relation as one of opposition and hierarchy, and in this Wolff was to follow Descartes more than Leibniz. Leibniz challenged precisely their hierarchical relation when arguing "that at bottom confused thoughts are nothing else than a multitude of thoughts which are in themselves like the distinct," as we read above. Already in *terminological* distinction to Descartes Leibniz speaks of *perception* and *apperception*: That which confusedly represents a rich multiplicity of marks he calls perception, and its transformation into a conscious enumeration of these (abstracted) marks apperception. The *Monadology* (1714) states (§14): "The passing condition, which involves and represents a multiplicity in the unit or in the simple substance, is nothing but what is called Perception, which is to be distinguished from Apperception or Consciousness...."[50] By arguing for their difference, yet also for a relation—a movement of endless passing, evolving, and enfolding—between them, Leibniz distances his notion of perception from Cartesian rationalism. The *Monadology* contends that "[i]n this matter the Cartesian view is extremely defective, for it treats as non-existent those perceptions of which we are not consciously aware."[51] Leibniz makes his own "rationality of the relative"[52] part of the philosophical endeavor to open alternatives to the

Cartesian division of body and mind and the attribution of thinking only to reason. Leibniz's notion of the fold designates the endless "passing" and relating, whereupon Leibniz bases his theory of perception and affirms, as Deleuze notes, "the relativity of clarity…, the inseparability of clarity from obscurity, the effacement of contour—in short, the opposition to Descartes, who remained a man of the Renaissance."[53] For Leibniz, Deleuze writes, clarity "endlessly plunges into obscurity. Chiaroscuro fills the monad following a series that can move in either of two directions: at one end is a dark background and at the other is light, sealed" (F, 32). The affirmation of a zone of chiaroscuro, from which two series spring forth and come to pass as the differentiated states of a more or less dark background and a more or less lit foreground, is the significant revision that Deleuze attributes to Leibniz. It is this affirmation of two similar series, their analogy yet difference, that Baumgarten—as I would like to suggest here—took from Leibniz.[54] To point to the fact that the more or less dark background passes into clarity as soon as it is conceptualized, explicated, or defined, means, on the one hand, *not* to attribute it to nothingness, and, on the other hand, to *account for* its different modality: a modality we have to think more as the "insistence" of a dark background, and not so much as an expressible, graspable existence.

The difficult question this poses is how something that is inseparable (and in that sense continuous or gradual), can be or become really distinct (in the sense of different); or, as Deleuze puts it, "the point is one of knowing how we move from minute perceptions to conscious perceptions" (F, 87), from perception to apperception. In the *Discourse on Metaphysics* Leibniz gives a well-known example intended to illustrate this paradoxical relation of something inseparable, yet really different. Arguing against the nothingness Descartes attributed to confused idea, Leibniz explains:

> [O]ur confused sensations result from a really infinite variety of perceptions. This is somewhat like the confused murmur heard by those who approach the seashore, which comes from the accumulation of innumerable breaking waves. For if out of several perceptions, which do not harmonize so as to make one, there is no single one which surpasses the others, and if these perceptions make impressions that are about equally strong and equally capable of holding the attention of the soul, it can perceive them only confusedly.[55]

As long as none of the many small perceptions stands out from among the others, they receive the same attention and their effect is of equal power. Their perception is confused. However, as soon as at least two waves are perceived as "heterogeneous enough to become part of a relation that can allow the perception of a third, one that 'excels' over the others and comes to consciousness" (F, 88) the differential relation between them allows the third to pass the threshold of attention. In §17 of the *Aesthetica*, Baumgarten accordingly notes that "sensate thinking is, according to its main designation, the entirety of representations remaining below the threshold of logical distinction" (*Ä*, 10). Or, we could say, the threshold of the excitement of attention. The coming to consciousness—as for example in the case of someone approaching the seashore—is not due to a selection *made by* consciousness. Rather, it is the differential relation that produces the selection, and thereby produces consciousness, or distinct ideas. It is not the conscious mind that selects perceptions and produces understanding, but "[d]ifferential relations always select minute perceptions that play a role in each case, and bring to light or clarify the conscious perception that comes forth" (*F*, 90). Likewise, this does not imply that by crossing the threshold confused perceptions become distinctly cognizable. Rather, the moment they are distinctly cognized, they have already ceased to be confused. But at the same time, and this is all-decisive, as long as they are confused, they are—albeit not consciously enumerable—not nothing, but rather a different modality of cognition, which Baumgarten calls sensate thinking, and which operates by confused ideas: ideas that are—as Jeffrey Barnouw aptly puts it— "taken simply as they are given in experience; a sensuous idea is an unanalyzed whole that may include a number of undifferentiated elements *fused* together."[56] In this sense, they are con-fused, forming blocks, which Barnouw associates with simplicity here. This is where the present study intervenes and from where it begins to pursue an exemplary set of figures of simplicity, whose thinking implies many of the elements discussed here as con-fusion. When speaking of an undifferentiated whole here, we must by no means forget that the relation of small perceptions to apperceptions is not one of parts to a whole, or of a negatively construed opposition. For Leibniz, "the relation of the inconspicuous perceptions to conscious perception does not go from part to whole, but from the ordinary to what is notable or remarkable" (*F*, 87), from a conglomerate of perceptions beneath the threshold of attention to marks or clear-distinct ideas, which have come to awareness. "Inconspicous perceptions are...not parts of conscious perception, but requisites or genetic elements, 'differentials of consciousness'" (*F*, 89). It is this relation of continuity that Baumgarten takes up, and which forms the basis of his *scientia cognitionis sensitivae*.

At the beginning of the *Aesthetica*, Baumgarten thinks of likely objections against this new *scientia cognitionis sensitivae*, one of the main ones being an objection to confusion. He states and begins to refute it as follows:

> Against our science it could further be argued that...§ 7 5) Confusion is the mother of errors. My answer: a) But it is an indispensable prerequisite for the discovery of truth, since nature does not leap from darkness into the clarity of thinking. From night the path only leads through twilight to noon. b) Due to this one precisely

has to trouble oneself with confused knowledge, so that no errors arise, as they do plentifully and in wide range with those, who do not attend to it. c) This is not to recommend confusion, but to improve thinking, in as much as something confused is necessarily admixed to it. (Ä, 4)

In clear lineage with Leibniz, Baumgarten insists here on the *continuity* of confusion and clarity, sensation and reason, and in one of the most insightful recent rereadings of Baumgarten's aesthetics, Caygill repeatedly emphasizes that it was this principle of continuity that Baumgarten stressed throughout his work: "The fundamental principle which Baumgarten developed between 1737 and 1750 was continuity—between sensibility and reason, intuition and concept, sensitive and rational perfection."[57] Caygill views precisely this as his "rather Leibnizian than Wolffian (or Kantian)"[58] heritage. With this principle of continuity, Baumgarten's aesthetics, on the one hand, stresses that conscious apperceptions are bound to their grounding in perception, in the indefinable multiplicity of small perceptions. In that sense, aesthetics, far from claiming a return to an originary sensibility or feelings, exposes and discusses the constitutive, engendering relation between small perceptions and apperceptions, and accounts for their continuous *chiaroscuro*—the fact that "[c]larity emerges from obscurity by way of a genetic process, and so too clarity plunges into darkness" (F, 90). In this sense, aesthetics is meant to "improve thinking, in as much as something confused is necessarily admixed to it" (Ä, 4), that is, become the discipline that occupies itself with this logic of a folded relation between perceptions and apperceptions. Such a continuous, folded relation is a prerequisite if we want to conceive of two *analogous* modes of thinking: that is, conceive of them not as a similarity, where one side (sensation) is modeled after the other (privileged) side (rationality), but as an analogy, where "two things can be thought as being really distinct without being separable" (F, 55).

On the other hand—and this is why many readers have rightly pointed to the doubled agenda in Baumgarten's work[59]—aesthetics as Baumgarten envisioned it was to occupy itself with *one* side of this folded relation in particular: with "confused" or sensate thinking. It was to analyze its specificity, its operations on the basis of an ambiguous richness of phenomena that is only given under the condition that their marks cannot be made distinct. It was to be not only the "doctrine of lower cognition"—making a more general epistemological claim for sensation as thinking—but also "a theory of the liberal arts," as we heard earlier. To these two dimensions, Baumgarten adds a third—also in the very first paragraph of the *Aesthetica*: aesthetics was to foster at the same time "the art of beautiful thinking,... the art of thinking analogous to rational thinking [*ars analogi rationis*]" (Ä, 2). On the basis of Baumgarten's and Leibniz's fundamental claim of a continuous relation between sensation and thinking, it is this "art of thinking analogous to rational thinking" (that is made possible by *and* demanded by this fundamental epistemological claim) that I pursue in the figures of simplicity sketched by Kleist and Melville. Their figures expose what might come close to such a "thinking analogous to rational thinking" and with them, Kleist and Melville continue, experiment with, and test the assertions made by Leibnizian and Baumgartian aesthetics. Before we can look at the different dimensions of such sensate thinking their figures display, we need to briefly look at how Baumgarten—who is far more explicit in this than Leibniz—sketches such a putting into practice of the continuous relation between sensation and thinking.

## Sensate Thinking

When Hannes Böhringer begins his reconsiderations of aesthetics in his 1985 text *Attention im Clair-obscur: Die Avantgarde* with the assertion that "the world is chiaroscuro"[60] he echoes many of the concerns discussed above. Not only is a reevaluation of the potential of aesthetics at stake in such an assertion, but its relevance to how we approach knowledge and thinking. What Böhringer asserts—prosaic as it may sound—is that "[s]ome things are clear, many are unclear. At closer inspection, what is clear becomes diffuse, the dark by and by a little clearer.... Reality is mixed, chiaroscuro."[61] The challenging problem that arises from such a basic claim, however, is how one can "know" under those circumstances. To account for this chiaroscuro of the world *and* to sketch an *ars*—an art of thinking and acting—vis-à-vis this chiaroscuro was the aim of Baumgarten's aesthetics, and might be one of the reasons for the recently renewed interest in it. The dimension of his aesthetics that addressed the "art of thinking analogous to rational thinking" was to enhance our thinking of this mixed reality, something philosophy promises (or Baumgarten felt it did or should), only to restrict itself to conceptual-mathematical thinking. His discontent arose from the conviction that distinct enumeration and definition of attributes comes at the cost of losing the multidimensional and rich complexity of the whole. What distinctness establishes is the concept and definition of an object, which only comes about by way of abstraction. "§ 560 ... But what is abstraction, if not a loss? For similar reasons, one can only carve a marble ball from an irregular block of marble if paying the dues of a loss of material substance...." (*Ä*, 539) Thus, when attending to the perception of the whole (that is, when we are interested in *phenomena*, as given to the senses), the striving for enumeration of marks in view of distinctness misses the point. Accordingly, Baumgarten saw, a transformed notion of truth is relevant in these cases—an "aestheticologic truth": "§ 561 Thus, we presuppose that the striving for aestheticological truth first and foremost addresses material perfection (§ 558) and therefore tries to grasp the objects of a *singularly* determined metaphysical truth" (*Ä*, 539; emphasis added). Such an approach departs from measuring knowledge according to its universal applicability, and speaks for an assessment of singular phenomena. Without going into the implications for a thought of singularity here, it is crucial in our present context that Baumgarten ascribes a particular force to this type of aestheticological truth, which sensate thinking can arrive at, and thereby expands Leibniz's revaluation of obscure and confused ideas.[62] While Leibniz had advanced the possibility that clear-confused ideas can (re)cognize something, without its concept being clear-distinct, Baumgarten claimed not merely that, but attributed a specific force to this aesthetic mode of cognition. What is lost in terms of conceptual distinctness is gained in terms of sensate effect. Already the *Metaphysica* (1742) pointed to the greater effect of confused ideas, which his aesthetics would later turn into one of its crucial aspects. The *Metaphysica* notes that confusion is valued for heightening the force of a perception:

> § 517 The more marks a perception (idea) enfolds, the more powerful it is (§ 23, 515). Thus, an obscure perception including more marks than a clear one is more powerful than this latter, as much as a confused one including more marks than a distinct one is again more powerful than this latter one. PERCEPTIONS (ideas) that include more in themselves are called PREGNANT. Therefore, pregnant perceptions are more powerful.[63]

Being pregnant with marks or meanings, they have a greater force. They move. Or as Christoph Menke notes in his recent work on force as a central concept of aesthetics: "The sensate-beautiful image is in its ground and content indeterminable, but just in this manner it moves 'the whole world.'"[64] Baumgarten speaks in this context of the richness (*ubertas aesthetica*) of poetry, works of art, and phenomena in general; a richness due to the confused multiplicity of marks and lost as soon as these are conceptually cleared. Once individual marks are distinctly grasped, consciously enumerated, and the manifold implications conceptually dissolved, the very power and clarity of sensate thinking vanishes. Far from the deficiency attributed to clear-confused ideas by Descartes and Wolff, Baumgarten's aesthetics argues for the specific clarity of sensate thinking as an analogous mode of cognition. Solms points to the slight but significant difference between Baumgarten's notion of a pregnant perception (pointing to the translation of *praegnans* as meaningful),[65] and Kant's notion of an aesthetic idea as an idea that "occasions much thought, without, however, any definite thought, i.e. any concept, being capable of being adequate to it" (*CJ*, 197). Transcendentally framed, the Kantian aesthetic idea remains tied to intuition (*Anschauung*) and is of no epistemological import. It can only *occasion* thought. Baumgarten, on the contrary, holds that sensate thinking is, within its own fields, which are primarily art and life, an autonomous form of thinking. This link between art and life is crucial, as it broadens the scope of Baumgarten's aesthetics to a certain condition of thinking in life—a certain "life-knowledge," a thinking appropriate to the fact that "reality is mixed," as Böhringer phrased it. The assumption of the fields of art and life as comparable are a common trait of aesthetic thinking. Derrida remarks this link when speaking of reflective judgment in Kant: "In art and in life, wherever one must, according to Kant, proceed to reflective judgment and assume [by analogy with art] ... a finality the concept of which we do not have, *the example precedes*."[66] For Kant, reflective judgment, however, remains a self-reflective process, a moment, in which a subject experiences the free play of the faculties and the pleasure *in* self-reflection. It does not contribute in any way to philosophical, or cognitive, reflection. This is different for Baumgarten. His *Aesthetica* makes one of its aims to think about the *ars* that consists in thinking in a sensate manner. Sensate thinking is thinking, but its method, so to speak, is different from conceptual, rational thinking: its method is that it is without deductive method. It does not enumerate, test and clarify—Descartes was right to see this, but he unduly made it the criterion to deny it epistemological import. Instead, sensate thinking grasps at once, "without any discussion" as Menke puts it.[67] In that, it has its own clarity, conveying the complexity of the whole without distinguishing and enumerating its different marks, giving the complexity in one "simple" block. Its precision, its quality and value as an autonomous mode of cognition, can, however, only be "had" in a state of confusion.

The stress on the effect of the whole requires a certain "comportment" toward it. One can, but must not attend to the effect of the whole. It can easily be missed, if one strives for explication, and clarity in the sense of a dissolution of confusion. In chapter 2 we will observe two characters that perpetually miss what is before their eyes by striving for too much clarity. To think "analogous to rational thinking"—that is, to think sensately—requires a certain disposition. This disposition is not, as Baumgarten takes much care to stress, innate to particularly sensitive characters, beautiful souls born as aesthetes, but the result of aesthetic training and practice. By calling it an *ars* (*ars analogi rationis* (§1) *Ä*, 10), Baumgarten already stresses the fact that it *has* to be, and therefore *can* be, practiced. Practice is to improve our natural disposition to sensate thinking: It means training our "disposition" (as we will see Melville call it, too), or a "comportment"[68] vis-à-vis thinking, and refraining from conceptually grasping the object of knowledge, from testing and deducting. We will see especially Michael Kohlhaas and Billy Budd as two figures with which Kleist and Melville both sketch the process of such a *practice*. We will see in both that it has none of the lightness of theatricality or play; it is not practicing a role that would remain without consequences, where one could test a certain comportment in the realm of the art without any bearing on reality. When thinking of Kohlhaas and Billy Budd, we immediately see the earnestness of such practice. But it is an aesthetic exercise (*ascesis et exercitatio aesthetica* [§47]) (*Ä*, 38), one that forges and flexes the general, natural disposition to sensate thinking. The entire second section of the *Aesthetica* (§§28–46) speaks of this natural disposition to beautiful, or sensate, thinking (*dispositio naturalis animae totius ad pulcre cogitandum* [§28]) (*Ä*, 26), a natural disposition that needs to be enhanced, perfected, disciplined, we might say, to which the third section of the *Aesthetica* is dedicated (§§47–61). The state or character that Baumgarten sees at the horizon of such a process of training is what he calls the *felix aestheticus* (esp. §28 and §47): the effective, prosperous or happy (*felix*) sensate thinker (*aestheticus*). In order to see the potential of this for questions of affective, or sensate thinking, we should rather associate it to the athleticism of Kafka or Bacon, not to the theatrical enactment of a role. It is a bodily exercise, a training of habits. Certainly, Baumgarten did not envision this practice with the same forces and tensions involved as Kleist and Melville, or Kafka and Bacon will. Baumgarten phrased this in the relative calm of the 1750s, when the uncertainties, contingencies, and tensions of the modern experience had not yet been an issue. But the move is the same—it is a bodily practice of sensate or affective thinking that furnishes a different type of knowledge, for different purposes than logical, rational thought.

By looking at Kleist and Melville, this book pursues this disposition or state of mind under modern conditions. The most suitable term for it—in the cases studied—seems to be "simplicity." The term pays tribute both to the folded relation between perceptions and apperceptions—having the *pli* written into the very term—but also and more importantly to the simplemindedness with which this disposition might at first seem to be endowed. However, in all the cases displayed by Kleist and Melville, simplemindedness is far from mere stupidity. These figures think, but their thinking cannot be accounted for within our habitual registers of deduction, rationality, distinctness, etc. They expose and epitomize the type of sensate thinking sketched by Baumgarten, but take its implications far beyond Baumgarten, once again with incalculable, and very powerful, effects.

## Figures of Simplicity

Before turning to the different types of simplicity suggested in the next three chapters, I would like to close this one with a brief look at Melville's novel *Pierre; or, The Ambiguities* (1852), written shortly before Melville was to turn to tales in that same year. *Pierre*, Melville's most enigmatic and critically only recently appreciated novel,[69] phrases many of the aesthetic and poetological concerns discussed in this chapter, and it would be necessary at another occasion to read it in detail as almost Melville's program for writing tales. *Pierre*'s poetological passages and Pierre's interior monologues largely *state* what the tales will then *do*.

Much like *Moby-Dick*, *Pierre* satirically mocks the philosophers. After the main character, Pierre, a writer, has left his mother's substantial inheritance and his fiancée Lucy behind to prove his loyalty to his recently come forth, illegitimate, and unacknowledged half-sister Isabel, toward whom he feels a

## Aesthetics

spontaneous and mysterious sympathy, both move to the city and live poorly in an old warehouse occupied by an intellectual crowd of people, "mostly artists of various sorts; painters, or sculptors, or indigent students, or teachers of languages, or poets, or fugitive French politicians, or German philosophers."[70] With ironic undertone, the narrator notes that although

> very fine and spiritual upon the whole... the vacuity of their exchequers leads them to reject the coarse materialism of Hobbes, and incline to the airy exaltations of the Berkelyan philosophy. Often groping in vain in their pockets, they can not but give in to the Descartian vortices; while the abundance of leisure in their attics (physical and figurative), unites with the leisure in their stomachs, to fit them in an eminent degree for that undivided attention indispensable to the proper digesting of the sublimated Categories of Kant; especially as Kant (can't) is the one great palpable fact in their pervadingly impalpable lives. (*P*, 267)

The airiness of these characters—to whom Pierre feels drawn as much as to the mysterious darkness of Isabel—and their impalpable lives stand in stark contrast to the steadfast characters of the tales; even Bartleby is palpable to the extent that he appears solid (although perhaps not understandable) compared to the lofty and wavering Pierre, despite the stony solidity his name announces. Pierre is torn between his penchant for philosophy and skepticism, and his will to abide by his inexplicable sympathy for Isabel, a sympathy that remains as unexplained as Isabel's exact background. It foreshadows the inexplicable antipathy Claggart feels for Billy Budd, as we will see in chapter 3. But he is much less of an affective character than Claggart; we see Pierre, the skeptic, entangle himself in helpless and bottomless ruminations, endlessly deliberating on the justice of his behavior, on the nature of his affection for Isabel, on his moral justification to abandon "his hereditary duty to his mother" (*P*, 106) and on his worth as a writer. The novel ends tragically, and his skepticism has led Pierre nowhere. The joke is certainly partly on "Kant," or philosophy intending to excavate a priori concepts free from skepticism, but whose—for that purpose indispensable—restriction of thinking to conceptual thinking eliminates the realm of the affective and destabilizes what it was meant to solidify. From among the miscellaneous variety of philosophies that are touched on, *Pierre* returns to Kant repeatedly, and always in a satirical fashion similar to that we read in the passage above (*P*, 293, also ch. 20, 22).

More interestingly for this context, Melville's ironies concerning philosophy's fixation on clarity reach their peak in *Pierre*. The novel intensely engages with philosophy, by having in Pierre one of its greatest zealots and admirers, yet also ridiculing him for it, by mimicking philosophical tone and discourse, whereby Pierre wishes to get at the bottom of his affection for Isabel, yet turning the novel into the self-contradictory, intensely twisted narrative it is. But the novel also already foreshadows narrative projects to come, in which this engagement will take a different "generic" form. After 1852, Melville turned to tales, and *Pierre* stands at the threshold of this. The tales, as we will see, engage much less explicitly with philosophy and the pool of names so frequent in *Moby-Dick* and *Pierre*, yet perform philosophical moves all the same. Although Pierre remains entangled in his endless ruminations—"ineffectual speculations" (*BBS*, 84) from which Billy Budd, as we shall see, opts to refrain—Melville also has him make attempts toward the affirmation of the inexplicable as inexplicable. Pierre never follows through, but we feel that he knows what he is missing. After an initial meeting with Isabel, when he is intrigued by her and her mysterious ways, he assures himself that he will refrain from unraveling the enigma of Isabel. We hear him meditate on it—hearing echoes of the debate on clarity and obscurity discussed in this chapter:

> In her life there was an unraveled plot; and he felt that unraveled it would eternally remain to him. No slightest hope or dream had he, that what was dark and mournful in her would ever be cleared up into some coming atmosphere of light and mirth. Like all youths, Pierre had conned his novel-lessons; he had read more novels than most persons of his years; but their false, inverted attempts at systematizing eternally unsystemizable elements; their audacious, intermeddling impotency, in trying to unravel, and spread out, and classify, the more thin than gossamer threads which make up the complex web of life; these things over Pierre had no power now. Straight through their helpless miserableness he pierced; the one sensational truth in him, transfixed like beetles all the speculative lies in them.... [H]e saw that... while the countless tribes of common novels laboriously spin veils of mystery, only to complacently clear them up at last; and while the countless tribes of common dramas do but repeat the same; yet the profounder emanations of the human mind, intending to illustrate all that can be humanly known of human life; these never unravel their own intricacies, and have no proper endings; but in imperfect, unanticipated, and disappointing sequels (as mutilated stumps), hurry to abrupt intermergings with the eternal tides of time and fate. (*P,* 141)

Pierre asserts that he no longer wants to systematize the unsystematizable, the complex web of life, and rejects, as a writer, the novel as a literary genre, because he sees it tending toward such systematization, trying to spread out the reasons of things, to unravel darkness into clarity. *Pierre*, the text, certainly counters these "audacious" yet "impotent" attempts by forgoing character development, linear narrative structure, and closure—challenging the very genre of the novel, due to which it was largely unsuccessful and remains even critically fairly little examined. Melville's last novel *The Confidence-Man* (1857)—reemerging from tale writing, which had occupied him from 1853 to 1856 exclusively, with the exception of *Israel Potter* (1855), published in installments largely to secure an income—will return to this poetological point and claim the right of the novel to keep unexplained what life itself could and would not explain. It is this claim in *The Confidence-Man* of a "superior irrationalism" that Melville embodies in his tales, written between 1853 and 1856 (with the belated addition of *Billy Budd*, unfinished at his death, and posthumously published in 1924), as we will see exemplified in three of them. The same idea of the vanity of attempting to classify, clarify, and unravel the complexity of life also drives *Pierre*. Yet, while the novel refrains from clarification, we find Pierre—despite his earlier affirmations of unraveled darkness—unable to refrain from deliberating on the nature of his affection for Isabel and the rights and wrongs of his loyalty to her. He is continually struck by the vanity in seeking to come to a clear and final stance by way of deliberation, but is incessantly drawn into it again. At one point, when seeing the futility of it, Pierre pitches "gray philosophizing" against "life":

> For there is no faith, and no stoicism, and no philosophy, that a mortal man can possibly evoke, which will stand the final test of a real impassioned onset of Life and Passion upon him. Then all the fair philosophic or Faith-phantoms that he raises from the mist, slide away and disappear as ghosts at cock-crow. For Faith and philosophy are air, but events are brass. Amidst his gray philosophizing, Life breaks upon a man like a morning. (*P*, 289)

The "real impassioned onset of Life" that is held up against gray philosophizing is not to be understood as a turn away from philosophy. For that, Melville's writing is too strongly engaged with it and this widely tentacled engagement—Melville's oft-noted eclecticism—also preempts any reduction to one philosophical source or adversary. Only one of these critical interlocutors for Melville was Kant. But in response to philosophy's—among others, Kant's—striving for clarity, which *Pierre* thematizes, his tales insist on the inexplicable. And at the same time, the figures they invent—Benito Cereno, Captain Amasa Delano, Billy Budd, John Claggart, Bartleby—tackle the problem of an affective mode of thinking that rests on the assumption of a relation between thinking and sensation. While the skeptic Pierre is laughable and lovable for his endless ruminations, showing the failure of, and perhaps inescapability of, the attempt to reasonably come to well-weighed judgments, Melville's tales demonstrate a different disposition toward thinking in view of the complex web of life. Where Pierre is overly complicated, we will find especially Billy Budd and Bartleby—and their astounding matches Michael Kohlhaas and Käthchen von Heilbronn—to be of stunning simplicity. They practice a sensate thinking that adheres, as best they can, to the "profounder emanations of the human mind, intending to illustrate all that can be humanly known of human life" (*P,* 141), what we saw Pierre hope for. As noted in the same passage for these profounder, un-novel-like emanations of the human mind, the figures of simplicity of the tales "never unravel their own intricacies, and have no proper endings; but in imperfect, unanticipated, and disappointing sequels (as mutilated stumps), hurry to abrupt intermergings with the eternal tides of time and fate" (*P,* 141). In contrast to the unraveling writing of novels that takes the space and time to explicate, the tale might answer best to this. In what follows, focus will be laid on the sensate thinking displayed by these figures of simplicity, which is inseparable from the form of their narration. This is what—despite everything—the subsequent chapters hope to unravel.

## Chapter 2

# Sentimentalities

Coming out of these discontents with Kant, a name that for better or for worse came to stand in for philosophy's striving for clarity of conceptual thinking, Kleist and Melville devised in their writings an approach to thinking and knowledge that takes the "complex web of life"—its contingencies and obscurities, the preliminarity and precariousness of all judgments taken under its conditions—into account. This is certainly an endeavor of modern literature at large, if we think of Caygill's list of para-philosophical reactions to the epistemological shifts around the time of 1800.[1]

What, then, is specific to Kleist and Melville? I would like to suggest here that it is precisely their figures of simplicity, and the mode of thinking they are asking us to consider and explore. They ask how, without the yardstick of Enlightenment reason that had vouched for or at least held out the promise of certainty, clarity, and last grounds, and when being immersed in the uncertainties and contingencies that emerge as a result of this, how (and what) we can know. What is a mode of thinking adjusted to the uncertainties of life? Kleist and Melville pursue this question in the tests to which they put their protagonists, in the experiments they conduct with the latters' capacities to assess a situation and their ability to operate on the basis of that assessment. The compelling aspect of these experiments is not so much their outcome—they do not really deliver "positive" results and reliable insights. At times, we see them fail in their endeavors to figure out the situation. Circumstances get in the way, or their own rashness. At other times we sense that they do succeed, but in a way that we might call success only with great reserve. To what extent do Michael Kohlhaas or Billy Budd succeed, given their death at the end? Or can we even say that knowledge is a concern of theirs at all? Certainly not, if we understand by knowledge a graspable and perhaps even generalizable body of acquired certainties and verified facts. What is compelling is rather *how* all of these textual experiments pursue the processes that go into assessing a situation: how they dissect the registration of minute impressions and the turns taken by the protagonists to preliminarily evaluate what they find themselves immersed in. What is compelling is how they put the affective dimensions of these impressions and turns to the fore. We might suggest at this point—something that is to be tested throughout the next three chapters—that Kleist and Melville deliver an argument, in literary garment, on the *subterranean* processes that go into that which surfaces as "thinking." They display with great textual care the minute observations, the bodily twitches, the incalculable turns of bodies and events that guide their figures' conduct, their "conclusions" and their "reasoning." In that sense, their texts are considered here as a series of *études* on consciousness, knowledge production, and thinking. Within a post-Kantian epistemological framework, fully affirming contingency and epistemological uncertainty as modern conditions, Kleist and Melville ask after the relation between affectivity and thinking and implicitly respond to the aesthetic debates we considered in the last chapter on the relation between affectivity and rationality. What is specific to their positions within these debates is that their texts demonstrate the epistemological operations of affectivity, rather than merely expose the instabilities of rationally acquired understanding. On the one hand, these operations are shown to be bound to a complex web of infinitely small perceptions, to which the figures are exposed when situated within a widely ramified network of coincidences; a network that continuously branches out and diversifies, and incessantly complicates and redefines the situations they are in. On the other hand, the texts also present the figures as *maneuvering* these situations, as responding to these pressing situations with lesser or greater efficiency and success. The figures operate—to a lesser or greater degree, as we will see in the preliminary (and somewhat ironic) "classification" of three "types" of simplicity—with a state of mind, or a mode of understanding that I suggest be called *affective* or *sensate thinking*.[2]

In a letter to his sister Ulrike, Kleist suggests that life is such a difficult thing, because "incessantly and always again anew one has to draw a card without knowing which is trump; ... incessantly and always again anew one has to act without knowing what is the right thing" (*SW IV/1*, 490; my translation). One is forced to act upon the basis of assessments, and knowledge that is immersed in the complexities and instabilities of life, without being certain which way to turn. Yet turn one must. Kleist and Melville dwell on this problem with their extraordinary figures, whose predicament it is—within the uncertainties of *life*, which no certainty of Enlightenment reason comes to clear up—to draw a card without knowing which is trump. Realizing knowledge to be open-ended, experimentally gathered, procedural, and always reevaluated, they stand at the threshold of modernity, and their figures of simplicity are the response to this insight: They do not lament the loss of certainty, but affirm a preliminary, "simple" assessment. They do not strive for objective truth, but rather for a perspective, for a pragmatic positioning within the web of circumstances. What motivates and propels their efforts is not to achieve a distance from where to *judge* the situation, but to remain immersed and find an answer to the pressing questions: How to react to a given situation; or, how best to maneuver in a given turn of events? How to respond to a demand made, a blow dealt? How to "understand" things in the forward-rushing state of affairs?

In our first pair of tales—Kleist's *The Betrothal in Santo Domingo* (1811) and Melville's *Benito Cereno* (1855)—these circumstantial challenges are clearly determining the course of the narratives. The problem both main characters are faced with is: What is going on?—and of the three "types" of simplicity, they are without doubt the ones most striving for clarification. What Kleist and Melville examine in these two tales is how the circumstantial challenges are not really faced but, rather, are fitted into ready-made, preconceived schemata, and thus circumnavigated. Both tales expose largely the same problem, namely, how in a situation of epistemological uncertainty, one is likely to slip up, to cloud the situation and avoid the challenges it poses. Both figures remain very much immersed in it and are subject to a perceptive and affective assessment of it. They affectively register that something is not quite what it seems, that something calls for being figured out, and respond to this with over-attentively registering every move and minor detail. But we see them fall back on ready-made images and preconceived notions to explain to themselves what is going on. Overly quick to place all they see within black and white schemata, and mistaking these for well-weighed conclusions, they neither arrive at the desired clear picture of the situation, nor at a position toward it. Ready to avoid the volatility of sensate thinking, they evoke sentimental images and reconfigure what they see according to the pathos they muster.

Let us look at how this comes about. Unraveling against the background of the slave revolts on Saint Domingue (contemporary Haïti) shortly after the French Revolution,[3] both narratives employ this historical setting as experimental terrain to examine how their main characters attempt to figure out the situation they find themselves in. At a moment when established power relations are challenged and the established (racist) frames of reference contested, the two white men—in complicated circumstances, so to speak—are required to figure out if they can trust their black interlocutors. Throughout the entire narratives, both remain occupied with understanding the situation and ask themselves incessantly what is going on. In *The Betrothal of Santo Domingo*, we find Gustav von der Ried, a Swiss officer serving in the French colonial army on Saint Domingue, who, at the time of the revolts under General Dessalines, at night, knocks at the gate of a plantation. Formerly owned by the French planter Monsieur de Villeneuve, it is now ruled by de Villeneuve's former slaves, as the reader learns at the opening. Gustav seeks food and shelter for himself and his uncle's family who stayed behind in hiding, fleeing Dessalines's advancing troops. Upon entering the house, he only finds the black housekeeper Babekan and her daughter Toni, with the new master of the house, Congo Hoango, gone on a foray, and Gustav embarks on a series of attempts to verify if he can trust the women. In *Benito Cereno*, one day in 1799, Amasa Delano, captain of the

American trader *The Bachelor*, boards the Spanish slaver *San Dominick* to offer his nautical assistance as the vessel's rigging is badly torn and the ship appears to be in distress. With growing unease, he registers the disarray on board, the bizarre behavior of the Spanish captain Benito Cereno, the hovering sense of threat, and wonders what is going on. We see these attempts to evaluate the situation fail in both cases. To a certain extent, we have to grant them that they are framed. The fact of a successful slave revolt is skillfully disguised by the Africans on the *San Dominick*, and Gustav is led to believe that Babekan and Toni are genuinely hospitable, while in fact they have orders to keep anyone white detained until Hoango's return. But the ingenious theatrical camouflages—these exceptionally difficult test environments Kleist and Melville devise—do not satisfactorily explain why the men fail to get what is going on. In addition to the difficult setup, to them being literally set up, we see them continuously fall back on preconceptions and sentimental images that foreclose the understanding they strive for. They sentimentally reduce the complexity of what goes on before their eyes, and are of a simplicity that largely misses the plot.

On a second level, Kleist and Melville also make use of the historical scenario to test the reader's sentimental resolutions. Just as the rebels ingeniously camouflage the reality of a revolt for Gustav and Delano, Kleist and Melville explicitly dress their tales as realist prose: with references to historical events, historical figures, dates, and places. We are strongly invited to situate the narrative within real historical events, when *The Betrothal in Santo Domingo* announces in a first sentence that the ensuing story happened "at the beginning of this century, at the time when the blacks were murdering the whites" (*BSD*, 231/*SW II/4*, 7),[4] a reference that is narrowed down a few lines later to "the year 1803," supported by reference to the historical figures involved in the struggle: "general Dessalines ... advancing against Port-au-Prince at the head of thirty thousand negros" (*BSD*, 232/*SW II/4*, 10). The opening of *Benito Cereno* places the narrated events in "the year 1799" (*BC*, 46) and references the Haitian slave revolts by christening the vessel that Delano boards *San Dominick*. In both cases, these clearly marked historical references, combined with the racial prejudices the protagonists display, have confused the critical reception. Due to the realist depiction of historical events, doubts arose about the authors' political opinions on race and slavery. And when it was discovered that in Melville's case *Benito Cereno* builds on the historical Captain Delano's *Narratives of Voyages and Travels* of 1817, the tale's aesthetic value was contested also on the grounds of being a mere rewriting of historical sources.[5] It has been shown that both tales are not unambiguously depicting a historical reality, although they ostensibly purport to do so with their frequent references to dates, places, and historical figures. Tracing the different dates and references in Kleist's *The Betrothal in Santo Domingo*, Christine Lubkoll is right to argue that the text is no unambiguously realist depiction of historical events, and rather works with a rich layering of different historical dates, which induces fundamental irritations in the reading process.[6]

Such dense referential layering has also been demonstrated for *Benito Cereno*.[7] Thus, when reading these tales we have to take the complications into account that result from an explicit pretense to realist aesthetics while distorting it at the same time with ambiguous, sometimes contradictory references. Instead of presenting allegedly realist (and therefore potentially racist, and politically problematic) accounts, the tales rather *subject* the reader to the chauvinistic and at times sensationalist tone of the narrative voices and thereby *challenge* us to deal with the straightforward assumption of realist representation. As much as they conduct experiments in perception with their main characters *in* the narrative, their rhetorical strategies equally inflict these experiments of understanding and the treacherous mixture of readings, perceptions, and preconceptions upon us as reader. Even before we begin reading, the titles already do their best to insinuate that we should expect a love story in Kleist's case and the story of the (mis)fortunes of the Spanish captain Benito Cereno in Melville's case. If we are ready to remain there, we fall prey to the same blindness as Gustav and Delano, as I will show. We must beware not to base our assessment of the tales' aesthetics on mimetic accuracies or even the writers' alleged opinions, as has been the fate of both tales. Rather, we have to take the rhetorical strategies of both—their experimenting with formations of knowledge and with the pitfalls of clichés, and the way these experiments are textually conducted—as the yardstick of their aesthetics.

## Befuddling the Senses

### *(The Betrothal in Santo Domingo)*

Kleist's tale was first published in August von Kotzebue's journal *The Ingenuous or Berlin Gazette for Educated, Unbiased Readers* (*Der Freimüthige oder Berlinisches Unterhaltungsblatt für gebildete, unbefangene Leser*). With one of its last contributions—*The Betrothal in Santo Domingo*—the journal lived up to its name by putting its readers' biases—the absence of which was postulated in the journal's title—to an intricate test. At the opening of the tale, the narrative voice immediately sets the tone for this, in that it rings with unmistakable sensationalism, when it notes the deceitfulness and bloodthirst of Congo Hoango. "Such indeed was his inhuman thirst for revenge that he even insisted on the elderly Babekan and her young daughter, a fifteen-year-old mestiza called Toni, taking part in this ferocious war" (BSD, 232).[8] Throughout the tale, the narrator's voice, "ideologically distorted and politically incorrect, without a doubt,"[9] continues to have a sensationalist ring to it, and we can feel the excitement mixed in with imminent danger and fear. What it resonates with is the "sound effect of white reactionism, white noise in the truest sense of the word, obfuscating the political senses."[10] This obfuscation of Gustav's metaphorical (political) senses ultimately drives the plot and underlies the uncomfortable narrative tone we pick up. It is, however, masterfully contrasted by Kleist with Gustav's incessant yet unsuccessful attempts to clarify the situation by employment of his literal (physical) senses. This second level is also introduced right at the beginning of the narrative, when all three main characters—Gustav, Toni, and Babekan—repeatedly and explicitly pose the question, "Who are you?" It initiates an investigative process that mobilizes the literal senses and alternates throughout the narrative between sight and touch as its two main devices. Visual and haptic senses are equally employed to furnish perceptions that are intended to clear up the obscure situation. "You are someone I can trust; in your face, like a gleam of light, there is a tinge of my own complexion" (BSD, 236/SW II/4, 18). With this, Gustav begins to tell Babekan who he is and what he wants from them. The whole of *The Betrothal in Santo Domingo* works to unravel this assertion and the complications it is already shown to contain. Gustav postulates that he can trust Babekan and explains this with her relatively light complexion. Because there is a tinge of Gustav's own complexion in Babekan's, he decides (for the time being) to trust her. The semicolon between postulating (You are someone I can trust;) and explaining its motivation (in your face ...), however, marks the break between the two registers that are continuously pitted against each other with the positivist belief that one follows from the other: that of trust and that of empirical observation. Toni will later confirm this break, announced already at this point by the semicolon, in her dying exclamation that Gustav should have trusted her, realizing that trust cannot be deduced from "empirical" evidence of skin color, as Gustav seems to believe. To assume that it can is Gustav's fatal mistake, and *The Betrothal in Santo Domingo* exposes the pitfalls of such a simple understanding of reading processes. Nevertheless, the tale pursues Gustav's flawed attempts to understand whom he is facing and what the situation is on the plantation. And in order to assess if he can trust Toni, Gustav closely examines every minor move. As already mentioned, Kleist creates an exceptionally difficult environment for him to succeed in doing so.

> Babekan, who suffered from consumption as a result of a cruel flogging that had been inflicted on her when she was a girl, used on these occasions [of a stranger seeking shelter] to dress up her young daughter in her best clothes, for Toni's yellowish complexion made her very useful for the purpose of this hideous deception; she urged her to refuse the strangers no caresses short of the final intimacy, which was forbidden her on pain of death; and when Congo Hoango returned with his negro troop from his expeditions in the surrounding district, immediate death would be the fate of the wretches who had allowed themselves to be beguiled by these stratagems. (*BSD*, 232)[11]

When feigning trustworthiness, Babekan counts on the "black and white" imagery in Gustav's head, and his readiness to go by complexion and to in fact allow himself to be beguiled by these stratagems.

But let us begin with the processes of observation and experimentation, the perceptive processes by means of which Gustav struggles to confirm his proclamation of trust. A key scene in this respect is the footbath scene. After Gustav has entered the house, introduced himself to Babekan, and been invited to stay the night, Toni is asked to prepare a footbath for him. Bowl in hand, she shows him to his room. A scene ensues that is orchestrated by Toni to mollify his worries of betrayal. Up until this point a very outspoken and clever young woman, Toni kneels before Gustav to prepare the bath. She suddenly turns rather shy and passive, showing all signs of feminine modesty and gentleness, quite unlike her rather forthcoming character until now. Accordingly, she appears coy and lovely to Gustav, who still fears betrayal and for his life, and, seeing her so lovely, decides to take the opportunity and test her heart. He goes about it by first noticing her well-arranged attractive looks, and his eyes slide from one eroticized body part to the next. "Her hair, in its abundance of dark curls, had rolled over her young breasts when she knelt down; there was something extraordinarily graceful about her limbs and about the long lashes that drooped over her lowered eyes" (*BSD*, 243/*SW II/4*, 35–36). Despite being repelled by her dark complexion, he pulls her onto his lap, and inquires about her marital status, teasingly asking "whether she was already engaged to be married" (*BSD*, 244/*SW II/4*, 36), noticing not only her barely murmured negation, but also how she lowered "her great black eyes with a sweet air of modesty" (*BSD*, 244/*SW II/4*, 36). When she shyly names a young suitor, explaining that she refused him due to her young age, Gustav dismisses this hint about being underage with a far-fetched Swiss proverb, which counts girls as young as fourteen years and seven weeks fit for marriage. Insisting on the topic of her betrothal, he "tenderly stroked the hair back from her forehead and said: 'Perhaps he didn't attract you?'" When she responds evasively with laughter, Gustav persists and he whispers jokingly into her ear, "whether it was necessary to be a white man in order to gain her favour." Again she evades an answer, and "suddenly, after a fleeting pensive pause, and with a most charming blush spreading suddenly over her sunburnt face, sank against his breast." She seemingly lends him her ear and as her replies of laughter and blushing meet his expectations, he allows himself to be beguiled. The narrator is quick to confirm that hardly has Toni leaned against Gustav's chest than his doubts have vanished and, "feeling that the hand of God had swept away all his anxieties," he takes her in his arms. She is now his "darling girl" (all *BSD*, 244/*SW II/4*, 38) and it is impossible for him to believe that she means to deceive him.

> He could not possibly believe that all these signs of emotion she showed him were merely the wretched antics of cold-hearted,

hideous treachery. The thoughts that had preyed on his mind were dispersed like a host of ominous birds; he reproached himself for having failed even for a moment to appreciate her true feelings, and as he rocked her on his knees and drank in the sweet breath that rose from her lips towards him, he pressed a kiss on her forehead, as if in token of reconciliation and forgiveness. (*BSD*, 244–45)[12]

Seeing a tender woman, he cannot believe that she feigns such devotion and now believes to no longer misconstrue (*verkannt*) her true intentions. This allows him to recognize her, in a second move, as the double of his former fiancée Marianne, a misfiring recognition that ultimately leads to the betrothal. Christian Moser rightly calls Gustav's examination of Toni's heart a process of projection, in which Gustav labors "with blind pertinacity"[13] to turn the figure in front of his eyes into the appearance of Marianne. What started as fear of hideous deception is transformed at this point into the belief in recognition and leads momentarily to the second "recognition" of the betrothal.

The text signals to us that this is no full elimination of doubt: Gustav could only "not possibly believe" (*es war ihm unmöglich zu glauben*) that she betrayed him, so that the negation of what he cannot believe bars doubt for the moment, yet without installing trust. The fear of "wretched antics of cold-hearted, hideous treachery" are still ringing through Gustav's assertion that *this* it could not possibly be. The same goes for his reproach to have misconceived (*verkannt*) her true feelings. The text gives us the negation and his reproach for it, not any affirmative quality in its place. Gustav's uneasiness is alleviated precisely by finding traces of familiarity and resemblances. The remote resemblance he had noticed in Toni's face at the beginning of the scene has grown into an "extraordinary" (*BSD*, 245) one, and makes Toni Marianne's double. Unable to work with the ambiguity of Toni's brown face, yet wishing to resolve its ambiguity, Gustav covers it by projecting white images on it. Upon "recognizing" Marianne in Toni, he begins to tell the story of Marianne's sacrifice—more as an address to himself than to Toni. His recollections move him to shed tears for Marianne's true love, which caused her on her way to the guillotine strategically to refuse to recognize Gustav in the crowd, to prevent him from sharing her fate. Toni, at this junction, is "overcome by a sense of human compassion, and impulsively followed him, throwing her arms round his neck and mingling her tears with his" (*BSD*, 247/*SW II/4*, 43). Leaving the nature of her compassion aside for the moment—we will see later that her tears correspond to her own sentimental resolution of the situation—we have arrived at the critical moment where Toni's art of deception meets Gustav's readiness to be beguiled by it, and at which in turn his readiness opens up new options for her. Right after this nanosecond of mixing tears, however, things get out of hand again and a scene ensues whose sexual nature is suggested, but whose exact quality is left unspoken. The reader is instead confronted with a gap in the narrative: with ostensible sobriety we are told that "[t]here is no need to report what happened next, for it will be clear to anyone who has followed the narrative thus far" (*BSD*, 247/*SW II/4*, 43). Faced with this crucial challenge to readability, we are implicitly invited to fall back on the interpretation that the title had already offered: this is the moment of the betrothal in Santo Domingo. If we opt for such a (ultimately sentimental) resolution of the obscure knot in front of us, we underread, as I would like to suggest, what ensues after this turning point. All that becomes clear, really, is that afterward we hear rather pragmatic considerations rule. Gustav "for the time being at least... understood that he was saved, and that... there was nothing for him to fear from the girl" (*BSD*, 247/*SW II/4*, 43), and Toni from then on prefers to be a white girl, as this seems her best bet. Later, when she is trying to side with Gustav's party, and is about to leave the plantation with them, she tells her mother: "'I have not betrayed you; I am a white girl and betrothed to this young man whom you are holding prisoner; I belong to the race of those with whom you are openly at war'" (*BSD*, 267/*SW II/4*, 81–82). But when we get there, Gustav's (politically and sexually) giddied senses will get it all wrong again, with fatal results.

Let us remain for a moment longer with the crucial footbath scene. Sight has been evoked as a means to evaluate the situation, but proved an unreliable method. Gustav's incapacity to see Toni without assimilating her to familiar images had already been noted explicitly by Toni herself, when Gustav was received in the beginning in Babekan's room. Relating their first encounter at the door, Toni alludes to Gustav's incapacity to see anything but his own preconceptions, when telling her mother "how she had held the lantern in such a way that its full beam had fallen on her face. 'But,' she said, 'his imagination was obsessed with blackamoors and negroes, and if a lady from Paris or Marseilles had opened the door to him, he would have taken her for a negress" (*BSD*, 239).[14] This is a moment of intense irony, to which Gustav remains entirely ignorant. In Old German, Gustav's surname "Ried" means "Moor" (swamp), and in a sense, he is literally from the swamps, walking on highly treacherous ground that might give way at any moment. On a second, even more significant level, the German "Moor" is phonetically identical to "Mohr," a term for African commonly used in Kleist's time. When Toni accuses Gustav's imagination to be filled with *Mohren und Negern*, she accuses Gustav of being full of himself and unable to see her. Additionally, her seemingly exaggerated assertion that his racially tainted imagination would have even turned a lady from Paris or Marseille into a black woman is the second ironic moment that Kleist plays out here. Although it escapes Gustav, the irony resonates with the reader, when we learn a few lines later that Toni is in fact a French-Caribbean woman precisely from Paris or Marseille. When asked after her daughter's parentage, Babekan reveals that Toni's father was a merchant from Marseille, and that Babekan's pregnancy and Toni's birth took place in Paris. Not an exaggeration on Toni's side, thus, but rather hitting the nail on the head, knowing full well that with the color of her skin, whether a lady from Paris or Marseille, she will look all the same, that is, black, to Gustav.[15] Again, Toni rightly notes that no matter how carefully she illuminates her face, he would not be able to see. Faced with her reproaches, he exonerates himself by blaming his blindness on the empirical obstacle of her hat, which was drawn too deeply into her face for him to see, and tries to do better this time by pulling her toward him. "The stranger, putting his arm round her gently, said in some embarrassment that the hat she had been wearing had prevented him from seeing her face. 'If I had been able,' he continued, pressing her ardently to his breast, 'to look into your eyes as I am doing now...'" (*BSD*, 239/*SW II/4*, 26), he would have trusted her. Touch is evoked here as supplement for the unreliability of sight and in a permanent back and forth, the narrative continuously employs these two modes of perception—sight and touch—as means of understanding. Both, however, prove to be unreliable and inconclusive.

The haptic, however, recurs in the narrative with a specific force. The grasping of hands in the face of the dark is a recurring motif throughout, and alludes to a mode of understanding and of assessing the possibility of trust by the touch of hands, with the haptic supplementing the gaze. The motif oscillates in *The Betrothal in Santo Domingo* between the promise of immediate or unadulterated perception, and the threat of erupting violence. On the one hand, hands imply bodily immediacy. The clasp of a hand promises access to information, such as body temperature, transpiration betraying anxiety, tension, and pressure, that escapes the eye. On the other hand, hands also—and significantly for this tale—have the potential for violence; where looks *could* kill, hands do. They enforce, drag along, and are raised against. Throughout the narrative, hands mark the striving to get beyond treacherous imagery, to get out of the structures of racially biased perceptions, but at the same time are shown to harbor and exert the violence whereby fear and bias are fuelled. In a way, they produce the "matters-of-fact" faster than their promise to understand these "matters-of-fact" can be kept. We find such a rush of precipitating occurrences, for example, in the scuffle (*Handgemenge*) that ensues after Gustav first enters the plantation. While Toni is about to open the door for him, the young boy Nanky closes the yard gate behind him, as he is instructed to retain any white person on the premises.

> The stranger was puzzled by this and asked the boy, whom to his horror he recognized at close quarters as a negro: 'Who lives in this settlement?' And on hearing his answer that since Monsieur de Villeneuve's death the property had been taken over by the negro Hoango, he was just about to *hurl* the boy to the ground, *snatch* the key to the main gate *from his hand* and escape into the open, when Toni, *holding* the lantern, came out of the house. 'Quick!' she said, *seizing his hand* and *drawing* him towards the door, 'come in

here!' As she spoke she was careful to *hold* the lantern in such a way that its beam would fall full on her face. 'Who are you?' exclaimed the stranger, *struggling* to free himself and gazing, surprised for more reasons than one, at her lovely young figure. 'Who lives in this house in which you tell me I shall find refuge?' 'No one, I swear by the heavens above us, but my mother and myself!' said the girl. And she renewed with great eagerness her efforts to *draw* him in after her. 'What, no one!' cried the stranger, *snatching his hand from hers* and taking a step backwards. 'Did this boy not tell me just now that a negro called Hoango is living here?' 'No, I tell you!' said the girl, stamping her foot with an air of vexation, 'and although the house belongs to a monster of that name, he is absent just now and ten miles away!' And so saying she *dragged* him into the house *with both hands*, ordered the boy to tell no one who had arrived, *seized* the stranger *by the hand* as they passed through the door, and led him upstairs to her mother's room. (*BSD*, 234; emphases added)[16]

This scuffle and the ensuing sense of vexation and surprise on both sides sets the plot in motion. The incident occurs between two scenes where hands figure less forcefully, and rather as means of perception, as emblems of an attempt to understand better. Before Babekan orders Toni to open the door to Gustav, she herself has already answered his knock. Opening a window, she asked him to identify himself, whereupon he returned the question and extended his hand to grasp hers. "'By the Blessed Virgin and all the saints,' said the stranger in a low voice, placing himself under the window, 'before I tell you, answer me one question!' And reaching out through the darkness of the night to grasp the old woman's hand, he asked: 'Are you a negress?'" (*BSD*, 233/*SW II/4*, 11–12). As if to see in the dark, he extended his hand to touch hers. The same hand that Gustav fears might kill him is touched in the promise of an understanding that can bypass the unreadability of the face. Seeing him through, however, she answered: "'Well, you must surely be a white man, since you would rather look this pitch-black night in the face than a negress!'" (*BSD*, 233/*SW II/4*, 12), and left his question unanswered. Once the scuffle gets Gustav inside the house, Babekan worries about Gustav's trustworthiness and asks him with reference to his rapier whether he intends to repay their hospitality with betrayal. He again grasps her hand, as if to dispel her doubts and convince her of his good intentions. "He seized the old woman's hand, pressed it to his heart... saying: 'You see before you the most wretched of men, but not an ungrateful villain!'" (*BSD*, 235/*SW II/4*, 16). Uncertain, however, whom she sees, despite having just put her glasses on, Babekan merely repeats the question she addressed to him earlier: "Who are you?" The multifaceted ways, in which hands are being grasped, held, torn away, pressed, or wiped across foreheads epitomize the mutual, but particularly Gustav's attempts to determine the possibility of trust, only to find it destabilized and yielding to distrust again. The ambiguity of the employment of haptic perception is the emblem of this endless testing. The touch of skin, whose color is the taint in Gustav's perception, is drawn on to verify haptically what cannot be ascertained visually, but at the same time, each touch harbors the potential threats it is sought out to dispel. Gustav's quest proves only the inevitability of endless testing and the endless deferral of trust, if one wishes to establish it on the basis of "evidence." In Gustav's case, it leads to nothing but misconception.

The attempt to verify trust in the way Gustav intends it returns us to the critical omission in the text. It is Gustav's test of Toni that leads to the betrothal (*Verlobung*), which the title had invited us to expect. Gustav begins the test by sleight of hand—"knowing that there was only one way of finding out whether the girl had sincere feelings or not *he drew her down* on to his knees" (*BSD*, 244/*SW II*/4, 36; emphasis added). And he also ends it thus, literally wiping the distrustful thoughts off his forehead, which enables him to realize Toni's distant resemblance with Marianne: "The stranger had passed his hand across his brow ... and replied: 'An extraordinary resemblance between you and a friend of mine!'" (*BSD*, 245/*SW II*/4, 39). However, his attempts to handle his trust and truly (re)cognize Toni are bound to fail. Based on the ambiguous "material" of perceptive evidence, his desire to verify drives him to sentimentally resolve what can otherwise not be definitely resolved. It is emblematic for this structure that, at the moment of recognizing Marianne in Toni, sentimentality overwhelms him. Retelling Marianne's story to himself moves him to tears, as we heard earlier.

> With these words [closing his account of Marianne's sacrifice] the stranger, letting go of the girl, returned to the window, where she saw him, in deep emotion, bury his face in a handkerchief; at this, for more than one reason, she was overcome by a sense of human compassion, and impulsively followed him, throwing her arms round his neck and mingled her tears with his. There is no need to report what happened next, for it will be clear to anyone who has followed the narrative thus far.
>
> When the stranger regained possession of himself and realized what he had done, he had no idea what its consequences might be; but for the time being at least he understood that he was saved, and that in this house he had entered there was nothing for him to fear from the girl. Seeing her sitting on the bed, with her arms folded across her and weeping, he did everything he could to console her. (*BSD*, 246–47)[17]

Toni's tears then in turn call forth various attempts to console her: Gustav offers her a present, caresses her, promises to marry her, and tells her of his property in Switzerland. When all promises of material advantage fail to console, he vows that "it had only been the turmoil and confusion of his senses, the strange mixture of desire and fear she had aroused in him, that had led him to do such a deed" (*BSD*, 247/*SW II/4*, 44). This confusion of the senses, in which Gustav finally takes refuge to exonerate or explain his unnamed deed, is precisely what is at stake here, and the gap in narration, covered over by a garrulous refusal of the text "to report what happened next," inflicts a similar moment of blindness and confusion upon our reading of the scene as well. The gap forces us to reread, and in fact, it commands us to. The German original claims at this point: *Was weiter erfolgte, brauchen wir nicht zu melden, weil es jeder, der an diese Stelle kommt, von selbst lies't.* The idiosyncratic spelling of *"lies't"* incises the verb by an apostrophe and almost turns it—also visually—into a command to the reader to read: *"lies!"* Keeping the deed implicit in the omission, the text at the same time demands us to read and explicate it. Chances are that our own desire for a sentimental reading gets the better of us, and we gladly accept the title's offer to read what is omitted here—as if automatically (*von selbst*)—as a betrothal. An offer that the tale's reception has largely taken up, but that it has also struggled with. Different suggestions have been made that read what is omitted as a moment of loving fusion (*Verschmelzung*), the seduction of a minor (*Verführung*), or even rape (*Vergewaltigung*).[18] But it remains uncertain if the text omits a promise (*Versprechen*) or a crime (*Verbrechen*), and the point here is not to ascertain one option over the other. It is rather to note that the text does not sustain any, however sentimental, resolution of the gap in narration. It rather destabilizes the projections, which both Gustav and Toni, as well as the reader would perhaps like to settle on. To interpret the omitted occurrence as consummation of a (doomed) love, that much can be said, reconstructs the omitted deed along the sentimental lines of Gustav's and Toni's mutual projections. Unable to face the violence, they rather hope, somewhat pragmatically, for sentimental resolutions, while the text shows the constant entanglement of the attempts to clear up the situation and speaks, beyond the mustered pathos, of fear of betrayal and death on both sides. But why speak of pragmatism in relation to Toni and Gustav? If we look at the interest, with which Gustav tested Toni's heart—a test he validated on the basis of the sentimental images that have sprung to his mind—we find, when reading on, that it was first and foremost to establish that "in this house he had entered there was nothing for him to fear from the girl" (*BSD*, 247/*SW II/4*, 43). And only after her tears do not stop flowing, does he try "everything he could to console her" (*BSD*, 247/*SW II/4*, 43). And again, when neither the present of Marianne's golden cross, nor further caresses have any effect, he promises to marry her, which sounds more like a last resort than romantic infatuation. "As she went on weeping and did not listen to him, he sat down on the edge of the bed, and told her, stroking and kissing her, that he would tomorrow morning seek her mother's permission to marry her"

(*BSD*, 247/*SW II/4*, 43–44). And Toni, likewise interested in maneuvering the situation, collects herself and sees that her best bet is to trust the stranger's promise. Although, for fear of her mother, she keeps him from immediately revealing their intention to marry, she promises herself that once his party has gained the upper hand—"as soon as he was strongly enough supported in the house by his followers" (*BSD*, 254/*SW II/4*, 58–59)—she will. The (albeit sentimentally disavowed) pragmatism at work here inhibits us to follow the title's suggestion and read the omitted deed, sentimentally, as a betrothal. Instead, when attending to the text carefully, we notice the pragmatics at work: to find out "what is going on," to see "what is to be done" under threat of violence. And we notice that Toni and Gustav do come together precisely in disavowing their pragmatism. The basis of their rapprochement lies in the sentimental compassion that both allow themselves to be charmed into by the impression of "true feelings." This is even at work when Toni is charmed by Gustav's anecdote of Marianne's sacrifice. She sees Gustav moved to a display of deep emotion by it, and right before the crucial omission, is moved to tears herself and flings her arms around his neck. The German text significantly notes that Toni "*übernahm*... von manchen Seiten geweckt, ein menschliches Gefühl, sie folgte ihm mit einer plötzlichen Bewegung, fiel ihm um den Hals, und mischte ihre Tränen mit den seinigen" (*SW II/4*, 42–43; emphasis added). The English translation tells us that she was "overcome by a sense of human compassion" (*BSD*, 246), and translates what we would, according to syntax and context, also expect to read in German, namely: "so *überkam* sie ein menschliches Gefühl". But what we find there is that she "*übernahm*... ein menschliches Gefühl": She "adopts a human sentiment," which makes her mix her tears with his. With the surprising verb *übernahm*, Toni is not so much portrayed as emotionally overwhelmed or falling in love, but rather as *adopting* his human sentiment of compassion and sentimentality. In a reciprocal movement they settle on compassion—and in an equally reciprocal movement they turn to sentimental projections, when he obliterates her brown face by recognizing Marianne in her, and she from then on prefers to be a white girl and to believe in his promise, opting—like him—for a sentimental release of the tension.

Despite closely pursuing these efforts to assess the situation and one's counterpart by incessant observations and sentimental interpretations, the text itself alerts us to the fact that these efforts largely misfire. It resonates with great frequency, if we read the German text, like a stutter, with words carrying the prefix *ver-*; with greater frequency even than the semantic field of touch and sight, whose purported understandings it eventually undermines. With unremitting repetition, *ver-* inscribes both the desire of understanding (*Verstehen*) and betrothal (*Verlobung*), and their incessant derailments of misconception (*Verkennen*) and betrayal (*Verrat*) into the ceaseless attempts to make sense of the situation by collecting sense-data and observations. The prefix echoes from every other sentence, and an exemplary assemblage of its recurrence illustrates that such *Verkennung* is no lack of understanding, but rather performs an understanding that misfires, and in misfiring nevertheless produces effects of its own. In his engagement (*Verlobung*) to Toni, Gustav constantly wavers between trust (*Vertrauen*) in Toni and a fear of betrayal (*Verrat*). He suspects a potential conspiracy (*Verschwörung*) because of the "racial" kinship (*Verwandtschaft*) that Toni and Babekan both share with him. He puts his trust (*sich anvertrauen*) in the two women, as he tells Babekan after entering the house, and revokes his trust due to the same "shadow of kinship with them which lies on our faces" (*BSD*, 237/*SW II/4*, 21), whereby Babekan means to confirm (*versichern*) what Gustav had asked: "Do you mean to say that you yourself... are condemned to the same fate as us Europeans?" (*BSD*, 236–37/*SW II/4*, 20). After the death of Gustav and Toni, Herr Strömli, Gustav's uncle, keeps his promise (*Versprechen*) to Congo Hoango and releases the two boys he held captive, and Kleist has him—with the remains of his small fortunes (*Vermögen*) and not without irony on Kleist's part—buy a quiet place to retire, and erect a memorial for his nephew and his fiancée ("*Vetter*, und der *Verlobten desselben*" [*SW II/4*, 91/*BSD*, 267; emphases added]). Thus, what we might prefer to read as promise (*Gelöbnis*), is marked in the text with literal precision as a misfired promise (*Ver-löbnis*). And although Neumann is right to describe the tale as "an experiment with the cognitive assessment of a situation by means of experienced and bequeathed pre-conceptions, emerging from the unconscious and its deceptive spaces,"[19] the tale equally displays the going awry of such a test, where, although an understanding of the situation is the aim, misunderstanding (*Verkennung*) is produced.

As we saw, Gustav engages in the (we may grant) well-meaning attempt to understand a complex situation in order to assess its potential for both danger and trust. In order to get a clear picture of things, to know what is to be done, he collects perceptions and close observations. What he misses is that his own resentments—taking shape as sentimentality and benevolent compassion—frame these perceptions. Although he believes himself to be but a neutral (Swiss) observer, who assesses the situation to the best of his knowledge and means no harm, such a shot at trust cannot but be haunted by mistrust, as the text teaches us. And such a betrothal remains haunted by betrayal. Hoping that it will be good enough seemed the best Toni could do.

## Spectacularly Simple: Well-willingly Seeing Nothing

### (Benito Cereno)

In Melville's *Benito Cereno* (1855), we find Captain Delano going about things in a similar fashion as Kleist's Gustav. The narrator informs us right at the beginning that Amasa Delano, American captain of the *Bachelor's Delight*, is a "man of such native simplicity as to be incapable of satire or irony" (*BC*, 63), and accordingly, Delano misses all the double entendres with which his Spanish interlocutor Benito Cereno, deposed captain of the Spanish slaver *San Dominick*, tries to communicate to him the situation on board. Although the "blunt-thinking American's eyes" (*BC*, 57) incessantly observe the strange circumstances on board, the American's blunt thinking ultimately prevents him, despite all observations, from understanding what he sees. Finding the ship in dismal disarray, and its captain Benito Cereno behaving very strangely, Delano increasingly suspects the other captain of scheming against him, or against his own ship and cargo. However, being a person of "a singularly undistrustful good nature" (*BC*, 47), as the narrator informs us, he repeatedly calls his mind back to its good senses, and "whatever in a serious way seemed enigmatical, was now good-naturedly explained away by the thought that, for the most part the poor invalid [Benito Cereno] scarcely knew what he was about" (*BC*, 69). Throughout his stay on board the *San Dominick*, Delano continually suspects that something is not quite right, but endowed with a great capacity to explain away all that is unwelcome, he dismisses all uncertainty and unease in the face of the spectacle before him and drowns suspicions in pity and benevolence—sentiments that habitually stand in for his racist preconceptions and prevent Delano from seeing any of the operations on board in their true light.

When first sighting the vessel, Delano's surprise at seeing no display of colors, "might have deepened into some uneasiness had he not been a person of a singularly undistrustful good nature, not liable, except on extraordinary and repeated incentives, and hardly then, to indulge in personal alarms, any way involving the imputation of malign evil in man" (*BC*, 47). The same lack of color (in the literal sense) reigns at the beginning of the narrative, with everything enveloped in fog, clouding the bay where Delano first sights the *San Dominick*. It was "not long after dawn," with "everything gray" and shrouded in "troubled gray vapors," the sea seeming "like waved lead" (all *BC*, 46). The tale closely pursues Delano's attempts to clear up this *chiaroscuro* and to develop the picture into a nicely contrasted black and white. But despite these efforts, his assessment of the situation will remain hazy and giddied, and his understanding vague. Already before boarding the *San Dominick*, Delano's efforts to interpret fall short. Upon approaching the vessel to offer assistance if needed, in a first venture of clarification we hear that he is "almost ... led to think" that the ship "appeared like a whitewashed monastery after a thunderstorm" carrying monks, because he perceived "what really seemed, in the hazy distance, throngs of dark cowls ... as of Black Friars pacing the cloisters" (all *BC*, 48). The *almost* alludes to the state, which Delano will remain subjected to until the end. Like Gustav, he strives to collect sense-data and visual impressions, and like him he is highly susceptible to minor moves and facial expressions of his opponents, always trying to get a grip on his suspicions of betrayal and to assess his counterparts by an overattentiveness to perceptions. But we hear him always to be only *almost* led to think certain things, or arrive at an understanding of what is at hand. His "blunt-thinking" disposition and his readiness to resolve things with his eyes alone arrest his thinking midway, and instead of sticking with the implications of his first impression, he dismisses them as moments of fancy and foolishness. Accordingly, when the "shreds of fog here and there raggedly furring" the foreign vessel lift a little, he happily corrects his allegedly premature, faulty impression of "a whitewashed monastery" and is convinced that "the true character of the vessel was plain." As if registering the information with the port authorities, he soberly reports: "a Spanish merchantman of the first class, carrying negro slaves, amongst other valuable freight, from one colonial port to another" (all *BC,* 48). He laughingly dismisses his first flowery impression of a whitewashed monastery after a thunderstorm as "fanciful resemblance" and registers the ship's official character with a relief. Ironically, the only thing that is plain is Delano himself. His sober assessment of reality prevents him from seeing that he indeed confronts precisely a whitewashed monastery after a thunderstorm—the secluded space of a ship occupied by men under (forced) vow to stage a whitewashed appearance, cleansed of the thunders of the black revolt that had just rolled across it. The fanciful illusion of a metaphoric reference, which Delano is relieved to soberly dispel, however, had hit the nail on the head, whereas by sobering up, the captain misses the plot and fails to see that what he takes to be plain reality, is in fact a staged illusion. As much as Gustav resolves the complexities of Toni's yellowish-brown complexion and tries to escape its indeterminacy by casting black and white projections upon her, Delano resolves the unclassifiable he encounters by soberly classifying the ship. This initial scene sets the tone for all the labors of understanding to come, the endless movement from observing to interpreting, from double entendres to their dismissal, that predominates the course of the narrative, in which we mainly follow Delano's perspective. After this first convoluted and ultimately misfiring attempt to "read" the *San Dominick,* Delano boards the ship and registers with vague unease that something is not quite as it seems. In order to figure out what is going on, he tries to be overattentive and register every move. In the process, however, Delano's attention is arbitrarily drawn hither and thither, echoing the helpless drift of the hull that desperately waits for favorable winds. Minor twitches and sudden whims call his attention from one observation to the next, and myriads of minor details, moves, and looks press upon him. They continuously impel his gaze to turn elsewhere, half drawn by sudden sounds, half directed by his preference to deflect from any mind-troubling observation. Unable to make sense of his perceptions, his thoughts drift along with his gaze, and prevent him from getting the drift of things. Despite his good intentions to take everything at face value, he immediately orders what he perceives according to his racist, chauvinistic notions of social order and foregoes any chance to see the theatrical nature of the spectacle that is staged before his eyes. Unwilling—or unable—to attend to its complexities, to the double entendres of Cereno's words and the ambiguous moves of Babo, Cereno's "personal servant", Delano projects his black and white certainties upon everything. These certainties are themselves mere reading-effects of the ambiguities he faces, and evidently readings that go off in the wrong direction, and the readiness to turn "reading" into comforting ease and the recurrence to preconfigured imagery is what the tale exposes.

But let us take a step back. On board the *San Dominick*, the former slaves stage a performance that serves Delano's idea of racial difference and racial relations well. During Delano's entire stay on board, Babo, leader of the revolt, directs a staging of the "normalcy" of a slaver with such rhetorical skill and efficacy that it works perfectly with Delano's preconceptions against Delano's understanding. Immediately upon boarding the ship, the American captain notices two different groups and registers them—in one "first comprehensive glance"—as "oakum-pickers" and "hatchet-polishers," which describes their immediate occupation. He fails to recognize the strategic positions they occupy to keep control of the ship, something the reader is equally unsure of at that point. But Delano is quick to place them within his frames of reference, seeing "the conspicuous figures of four elderly grizzled negroes, their heads like black, doddered willow tops ... couched, sphinx-like, one on the starboard cat-head, another on the larboard, and the remaining pair face to face on the opposite bulwarks above the main-chains" (all *BC*, 50). To him, they are not human, but half willow and half sphinx, and harmless in their apparently good-natured mindlessness, "a sort of stoical self-content," with which they "were picking the junk into oakum, a small heap of which lay by their sides. They accompanied the task with a continuous, low, monotonous chant; droning and druling away like so many gray-headed bag-pipers playing a funeral march" (*BC*, 50). Delano misses the fact that the oakum-pickers are arranged as part of a spectacle of obedience to Spanish rule, performing to be mindless at work and to be directed so by the Spanish, while in fact they are eyeing these latter carefully to prevent them from signaling the circumstances to Delano.

Throughout the narrative, the oakum-pickers will remain a point of reference and confusion to Delano. Musing upon the fact that "[t]rue, the old oakum-pickers appeared at times to act the part of monitorial constables to their countrymen, the blacks," he concludes that their monitoring can only be partially successful, since—although they themselves are "as little troublesome as crates and bales"—their harmless friendliness can never be of "so much avail as the unfriendly arm of the mate." Correspondingly, he attributes the ship's disarray and any other irregularity on board to the lack of "stern superior officers" (all *BC*, 54) and the natural leniency of Spanish Catholic authority. Although he suspects something awkward, he reassures and calms himself every time doubts arise. And despite phrasing his observations in theatrical terms, which could give the plot away—the oakum-pickers are thought to "appear ... at times to *act the part* of monitorial constables" (*BC*, 54; emphasis added) or "seem to *act the part* of old dominies to the rest, little heeded as their admonitions are at times" (*BC*, 60; emphasis added)—he quickly reassures himself of the slaves' inferior, almost nonhuman, status. The possibility of black rule is entirely beyond him. At most, he could believe that Cereno conspires with the slaves against him and his crew. When feeling menacingly observed by one of the oakum-pickers, he contemplates this possibility, but quickly pushes these worries aside by "concluding" that the blacks were too stupid for such conspiracy, and the whites "by nature, were the shrewder race" (*BC*, 75). Lost in these thoughts, Delano's gaze is drawn elsewhere and chances upon a sailor tying a knot.

> Captain Delano crossed over to him, and stood in silence surveying the knot; his mind, by a not uncongenial transition, passing from its own entanglements to those of the hemp. For intricacy, such a knot he had never seen in an American ship, nor indeed in any other. The old man looked like an Egyptian priest, making Gordian knots for the temple of Ammon. The knot seemed a combination of double-bowline-knot, treble-crown-knot, back-handed-well-knot, knot-in-and-out-knot, and jamming-knot. At last, puzzled to comprehend the meaning of such a knot, Captain Delano addressed the knotter:—"What are you knotting there, my man?" "The knot," was the brief reply, without looking up. "So it seems; but what is it for?" "For some one else to undo," muttered back the old man, plying his fingers harder than ever, the knot being nearly completed. While Captain Delano stood watching him, suddenly the old man threw the knot towards him, saying in broken English—the first heard in the ship—something to this effect: "Undo it, cut it, quick." It was said lowly, but with such condensation of rapidity, that the long, slow words in Spanish, which had preceded and followed, almost operated as covers to the brief English between. For a moment, knot in hand, and knot in head, Captain Delano stood mute; while, without further heeding him the old man was now intent upon other ropes. Presently there was a slight stir behind Captain Delano. Turning, he saw the chained negro, Atufal, standing quietly there. (*BC*, 76)

Delano being all knot, in hand and head, misses the message, even though it is transmitted in his own language. Any investigative interest is dropped immediately after "an elderly negro ... with a good-natured, knowing wink, ... informed him that the old knotter was simple-witted, but harmless; often playing his odd tricks" (*BC*, 76). A man of peculiar simplicity himself, Delano is reassured and happily attributes dim wits to others. Believing in the naturalness of social order, he fails to see that order is always fictitious, based upon narration and discursive construction, and thus he is ill-prepared to recognize the fiction before his eyes: the reality of black rule, and the theatrical performance of its absence.

Likewise, when Delano expresses his uneasiness and doubts about the proceedings on board, which he cannot quite get rid of, to Cereno and the latter assures him that all is done upon his own, Cereno's, orders, Delano registers but overlooks the double entendre in Cereno's "acrid tone, as if resenting some supposed satiric reflection" (*BC*, 60). Delano, as we heard earlier, a man of such "native simplicity as to be incapable of satire or irony" (*BC*, 63), does not read Cereno's tone and rather takes him at his word; just as he prefers to explain away Cereno's twitches and faltering as the expression of a melancholic, Catholic, and "morbidly sensitive" (*BC*, 63) mind. And while Delano musters benevolence and pity, rather than reading the undertones, Babo's skillfully stage-managed illusion continues to remain hidden to him.

How well Babo directs the communication between Delano and Cereno becomes apparent when Cereno gives his coerced, distorted account of what happened to the *San Dominick*. Presumably thus instructed, Cereno praises Babo for preserving him from harm, when the ship, on its way from Buenos Aires to Lima, suffered drastic damage and loss of men due to heavy gales off Cape Horn. When later many of the crew and slaves alike were killed by an outbreak of scurvy, and, thus decimated, the ship became unmanageable, Cereno thanks Babo for keeping peace on board, "pacifying his more ignorant brethren, when at intervals tempted to murmurings." Babo's reply—"'Ah, master,' sighed the black, bowing his face, 'don't speak of me; Babo is nothing; what Babo has done was but duty'"—is really aimed at Delano and it does the trick. "As master and man stood before him, the black upholding the white, Captain Delano could not but bethink him of the beauty of that relationship which could present such a spectacle of fidelity on the one hand and confidence on the other. The scene was heightened by the contrast in dress, denoting their relative positions." What Delano sees is a relationship based on fidelity and confidence, and exclaims—with a biting irony that escapes him: "'Don Benito, I envy you such a friend; slave I cannot call him.'" (all *BC*, 57) Babo's reply is an effective stratagem—much like Toni's—precisely because it articulates the biases of its indirect addressee, or as Phillipe Jaworski said: "Delano is fooled by the scenes staged by Babo ... because he is incapable of seeing the black man. Moreover, he fails to see him because, in his eyes, the Black does not exist."[20] Babo was saying just that: "don't speak of me; Babo is nothing" (*BC*, 57).

Inexplicably to Delano, Cereno pales, faints, bites his lips, and appears to be in pain, during his account. Delano does not see someone choking on the words he is forced to speak, but rather suspects the coughs to be either signs of physical weakness, or feigned in order to lure him into believing in Cereno's physical weakness. Uneasy, Delano ruminates on the fate of the *San Dominick* while listening to Cereno's account and watching Babo come to his master's help when the latter falters in his account, and tries to understand what happened. He misses that Babo's helping hand is in fact one that keeps Cereno under firm control, and that it was the successful revolt of the African slaves that had caused the damage to the ship and the deaths of men. When Babo pulls Cereno to the side, as he does many times when Cereno's insinuations that the official story is not true become too obvious, Delano is embarrassed and made uneasy by their whispers, and—partly so as not to intrude upon a relationship that appears so confidential to him—he turns his head. "[H]is glance accidentally fell on a young Spanish sailor" whose stare Delano registers, again with unease. But hearing Babo's and Cereno's whispers, he turns back and, "[h]is attention thus redirected to that quarter" (BC, 64), forgets all about the sailor. Accidentally gazing at the Spanish sailor and noticing his stare had allowed him to deflect from any troubling thoughts on what the whispers might mean. But running into a new problem—the sailor's uncomfortable stare—he turns toward Cereno and Babo anew, almost gladly registering the sound of their whispers again and redirecting his attention from the sailor to Cereno and Babo.

> His own attention thus redirected to that quarter, Captain Delano gave a slight start. From something in Don Benito's manner just then, it seemed as if the visitor had, at least partly, been the subject of the withdrawn consultation going on—a conjecture as little agreeable to the guest as it was little flattering to the host. The singular alternations of courtesy and ill-breeding in the Spanish captain were unaccountable, except on one of two suppositions—innocent lunacy, or wicked imposture.... The man was an imposter. Some low-born adventurer, masquerading as an oceanic grandee.... From no train of thought did these fancies come; not from within, but from without; suddenly, too, and in one throng, like hoar frost; yet, as soon to vanish as the mild sun of Captain Delano's good-nature regained its meridian. Glancing over once more towards his host ... he was struck by the profile, whose clearness of cut was refined by the thinness, incident to ill-health, as well as ennobled about the chin by the beard. Away with suspicion.... Relieved by these and other better thoughts, the visitor, lightly humming a tune, now began indifferently pacing the poop, so as not to betray to Don Benito that he had at all mistrusted incivility. (BC, 64–65)

Unable to entirely ignore the double entendres in Cereno's account, these ambiguities continue to bother Delano, and make Cereno "unaccountable" for him. At first, Delano thinks he can resolve this unaccountability by judging Cereno by the standards of his own anti-Catholic chauvinism. But these are half-thoughts; coming from without, they are partly generated by chance, depending on where the eyes happen to look, and partly draw on general ideas and clichés. These biased misconceptions of Cereno go hand in hand with Delano's racist resentments, and both make his simplicity highly problematic. No less problematic is Delano's good nature, which soon manages to get the upper hand and melts unease away in the mild sun of a humming indifference that thinks it can benevolently observe Cereno as a bizarre specimen. It is problematic, as Melville shows, in that this good nature maintains the dubious assurance to be free from resentment, and merely neutrally observing. We can hear this ring through, when Delano again misreads one of Cereno's silences as involuntary display of indignation. Explaining the silence with Cereno's excessive sensibility, Delano assures himself at this opportunity of his own freedom from resentment and from obstructive sensitivity. But from his denomination as a "good sailor," we also hear Melville's irony at such good-natured and undiscerning simplicity.

> [F]inding his companion more than ever withdrawn... by-and-by Captain Delano likewise became less talkative, oppressed, against his own will, by what seemed the secret vindictiveness of the morbidly sensitive Spaniard. But the good sailor, himself of a quite contrary disposition, refrained, on his part, from the appearance as from the feeling of resentment, and if silent, was only so from contagion. (*BC*, 63)

But despite these temporary assurances, Delano continues to ruminate, doubt and speculate on whom he is facing.

> He recalled the Spaniard's manner while telling his story. There was a gloomy hesitancy and subterfuge about it. It was just the manner of one making up his tale for evil purposes, as he goes. But if that story was not true, what was the truth? That the ship had unlawfully come into the Spaniard's possession? But in many of its details... Don Benito's story had corroborated not only the wailing ejaculations of the indiscriminate multitude, white and black, but likewise—what seemed impossible to be counterfeit—by the very expression and play of every human feature, which Captain Delano saw. If Don Benito's story was, throughout, an invention, then every soul on board, down to the youngest negress, was his carefully drilled recruit in the plot: an incredible inference. And yet, if there was ground for mistrusting his veracity, that inference was a legitimate one. But those questions of the Spaniard.... But, with ill purposes, to solicit such information openly of the chief person endangered, and so, in effect, setting him on his guard; how unlikely a procedure was that? Absurd, then, to suppose that

those questions had been prompted by evil designs. Thus, the same conduct, which, in this instance, had raised alarm, served to dispel it. In short, scarce any suspicion or uneasiness, however apparently reasonable at the time, which was not now, with equal apparent reason, dismissed. (*BC,* 68–69)

He contemplates the possibility of Cereno's story being an invention. However, focusing solely on Benito Cereno as potential plotter, and excusing him as a poor invalid, as we heard, Delano misses the plot again. "At last, he began to laugh at his former forebodings; and laugh at the strange ship ... and laugh, too, at the odd-looking blacks, particularly those old scissors-grinders, the Ashantees; and those bed-ridden old knitting women, the oakum-pickers; and almost at the dark Spaniard himself, the central hobgoblin of all" (*BC,* 69). He—the text is careful to tell us three times—laughs, and laughs, and laughs: the first laughter frees him from his ill thoughts, the second from his worries regarding the ship's mission, and the third laughter finally ridicules the Africans. Feminizing the oakum-pickers, Delano reduces what had formerly been "four elderly grizzled negroes ... sphinx-like" (*BC,* 50) to comic figures of whom he has nothing to fear. Only Cereno cannot be shaken off with a laugh. At him Delano laughs only "almost," but then hurries to pity him, which amounts largely to the same effect of overriding his feelings of uncertainty and unease by the reassurance of chauvinistic categorizations. From first judging Cereno as "some hypochondriac abbot" (*BC,* 52) and as "morbidly sensitive" (*BC,* 63), he moves to categorizing him as nothing but a Spaniard, and "as a nation—continued he in his reveries—these Spaniards are all an odd set; the very word Spaniard has a curious, conspirator, Guy-Fawkish twang to it. And yet, I dare say, Spaniards in the main are as good folks as any in Duxbury Massachusetts" (*BC,* 79). While at first the ascription of a general national character furnishes a classifiable image of Captain Cereno, this "certainty" is immediately destabilized again when Delano grants that largely they are as trustworthy as his own fellow countrymen. A preliminary conclusion that is contradicted once again by distancing Spanish monarchical decadence and capriciousness from American republican egalitarianism. Delano prides himself on such a "republican impartiality ... this republican element, which always seeks one level, serving the oldest white no better than the youngest black" (*BC,* 80). The tale proves the irony of such an assertion and shows such jovial "impartiality" to be a reading-effect: an effect of the ambiguity of an opaque reality that calls to be read, but in which the same observation can be used as evidence either way, since "the same conduct, which, in this instance, had raised alarm, served to dispel it" (*BC,* 69). What is demanded is a reading, and Delano goes about it by resolving these ambiguities regarding what he observes. What he evokes for this purpose are sentimental images and clichéd notions, which betray his fear and resentment, but are dressed as impartiality and benevolent generosity. These procedures become truly painful to pursue, when Delano's ruminations turn to the Africans, whom he denies even their essential humanity. He likens Babo's face to that of a loyal "shepherd's dog" (*BC*, 51) and reassures himself of his good disposition toward Babo by confirming to himself that "like most men of a good, blithe heart, ... [he] took to negroes, not philanthropically, but genially, just as other men to Newfoundland dogs" (*BC*, 84). Delano's simplicity becomes increasingly problematic. Delano is always ready to attribute "the unaspiring contentment of a limited mind" to the "indisputable inferiors" (both *BC*, 84) as he blithely designates the Africans, and he reduces them—in classic colonialist fashion—to props in a spectacle, which he suspects Cereno of performing. That the narrative voice remains intertwined with Delano's perspective forces the reader into an uneasy complicity with Delano, and challenges him or her to critically observe the processes whereby Delano ends up seeing nothing but weird Catholics and harmless wildlife. Melville forces us to follow these ruminations—these all-too-human fear-induced complacent reading-strategies—that pride themselves on reading carefully but fail to read anything, and asks us to see carefully ourselves.

Just like Gustav, Delano is spectacularly simple, so to speak: by going for the spectacle, that is, for the representation that embodies their racist preconceptions, they, ironically, miss the fact that it is a spectacle that is put before them. And like Gustav, Delano tries to understand what is going on by perceiving all the minor details. His attention is drawn hither and thither, in order to break the spell. But he misreads in a double movement: he *overreads* in the sense that he reads too much and perceives innumerable details in which he gets lost, and he *reads over* in the sense that he misses the significant signs and has his preconceptions readily step in to explain what he perceives before he can begin to think. All of his efforts, the narrator tells us, are to no avail: "Trying to break one charm, he was but becharmed anew" (*BC*, 74). In this sense *Benito Cereno*, as Peter Coviello notes, "pits gothic occlusion and opacity against sentimental modes of reading and response, and sentimental readers, the better to show how easily sentimentality consorts with a particularly American racism."[21] Sentimentality is shown as a way to misrecognize and misread the gothic text of race in America, especially at the time of the ideological propagations of Manifest Destiny, as Coviello argues. To this gothic text of racial imagery and violence—gothic "in its unyielding opacity, its resistance to easy legibility"[22]—the "blunt-thinking" Delano finds a sentimental resolution, and by exposing this as a violent misreading, Melville's "anti-sentimentalism"[23] responds to the rhetoric of texts such as Beecher Stowe's *Uncle Tom's Cabin*.

Contrary to Beecher Stowe, Melville operates by exposing the character's sentimentality. At a moment when Delano tries to settle once and for all the question of what all this means, he significantly ends up gazing out at the soothing sight of his whaleboat and collects himself with comforting images of familiarity. His whaleboat—affectively called "Rover by name, which though now in strange seas, had often pressed the beach of Captain Delano's home, and, brought to its threshold for repairs, had familiarly lain there, as a Newfoundland dog" (*BC*, 77)—had returned to the *Bachelor's Delight* to fetch provisions for the crew of the *San Dominick*. While waiting for its return, in the midst of his unease and confusion, "it was not without something of a relief that the good seaman presently perceived his whale-boat in the distance" (*BC*, 70). His boat, which Melville has approach incredibly slowly for more than twenty-five pages after the above first sighting, allows Delano to pitch its familiar sight and the "thousand trustful associations" (*BC*, 77) it evokes against the uneasiness that grabs him again and again. At one instance, for example, when the image of the old man with the knot unsettles him, Delano alleviates incomprehension by simply looking out to his boat—which is as helpless a solution to his confusion and unease as simply casting the knot, which is not to be disentangled, overboard.

> All this is very queer now, thought Captain Delano, with a qualmish sort of emotion; but, as one feeling incipient seasickness, he strove, by ignoring the symptoms, to get rid of the malady. Once more he looked off for his boat. To his delight, it was now again in view, leaving the rocky spur astern. The sensation here experienced, after at first relieving his uneasiness, with unforeseen efficacy soon began to remove it. (*BC*, 76–77)

Repressing the implications of the perceptions that he gathers, Delano prefers to look away and drown them in a sentimentality that covers over the insecurity and hides his resentment. Much as in Kleist's tale, we find this repression inscribed in the text itself. In *Benito Cereno*, it is the incessant recurrence of the grammatically unusual double negatives that inscribes this baring of understanding in the very fabric of the text, and reminds us of the instabilities, the inconclusiveness of Delano's reading of the situation. Constructions such as *not un-*, *not without*, or *undis-* proliferate with every move or observation Delano makes. He is "not unwilling" (*BC*, 51), "not without the idea" (*BC*, 52) and "not without humane satisfaction" (*BC*, 52), as well as "not uninfluenced by the peculiar good humor at present prevailing" (*BC*, 80). "Not unbewildered" (*BC*, 75), he gazes off for his boat, trying to disperse unpleasant thoughts. These double negatives suspend understanding without confirming its complete absence. Despite the text's dutiful pursuit of Delano's incessant attempts to understand, its very fabric arrests these attempts in midair. Already the first character description renders Delano as someone of a "singularly undistrustful good nature" (*BC*, 47), capturing this lingering, half-arrest of understanding, and a similar suspension of trust as we saw in Gustav, in the unusual double negation.

## Figures of Simplicity

Ultimately unable to figure out what all the insinuations and suspicious moves might mean, Captain Delano sticks to his preconceptions at hand. While Gustav and Toni in the footbath scene reciprocally assess each other, here we have Delano as the sole "interpreter." But we find the same entanglement in laborious investigations, which remain equally unresolved by the narrative voice, as in Kleist, since Melville's text also refrains from any clarifying comment or explicatory statement by a narrative voice. The text remains—until the three purportedly official testimonies on the case that are added as an appendix to clear up the story—reliant upon Delano's perspective, and recounts the situation on board through his eyes. What we follow are his efforts, and this close entanglement with Delano's perspective forces the reader into an uneasy, silent complicity with his account. Yet at the same time, the dramatic irony ringing from the narrative voice alerts us to the possibility that Delano is only giving us his confused projections and half-truths. The appendixed part of the tale then offers allegedly authentic "legal documents" that confirm how wrong Delano was. The transcriptions of the court proceedings, which report the court case that followed the overpowering of the rebels by Delano's crew, provide us with Cereno's declaration of what happened: a slave revolt. These transcriptions are explicitly attached in order to "shed light on the preceding narrative, as well as, in the first place, reveal the true port of departure and true history of the San Dominick's voyage" (*BC,* 103). Instead of clearing things up, however, they reiterate the obscurity, and are as unreliable as Delano's account was thwarted by his native simplicity. Fragmented into extracts, they are given as a translation from Cereno's Spanish, and upon a closer look his deposition is based on what the Africans have told him. The earnest declaration that facts are being presented is always accompanied by the phrase: "this is known and believed, because the negroes have said it" (*BC,* 111). As much as the report is flagged as a matter-of-fact account it remains narration and challenges the reader now in turn to stay aware of this fact. Instead of substituting Delano's perspective with a true and conclusive one, the allegedly factual legal appendices rather mirror Delano's account in vagueness, and ask us to consider that although Cereno's declaration is based on what "the negroes have told him"—as much as Delano's was based on what the African's orchestrated before his eyes—their voices are again not heard directly. In the end, "on the testimony of the sailors alone rested the legal identity of Babo" (*BC,* 116). The purported clarification of the case ultimately resists verification, and remains nothing but the echo of white narration, in which the other side remains unheard and silent. The text's last paragraph drives this home, when Babo, having been sentenced to death, is said to have "uttered no sound and could not be forced to. His aspect seemed to say, since I cannot do deeds, I will not speak words" (*BC,* 116). What remains is the narration of Benito Cereno, that is, a violently partial construal of the story. Melville alerts us to this fact by making us realize that we had implicitly expected no less by the offer of his title, and that this places us in an uncomfortable closeness to the American captain.

## Sentimentalizing Resentment

As we have seen, Kleist's *The Betrothal in Santo Domingo* and Melville's *Benito Cereno* perform experiments in perception. Both attend to the continuous and situated production of knowledge *in* and *about* social situations, and show this production to be linked to the incessant registration of sense impressions.[24] The attempts of both men to get a clear picture of the situation they are in by registering every minor move, by incessantly collecting sense impressions and perceptions, are shown to be at the same time continuously undermined by their fear and stereotypical simplifications. Trying to understand by interpreting the evidence their sense-data is thought to provide, their simplicity always gets the better of them. The closer Gustav and Delano look, the more enmeshed they become in an ambiguous fog of minor details, and their way out is to fall back on preconceived notions of "black" and "white." The texts display these relentless attempts to clear up the situation and to disentangle the unsettling ambiguities of the plot around them, and betray their "native simplicity" (*BC*, 63) in going about it. Their senses—so eagerly mobilized to arrive at a solid assessment—are befuddled in a double sense: giddied by too many small perceptions and by a sentimentality that covers for a preconceived, eventually racist framing of these perceptions. What the texts show—and ask us to consider—is, thus, not authorial opinion, but the derailing of processes of understanding by stiffened clichés, the "medial arrangement, the opinion-making that has been frozen to clichés, with many-folded breaks, trapped in and biased by unbelievable contradictions, as well as its agitation by white panic and white sensationalism."[25] The texts, for one thing, are insistent on small perceptions as the basis of understanding, but for another, they show how preconceived, ready-made images easily intervene and superinscribe themselves—sustained by resentment and opinions congealed to clichés—as "conclusions" from these observations and impressions. We get a clear sense, however, that they are a product of Gustav's and Delano's sentimental resolutions to a complex problem. Their native simplicity—in its all-too-human form—gets the better of them.

Despite their well-meaning dispositions, the (in Delano's case) exceptionally undistrustful simple nature, as well as their persistent attempts to understand by looking even harder, the result of their overattention to perceptions are clichéd readings, sentimental (mis)interpretations, and a spectacular simplicity that literally turns good Gustav at times into a *dummen* August,[26] and endows Delano with "knot in hand, and knot in head" (*BC*, 76). One might grant that they are put to a difficult task. The spectacles in both tales mimic images that are calculated to fit as neatly as hand in glove with the preconceptions of their beholders. The situational knots cunningly tied by Babo and Babekan and enacted by Cereno and Toni work so well precisely because they were contrived in view of Gustav's and Delano's biased "knots in head." But the crucial point here is not that they could have attended to their senses better, had they not been racist. Or that someone less "simple" could have found a more reliable truth from attending to sensory evidence. The point is that the material is always ambiguous, and calls for an eventually always inconclusive reading. It cannot but be attended to, but if what is perceived is positivistically trusted as straightforward evidence, the task of reading is disavowed, and, due to the ambiguity and inconclusiveness of any material, substituted by—in our case—sentimental imagery that overcodes what is seen, in the sense that Deleuze and Guattari give to the term in *A Thousand Plateaus*: these sentimental signifiers rearrange all the minor details into familiar frameworks, and cause to see only what was already known.[27] Gustav's and Delano's attempts to find out "what is going on" are stabilized by these overcodings—by the imposition of readings that work according to hierarchical, totalizing, unifying registers, which enables them to go after a conclusive judgment on the situation. In order to pursue this aim, they precisely need to turn a blind eye to the continuously changing myriad of minor details and impressions in the situation. However, as the texts alert us, this "whole microsegmentarity, details of details, 'a roller coaster of possibilities,' tiny movements that have not reached the edge, lines or vibrations that start to form long before there are outlined shapes"[28] at the same time constantly undermines this endeavor, and destabilizes what the clichés were called upon to consolidate.

    Accordingly, our two figures of simplicity here show characters who are not too stupid to understand, but prefer to opt for a "simple" (in scare quotes to differentiate this simplicity from the types to come) "understanding" (in scare quotes, because we are dealing with a product of assessment, yet one more akin to "willful ignorance" than "insight") in order not to disturb their mind-set; they manage to calm their (nevertheless unappeasable, and ever resurfacing) doubts by occupying their minds halfheartedly with close observation. The texts, as we saw, do not so easily allow us to laugh at their incapacities; too much do the narrative techniques submit us as readers to the same ambiguities and force us to face our own sentimental escape routes. Were we not also ready to give in to Kleist's enticement of reading what the text omits as a betrothal? Even more so, since we cannot verify and prove the scene's true meaning on the basis of textual evidence? And were we not won over by the immediate offer of Melville's title that Benito Cereno will be the figure of interest, not his almost imperceptible shadow? In order not to be beguiled by the crafty spectacle before our eyes—and to not read what we expect or would like to read—we have to point to the texts' rhetorical strategies on the one hand, and the narratives' skillful enactments of a peculiar simplicity on the other. In a situation of fear-induced resentment—such as the exceptional situations composed as background to the characters' efforts—this is an uneasily familiar, all-too-human, everyday simplicity, one from which the texts take an ironic distance and which they expose as a readiness to resolve opaqueness and the instability of minor perceptions by the hasty imposition of familiar images.

As we will see in the next chapter, with Billy Budd and Michael Kohlhaas simplicity takes effect as a similar exposure to small perceptions. However, Billy Budd, who seems strangely foreign to all forms of understanding, abides by minute perceptions, and his simplicity must be read differently than Delano's. And the same holds true, as I will show, for Kohlhaas, who assesses the situation that he becomes involved in at every turn anew, operating with an affective assessment of it and thereby also produces a somewhat "simple" way of understanding what is happening. Neither Billy Budd nor Kohlhaas, however, are after resolutions of opaqueness and a stable judgment of the situation. They are rather seeking to maneuver the situations from within. They certainly both do this in ways that gets them entangled with judgments by the law—judgments that themselves resolve none of the issues raised by the narratives satisfactorily, as has been noted in relation to both texts. It seems that Billy's and Kohlhaas's ways of crosscutting judgment—of abstaining from judgment—has to do with this, and that we can read their practices of "understanding" or "reading" as another instance of Kleist's and Melville's inquiries into the relation of sensation and thinking. Delano and Gustav misunderstood it as a return to the senses, which entangled them in an ambiguous opaqueness from which they found pathetic escapes. Billy Budd and Michael Kohlhaas take this same problem into a different, more affective direction.

## Chapter 3

# Affectivity

Much like Delano, Melville's Billy Budd never quite knows who he is up against. And yet, he is an entirely different figure. To couple him with Kleist's Michael Kohlhaas might seem surprising, as Kohlhaas, unlike Billy Budd, is fixed upon his opponent in obdurate pursuit. At first, they seem to be the most dissimilar characters, and their capacities to strategize and understand seem to be worlds apart. Billy is apparently unaware of the plotting against him, and Kohlhaas is the one who, to a large extent at least, plots. But despite these seeming differences, the tales—as much as their protagonists—are strikingly alike on a more subterranean level. Although Kohlhaas pursues the Junker von Tronka as the one who wronged him, he never really knows who he is up against—the law remains a (*avant la lettre*) Kafkaesque, evasive apparatus, and the state is everywhere, but is nowhere to be located. And although it seems that Billy is not aware of the evil eye Claggart has cast upon him, his fist manages to find the one who wrongs him. Also, both trouble or thwart our attempts to morally judge them, and they make it difficult to even pinpoint their intentions. Billy's intentions remain mostly obscure to us, his extraordinary farewell to his old ship ambiguous, and when he unexpectedly strikes his opponent Claggart dead, we are not entirely sure what he intended. These uncertainties make a judgment of Billy's alleged innocence—and its reversal into guilt—so difficult and troubling. Similarly, in the light of Kohlhaas's troubling chase of the Junker, criticism has been unable to settle the question whether he is after justice or revenge: Is he driven by relentless revenge, irrational fury, or the righteous, rational demand of justice? It is hard to tell, or even to judge by his demeanor. He is too rash and discomposed to be called rational and strategic in a pursuit of justice, yet he is at the same time too collected to impute that he is full of blind passionate rage and driven by a thirst for revenge. We are not altogether certain of what it is exactly that Kohlhaas wants.[1] And fittingly we hear at the tale's opening that Kohlhaas is both righteous *and yet* horrifying at the same time.

On the level of the plot, this problematic and disconcerting *yet*—a firm resolution of the case that yet leaves us unsettled in *Billy Budd*, or of a disturbingly relentless but futile pursuit of justice in *Michael Kohlhaas* that yet seems to bring justice about in the end—makes it difficult to resolve the question of justice that both narratives raise. Martin Greenberg has noted this in his comparison of the two tales. In *Billy Budd*, he writes, "[t]he troubling case recounted in that story is firmly resolved. Nevertheless the resolution leaves all concerned in a state of agitation: characters, readers and (you feel) the writer of the story himself." In Kleist's *Michael Kohlhaas*, on the other hand, "justice seems impossible to arrive at, so tangled the situation of its eponymous protagonist becomes. But in the end, involved and complicated though it is, justice is done and a calmness ensues."[2] By centering on the issue of justice, Greenberg continues a focus that has been central to the reception of both tales. Although he notes that such justice is a difficult one, complicated by the striking paradox that unsettles any conclusive reading of the tales, his reading continues to go after it. Contrary to this focus on justice, approached by Greenberg and others via the level of plot, this present reading will rather take the tale's titles as indicators—albeit they had been misleading our attention in *The Betrothal in Santo Domingo* and *Benito Cereno*—and trace the problem of unsettling paradoxicality on the level of character.

We have to begin by noting that both narratives ostensibly refrain from explaining their actions. Nor do they give them the psychological depth that might explain their motives. Their actions, at times drastic and unexpected, are presented as resulting neither from conscious reflection or clear intentionality, nor from the involuntary upsurge of repressed or unconscious desires. Instead of explaining them either way and presenting them as examples of moral or immoral conduct, both texts conduct with them, as I want to suggest, studies in affectivity: they study and experiment with a disposition that neither coincides with "feeling" or "sensibility" nor tries to arrive at rational, reflective thinking. What Kleist and Melville sketch in these tales is a disposition that operates affectively, and whereby Billy Budd and Michael Kohlhaas arrive at assessments of the situation they face—a disposition that we will pursue here as a type of simplicity. In both cases, this affectivity does not provide a true or unmediated understanding, an immediacy of feeling that would be more authentic or unadulterated than reflection. It rather allows, precisely by suspending "thinking" between (active) conscious deliberation, or reasoning, and (passive) sensitive receptivity, to furnish effective answers to the question "What is to be done?" Being more than mere receptivity or irrational emotionality, but also not reflection and reasoning, the affective thinking produced in this suspension has the air of simplemindedness, particularly if we think of Billy Budd. But Barbara Johnson has pointed our pursuit of this simplemindedness in a fruitful direction when in her important essay on Melville's tale she asks: "[I]s Billy truly as 'plotless' as he appears? Does his 'simplicity' hide no division, no ambiguity?"[3] We will ask after the ambiguity of this simplicity and see that it lies in the affectivity at stake here; an affectivity that is not altogether foreign to understanding and already precludes any straightforward simpleton.

For this endeavor, Kleist himself has provided us with the corresponding theory in his essay *On the Gradual Fabrication of Thoughts While Speaking* (*Über die allmähliche Verfertigung der Gedanken beim Reden*). Written in 1805, shortly before he began writing *Michael Kohlhaas*, the essay is generally considered, along with *On the Puppet Theater* of 1810, to be one of Kleist's major aesthetic writings. The earlier essay sketches a theory of affectivity that relates corporeality and affects to the fabrication of utterances and thoughts, and sketches the idea of "affective thinking," which Kleist then substantiates—as my reading here suggests—in his character Kohlhaas. Thoughts in the sense of ready-made tools, or ideas in the sense of preconceived formulas, may be ready at hand, but not effective and are employed by "[o]nly very commonplace minds, which memorize a definition ... one day and forget it the next" (*ADE*, 222/*SWB*, 324). They are not of interest to Kleist, but rather the fact that "it is..." not we who 'know'; it is rather a certain condition, in which we happen to be, that 'knows'" (*ADE*, 222/*SWB*, 323). What he endeavors with *Michael Kohlhaas* is to outline precisely this condition, this state of ours that knows, a disposition, a countenance that "knows," but knows in a way that does not necessarily articulate, conceptualize, or grasp in words, as we will see. The essay *On the Gradual Fabrication of Thoughts While Speaking* challenges an idea of thinking as an exclusively rational, cerebral, or conscious act, and it challenges the notion of a speaker who speaks merely preconceived thoughts. Rather, as the essay contends, thoughts are incited by the position of the speaker in a context, within a web of relations and incidents. For example, the essay's narrator describes how he attempts to tackle an algebraic problem, and how it helps to speak to his sister about it, how his ideas are sparked by her intervention. A first move is made "because I do start with some sort of dark notion remotely related to what I am looking for," and the mind, "being pressed to complete what it has begun, shapes that muddled idea into a form of new-minted clarity, even while my talking progresses, with the result that my full thought, to my astonishment, is completed with the period." In order to make time for this process, the narrator tells us, "I mumble inarticulately, drawl out my conjunctions, use unnecessary appositions" and use "all other dilatory tricks to gain the time required". In such a situation, we learn, nothing is more helpful than a "movement of my sister, as if she was to interrupt me; because my already strained mind becomes only more excited by this attempt to snatch the speech it was entertaining from it, and its ability, like a great general, when circumstances are pressing, is intensified by yet another degree."(all *ADE*, 218–19/*SWB*, 320)[4]

The sister's movement, although apparently meaningless or unintentional, increases the tension of the mind (*Gemüt*) and provokes it to fabricate the idea, which is fabricated in no other way than by being articulated. The essay implicitly questions the Cartesian understanding of thinking as an activity of a rational mind, which would result in clear and distinct ideas that are subsequently put into words, which in turn represent these thoughts. The possibility of an intentional matching of thoughts and words, of the addition of words to thought, and the notion of an autonomous mind thinking clearly in conscious reflection before using words to express the reflection, is put into question. But we do not find its complete reversal either, which might be imagined as either complete automaticity or machinicity, or as unconscious or mad slips of the tongue. Rather, both thoughts and words are fabricated gradually in conjunction with each other, a conjunction that is permitted by a state that Neumann describes as the limit between an *automaton* and an *allomaton*, between a self-animated, autonomous movement, and one animated from outside.[5] At this limit, movements and actions can neither be explained as self-induced, nor as externally incited, and the response given is neither fully one's own, nor entirely indebted to the other. The essay outlines this state between active (conscious) reflection and passive (sensitive) reception, lingering at the limit of consciousness, in a limit-zone or state that we might call—following Melville's term for Billy Budd's state of mind—"semiconsciousness" (*BBS*, 81). Rather than striving for rational explication of the occurrences around them, both Billy Budd and Michael Kohlhaas subsist in such a "semiconscious" state of mind. In his essay, Kleist illustrates the process of fabricating a thought while speaking in this state of "semiconsciousness" with one pivotal example: Mirabeau's thunderbolt speech at the French National Assembly on June 23, 1789, with which Mirabeau defied the king's orders and declared the immunity of parliament. Mirabeau's thunderbolt, as Kleist has it, was not the result of rational reflection and subsequent conscious transformation of premeditated thoughts into words, but was triggered, with Mirabeau slightly beside himself, in a state of agitation and urgency to respond. Kleist comically attributes the spark of Mirabeau's boldness to an involuntary twitch by the master of ceremonies who transmits the king's orders. It was perhaps, the essay suggests, an involuntary betrayal of nervousness on the master of ceremonies' side, or something in his aspect that spurred Mirabeau's revolutionary words: "Perhaps, after all, it was only the twitch of an upper lip, or the ambiguous fingering of a wrist frill, that precipitated the overthrow of the old order in France" (*ADE*, 220/*SWB*, 321). Pressed to respond to the master of ceremonies and beginning a reply at a venture, it may have been this fidgeting that made Mirabeau utter his thunderbolt speech.

> "Yes," answered Mirabeau [to the master of ceremonies], "we have heard the king's command...." I am certain that he made this affable start without the faintest prescience of the bayonet thrust with which he was to conclude. "Yes, Monsieur," he repeats, "we have heard it...." Clearly he still has no idea of what he is about. "But by what right," he continues, whereupon a fresh source of stupendous ideas opens up to him, "do you proclaim commands to us? We are the representatives of the Nation!" This was exactly what he needs.... (*ADE*, 219)[6]

This string of stupendous ideas was not premeditated and subsequently expressed in words, but rather sprung forth from the start made at a venture, a start that Mirabeau made with the words "but by what right." The narrator's inserted comments mark the fleeting moments, in which Mirabeau registered any fidgeting, and which increased the momentum of both thoughts and words on their parallel course, reciprocally productive of each other. These thoughts or ideas were not produced in order to arrive at the truth of things, the objective state of affairs, or to order and understand the situation (as Gustav and Delano had tried), but were produced in the midst of a struggle, and as a response to a demand. In order to exemplify the state of mind, this affective agitation, needed for such a production of effective speech the essay employs the surprising and revealing terminology of experimental physics. Between Mirabeau's speech and the speculation a few lines later that a twitching lip might have sparked the French Revolution, Kleist likens the relation of Mirabeau and the master of ceremonies to the friction between electric bodies, an analogy that is supposed to render intelligible what had just happened between Mirabeau and his opponent:

> If we try to imagine the condition of the Master of Ceremonies at that moment, it can be nothing but a total mental bankruptcy, just as, by a law of physics, an electrically neutral object entering the field of an electrified object instantly assumes the opposite charge. (ADE, 220)[7]

In analogy to the laws of electricity—familiar to Kleist from his studies of experimental physics with Wünsch in Frankfurt an der Oder[8]—the essay holds that the master of ceremonies must have suffered "total mental bankruptcy" after his encounter with Mirabeau's boldness, while Mirabeau's degree of tension or "voltage" (*Spannung*) was intensified in this charged encounter by the opponent's depletion, and pushed his courage to the boldest enthusiasm. The neutral master of ceremonies—as mere transmitter of the king's message—heightened the electric charge in Mirabeau by an involuntary twitch of the lip and triggered a thunderbolt. After the discharge both returned to a neutral position: Mirabeau "having in the manner of a Kleistian Bottle[9] discharged himself,... had once again become neutral, and, returning from audacity, suddenly gave way to prudence, and to fear of the Chatelet" (*SWB*, 321; translation is my own). By likening their encounter to the laws of electricity it does become evident that we are not referred to an outburst of emotions. This "speaking-thinking" is neither the expression of a deep feeling nor of a premeditated thought, but induced affectively by sparks between bodies.[10]

The essay *On the Gradual Fabrication of Thoughts While Speaking* and the 1810 essay *On the Puppet Theater* frame the writing of *Michael Kohlhaas*. *On the Gradual Fabrication of Thoughts While Speaking* was begun in 1804 and written during Kleist's stay in Königsberg in 1805–06.[11] *Michael Kohlhaas* was also begun in Königsberg between 1804 and 1805.[12] The first quarter—up until Kohlhaas's departure from Kohlhaasenbrück to sack Tronka castle—was published in *Phöbus* in November 1808, and the text was completed for inclusion in Kleist's first volume of tales published in September 1810, three months before the essay *On the Puppet Theater* was published on 12–15 December 1810 in the *Berliner Abendblätter*.[13] Given *Michael Kohlhaas*'s stress on frictions between bodies, and their susceptibility to minute perceptions, I would like to suggest that we have to read it as Kleist's literary presentation of the essays' sketches of an *aisthetics*, an affective assessment of complex phenomena. In the later essay, Kleist figures this affectivity in rather "inhuman" terms, when the narrator attributes the most perfect grace of movement and perception to a marionette and a bear. Their depletion of consciousness and conscious reflection allows the puppet to move gracefully and the bear to miraculously parry all the blows a fencer intends to deal him. Paul de Man's reading of the essay condenses this to the formula: "consciousness's loss is aesthetic's gain."[14] De Man compares Kleist's essay to Schiller's *Letters on Aesthetic Education* and notes that both are "concerned with the same articulation of the aesthetic with the epistemological" but he remarks that Kleist does so "by way of formal computation," by exposing the "formalization of consciousness [which], as in a machine, far from destroying aesthetic effect, enhances it".[15] In that sense, "consciousness's loss is aesthetic's gain" according to de Man, and he suggests formalization of consciousness, and the machinicity of the quasi-automaton as Kleist's aesthetic concern (something de Man likens to the machinicity of the operations of language). Kleist's image of the fencing bear certainly evokes the fencer as a well-known image of the skilled rhetorician, which resurfaces from Quintillian via Kleist and Baudelaire in Benjamin's and de Man's stress on the inscriptions of language on the speaker—rather than the use of language as an allegedly transparent tool. And while such rhetoric is at play in Kleist without a doubt, we find that—specifically in *Michael Kohlhaas* and the two mentioned essays—such a depletion of consciousness is marked by an increasing attention to the affective. We find less, I would argue, the formalization or automatization of movements and actions, but rather the close attention to a curious interlocking of a susceptibility to impressions and physical responses to them with an, as it were, absent-minded, yet very effective calculation of those responses. When Herr C recommends that the human dancer, certainly ever only approximating the puppet in grace, should nevertheless strive for a puppet's depletion of consciousness, it is less to restitute its machinic qualities and mathematical computation, but rather in order to avoid "finding the soul (vis motrix) in any other point than in the movement's barycenter" (*SW II/7*, 322; translation is my own). The labor, as it were, is undertaken in order to maintain a state of mind that keeps with the barycenter of the motion, depleted enough not to reflect (as the boy's imitation of the *spinario*, which disrupts the movement), and present enough to be adequately adjusted to the bodily motion required, without losing composure—for otherwise the soul might slip accidentally into the elbow, for instance, as the narrator comically remarks, and the movement would go astray, its effectivity lost. This is difficult, Herr C. notes, "since we have eaten of the tree of knowledge. But Paradise is bolted and the Cherub is behind us. We must make a journey around the world, to see if a back door has perhaps been left open" (*ADE*, 214/*SW II*/7, 322–23). With paradise locked, it is no use to muster the pathos of a return to innocence. De Man is right to stress that what the essay calls grace is "cleansed of pathos." It does not promise a redemptive synthesis of conscious and machinic, of postlapsarian and prelapsarian, of rising and falling. Rather, I agree with de Man, "one should speak of a continuity of the aesthetic form that does not allow itself to be disrupted by the borderlines that separate life from death, pathos from levity, rising from falling.... [T]he puppet inhabits both sides of these borders at the same time. The text indeed evokes the puppet's dance as a continuous motion."[16] We can find an attempt at such a continuous motion in the two characters under scrutiny in this chapter. They strive to suspend consciousness in order to inhabit both sides of its border and dwell there in a state of "semiconsciousness." Striving for the effectiveness of the fencing bear, these figures immerse themselves in a state of simplicity that does not absolve them from the human predicaments of the Fall, nor permit them to turn to any form of bestiality. The bear is no raging animal; on the contrary, he is a chained and trained bear, and remains supremely composed in his responses. He adapted to his situation much as Kafka's ape did in order to find a way out of his cage. And as Deleuze and Guattari stress in their reading of Kafka's *Report to an Academy*, such a way out is not an escape out of the situation, but rather a bending of the situation, a transformation of its parameters.[17] In this sense, Michael Kohlhaas and Billy Budd lose consciousness: to parry the occurrences, to stake out their ever-changing positions in the midst of the muddle of things. This disposition of remaining malleable enough to stay on course—the practice of a mode of affective thinking that remains set on "what is to be done next?"[18]—is what is at stake in my reading of both tales.

## Resolute Simplicity

### *(Billy Budd, Sailor. An inside narrative)*

In her book *Stupidity*, Avital Ronell implicitly links Kleist's essay *On the Puppet Theater* to *Billy Budd, Sailor*. When discussing de Man's work and its focus on the performativity and productivity of language, she stresses de Man's point—in reference to his essay on Kleist, which was cited above—that language outwits the subject, that "[l]anguage smarts; the subject necessarily dulls." Ronell continues:

> If one were asked to designate a single work in literature that had anticipated and monitored the gathering of these broken threads

of cognition, one might settle on Melville's great allegory of testing, Billy Budd—although arguably, all literary texts, exhibiting different levels of boldness and intimate with gaps in cognition, put the conditions of understanding on trial.... Billy Budd tests the presuppositions that hold together the knowing subject. Emblematic of the trials to which it submits itself, the eponymous hero reflects the predicament of the novel. He is essentially put forth as a saintly avatar of stupidity, forced to endure tests that can only be failed....[19]

With explicit reference to Johnson's reading of *Billy Budd*, which had already earlier pointed us in the direction of Billy's simplicity, Ronell argues that "the disruption of knowing cannot be understood in terms of absence, default, or deficiency, as if something could be filled, completed, or known by being brought out of its state of absence into unconcealedness."[20] However, Melville's text asks us to consider not only the discontinuities in knowledge, but also their productive performative force: "[T]he rush of interference that produces gaps and unsettles cognition must be seen as a force that weighs in performatively and must be read. The interruptive moment of interference itself calls for a reading."[21] If Billy is this "interruptive moment" we must respond to Ronell's demand and not just state the interruption, but read it, that is, not just show that it momentarily interrupts understanding or knowledge but also try to assess what is produced in the interruption. How does Billy test the presuppositions that constitute the knowing subject? How does he deal with the interference, and what has his simplicity got to do with it? And what do we make of Ronell's implicit suggestion that Kleist's essay corresponds to this figure? At no point do we hear Billy lament the inattainability of reliable knowledge or stable understanding. He does not mourn the loss of epistemological certainty. Nor does he, in diametrical opposition to his adversary Claggart, play with the instabilities of knowledge, or ironically unsettle our belief in its stability. But neither can we say that Billy—in his own way—possesses a shrewd mind and call him "intelligent." As we will see, Billy Budd rather maintains a disposition that unhinges cognition by settling at the differentiating limit of understanding and not understanding, of knowing and not knowing, a disposition that Melville suggests to be "semiconscious" or—I would argue—we could call "simple". Or, said differently, his simplicity suspends their opposition in a "semiconscious" zone that permits him to refrain from knowing—so that, in a sense, he does not know, and yet does not not know. By staying at that limit, which grants him a liminal, minimal space for a semiconscious, affective assessment of things, Billy Budd manages to respond to and ward off Claggart's insatiable lust for irony, and Vere's inevitable commitment to law and order. But we have to take it slow.

*Billy Budd, Sailor* is Melville's last prose narrative, written between his retirement from the New York Custom House in December 1885 and his death in 1891, unfinished and posthumously published not until 1924.[22] The plot is simple, and easily told. In the summer of 1797—a critical moment in British naval history during the French Revolutionary Wars, and shortly after several serious mutinies in the fleet—twenty-one-year-old Billy Budd, foretopman of the British fleet, is involuntarily impressed into service on the man-of-war *Bellipotent* under command of Captain Vere. On the *Rights-of-Man*, the merchantman where he had sailed up until his impressment, everyone took to Billy, the Handsome Sailor, and swarmed around him to please and delight him. By his innocent air and the musical chime of his voice he effortlessly restored order to the lower decks, the merchantman's captain reports at Billy's impressment, lamenting the loss of his peacemaker. Billy's striking beauty and sweetness have a similar effect upon the crew of the *Bellipotent*, except upon its master-at-arms John Claggart, who suffers an immediate aversion to Billy. Strange occurrences and allegations suggest that Claggart is after him, but it remains unclear whether he truly suspects Billy, as he claims, of plotting mutiny, or is "down on him" out of mere spite or dislike. Claggart's allegations of Billy rest on hearsay and Claggart's overinterpretations thereof. In order to press a confession from Billy, Claggart brings the accusation before the captain, at a moment when the *Bellipotent* is on a special expedition and farthest removed from the fleet. Captain Vere, intending more to test the words of the accuser than the alleged deeds of the accused, confronts Billy with Claggart in his cabin. Hearing the unexpected accusation from Claggart's mouth, Billy is struck by the stutter that afflicts him when under pressure, and unable to utter a word of explication or exoneration he punches Claggart and strikes him dead. Although Captain Vere believes Billy to be innocent and falsely accused of mutiny, he feels impelled to immediately pass sentence for the crime committed, all the more so as it involved killing a superior in rank. Anything less than hanging would prove a weakness of command, and increase the threat of mutiny. Instead of waiting, as custom would have it, to rejoin the fleet and hand the case over to the admiralty, Vere summons a drumhead court, which sentences Billy to death by hanging. After a conversation between the captain and Billy behind closed doors, whose subject remains unknown, Billy shows acquiescence to the sentence and at the execution the next dawn he blesses Captain Vere with the last words he utters before being suspended from the yardarm-end. Surprisingly, his body neither quivers nor contracts when dying, and only the murmur of the crew and the shrieks of sea-fowl are raised.

That is the plot, but it is not as simple as this summary suggests. The narrator indicates that instead of "coherence" of plot, the text begs the consideration of its arrangement, of its exposition of a baffling chiasmus. So, as said before, instead of asking what the tale is about, we should look at what the tale turns around. The narrative is given momentum by Billy Budd's strange way of being—"a nature that, as Claggart magnetically felt, had in its simplicity never willed malice or experienced the reactionary bite of that serpent" (*BBS*, 78)—a baffling nature to which Claggart reacts just as bafflingly, namely—as we just saw—"magnetically." Pointing to the momentum that these strange "natures" give to the tale, the narrator notes that "[t]he point of the present story turn[s] on the hidden nature of the master-at-arms" (*BBS*, 76–77). Their opposing, yet somewhat similarly unaccountable dispositions lead up to the troubling chiasmatic reversal of guilt and innocence that occurs when falsely accused Billy kills scheming Claggart.

Given the confrontation of Claggart and Budd, we will begin this consideration of Billy's simplicity with a look at his opponent and the aversion that it magnetically sparked in him. Although we learn nothing of the motives for his aversion, Claggart is presented as someone who incessantly reads and misreads Billy, and it is this reading that sets the plot in motion.[23] However, as he begins to support his readings of Billy by collecting evidence of Billy's misdemeanor—evidence that Claggart himself had ordered to be fabricated—we must assume that his main objective is not the truth-value of these readings. He is not after knowing what Billy is really up to. Rather, as the oracular Dansker suggests to Billy when the latter is confused and vexed about the minor troubles he runs into again and again, Claggart's incentive for his readings against Billy is that he is "at heart and for nothing…down on him, secretly down on him" (*BBS*, 73). What are we to make of such "for nothing"? This is what the narrator suggests:

> Now to invent something touching the more private career of Claggart, something involving Billy Budd, of which something the latter should be wholly ignorant, some romantic incident implying that Claggart's knowledge of the young bluejacket began at some period anterior to catching sight of him on board the seventy-four—all this, not so difficult to do, might avail in a way more or less interesting to account for whatever enigma may appear to lurk in the case. But in fact there was nothing of the sort. And yet the cause necessarily to be assumed as the sole one assignable is in its very realism as much charged with that prime element of Radcliffian romance, the mysterious, as any that the ingenuity of the author of The Mysteries of Udolpho could devise. For what can more partake of the mysterious than an antipathy spontaneous and profound such as is evoked in certain exceptional mortals by the mere aspect of some other mortal, however harmless he may be, if not called forth by this very harmlessness? (*BBS*, 73–74)

It would be easy, we are told—or at least not too difficult—to come up with an invented "something," to construct some explanation by going back to their private histories prior to the narrated events, in order to explain Claggart's dislike of Billy Budd. Although we are told—in a feigned claim of mimetic realism—that "in fact there was nothing of the sort", it is—if we read closely—

rather a question of poetic principle that forbids such a search or invention: it would be only "more or less interesting" to account for the story in such a romantic (Radcliffean) manner. Only the lurking enigma that is presented on site, not temporally prior to or imagined spatially exterior to the writing, is of interest. And the lurking enigma, which drives the tale precisely because it perpetually withdraws from being grasped, is that Claggart was down on Billy for no apparent reason, except the only one necessarily to be assumed "in its very realism": a spontaneous antipathy. No gothic mysteries or sentimental secrets implied, no psychology behind it—we only hear that this antipathy drives Claggart to orchestrate the petty troubles Billy runs into. When learning that it might perhaps be for "the good looks, cheery health, and frank enjoyment of young life in Billy Budd" (*BBS*, 78) that Claggart despised him, we surmise that what is suggested here is no all-too-human resentment due to personal interests or disagreements, but truly a spontaneously sparked antipathy, which is "evoked in certain exceptional mortals." Billy simply does not agree with Claggart, and we are bound to recall Kleist's Mirabeau here. It may have been merely a twitch, a fidgeting or something in Billy's aspect that set Claggart off.

Claggart takes the incident in which Billy spills the soup in front of his feet—their only crossing of paths before fatally meeting in the captain's cabin—as proof that there is likewise "a spontaneous feeling on Billy's part more or less answering to the antipathy on his own" (*BBS*, 79). This is an eventually lethal supposition, as Claggart misreads Billy according to his own ironic categories, suspecting double meanings and Billy to be a "man-trap ... under the ruddy-tipped daisies" (*BBS*, 94). Billy, however, refrains from both antipathy and sympathy, and his incapacity for irony will in the end knock Claggart out. Yet, while Claggart cannot refrain from reading opaque Billy, he also—just as much as Billy—reacts affectively, namely, "magnetically," to Billy's simplicity. Being a man of energetic build, Claggart is as similarly affective a character as Billy—"a nature like Claggart's, surcharged with energy as such natures almost invariably are, what recourse is left to it but to recoil upon itself and, like the scorpion for which the Creator alone is responsible, act out to the end the part allotted it" (*BBS*, 94). Claggart tries to resolve his own affective reactions by fabricating a second, allegedly truer layer to it, and tries to make sense of his own affective reaction by attributing ill will to Billy. Accordingly, Claggart thinks he smartly detected Billy's true intentions when Billy spilled the soup, and reads this as a harmless demonstration of Billy's antipathy, "a foolish demonstration" of Billy's alleged aversion toward him, "and very harmless, like the futile kick of a heifer, which yet were the heifer a shod stallion would not be so harmless" (*BBS*, 79). Smirking at Billy's foolishness, Claggart fails to see that what is at work here is merely his own supposition of a hidden meaning, and that Billy's "foolishness" is irreducible to such an allegation of hidden intentions. Billy Budd's simplicity involuntarily—magnetically—has triggered Claggart's aversion, but due to this simplicity Billy does not acknowledge this.

## Affectivity

Diametrically opposed to Claggart's proliferation of rumorous intelligence and permanent suspicion of double meanings, Billy takes things and words at face value, but to a very different effect than we saw in Delano. Being illiterate, Billy is not only literally unable to read, but also metaphorically described as a plain reader: someone who does not, unlike Claggart, "deal in double meanings." Claggart's ironies and insinuations escape him, and Billy, going by the surface of things, assesses Claggart on the basis of the kind words he always has for him. So at first sight, Billy might merely seem a fool, a simpleton. But when considering Johnson's point of Melville's confrontation of two diametrically opposed manners of understanding, the crucial twist for our present context comes to the fore: Billy's disposition neither lies outside of or before the reaches of Claggart's ironic intelligence nor is it a deficiency. Rather, it seems not too far from Claggart's own, but asserts a different mode of operating under the same affective predicament. When at a later point in the narrative, the afterguardsman, who—we may suspect on Claggart's behalf—tries to set Billy up as a mutineer must confess that "the man he had sought to entrap as a simpleton had through his very simplicity ignominiously baffled" (*BBS*, 89) him, we see that much as Claggart's "intelligent" search for double meanings is an option to read the opacity of Billy, Billy's simplicity is an option to baffle Claggart. And, if this simplicity is able to baffle, to perplex, if it is a manoeuvre, then it cannot merely be due to dim wits, and we must ask again with Johnson: "But is Billy truly as 'plotless' as he appears? Does his 'simplicity' hide no division, no ambiguity?"[24]

After beginning the pursuit of Billy's simplicity against the foil of his "opposite pole" Claggart, let us now begin again with the first words Billy utters. Upon his impressment, he famously bids farewell to the *Rights-of-Man* by exclaiming "And good-bye to you too, old Rights-of-Man" (*BBS*, 49), which leaves a lot to speculate about regarding his intentions for breaking so disrespectfully with naval protocol. It could be meant as a "slight slur at impressment" (*BBS*, 49), a way of ironically expressing his disagreement with being pressed into naval service, as the lieutenant believes. And, although this cannot be ruled out completely, as ironies never can, we are given a first description of Billy Budd that makes such an expression of disagreement unlikely.

> And yet, more likely, if satire it was in effect, it was hardly so by intention, for Billy, though happily endowed with the gaiety of high health, youth, and a free heart, was yet by no means of a satirical turn. The will to it and the sinister dexterity were alike wanting. To deal in double meanings and insinuations of any sort was quite foreign to his nature. As to his enforced enlistment, that he seemed to take pretty much as he was wont to take any vicissitude of weather. Like the animals, though no philosopher, he was, without knowing it, practically a fatalist. And it may be that he rather

liked this adventurous turn in his affairs, which promised an opening into novel scenes and martial excitements. (*BBS*, 49)

Possibly, then, no however slight slur at past impressment, but an expression of excitement at this promising turn of events. We cannot be certain, for no reason for the exclamation is given, and just for that reason it will trigger a whole set of readings. But aside from these reading effects that the narrative unravels and that Claggart performs, we are interested here in Billy's strange disposition of which his "hardly given" intentions speak, the type of simplicity he displays, and how it relates to Melville's aesthetics. In the above quote, we witnessed that with great care intentionality is barred in a way that does not attribute it entirely to its opposite of unintentionality either. If any double meanings were expressed by shouting good-bye to the *Rights-of-Man*, it was "hardly so by intention," because Billy does not "deal in double meanings." It is more likely that Billy did not mean anything by his verbal outburst but an excited farewell. We might still think Billy a simpleton, then, someone who lacks the capacity to read between the lines or caution against what others may read into his farewell. Many of the characterizations that follow tempt us indeed to take him as too blunt a reader, as both literally and metaphorically illiterate, and a little stupid. Following that temptation, we then might find his plain straightforwardness and simple innocence, whereby he takes every utterance at face value, to be his tragic flaw, which is—in unlucky conjunction with his "occasional liability to a vocal defect" (*BBS*, 53) and when challenged by Claggart—also his doom. However, Billy's simplicity does not entirely coincide with mere bluntness or straightforward absence of understanding, and we must reconsider. Only "more likely," it is not definite that Billy did not mean anything by his utterance; and "hardly" intentional it was neither fully unintentional nor fully intentional—it was only almost, or hardly so. Furthermore, we learn that Billy lacks the will to and sinister dexterity for satire. Although the lack of dexterity makes Billy a little too clumsy for satire, a little incapable to meet Claggart's methods of reading on an equal footing, at the same time he is said to lack the will to it. If Billy were plain stupid, or simply dumb, a lack of will would be an irrelevant question. It would merely be his intellectual or linguistic incapacity that prevented him from understanding. But as we follow the wording closely we find a state somewhere between intentionality and unintentionality. Billy Budd rather *refrains* from grasping, from understanding the situation; or, to take up Ronell's suggestive phrasing, he is a character of "*resolute* simplicity."[25] We will have to consider this resoluteness that exclaims utterances hardly by intention. In its oxymoronic alliance with simplicity, such a rare form of resoluteness cannot be accounted for as resulting from intellectual conviction, nor can such a simplicity be accounted for in terms of intellectual incapacities. Resolute enough to be the outcome of a manoeuvre, such a simplicity cannot be attributed to a merely plain mind, but might point toward an understanding that works differently. In order to pursue this, we can take the narrator's advice, who notes that it takes "something more, or rather something else than mere shrewdness...for the due understanding of such a character as Billy Budd's" (*BBS*, 90). We have to go about it differently than by measuring Billy up against intelligence, or gauging his degree of it.

In a way, Billy does seem strikingly stupid. His straightforwardness immediately hits the officer who enquires about Billy's background after Billy has been impressed into service on the *Bellipotent*.

> Asked by the officer, a small, brisk little gentleman as it chanced, among other questions, his place of birth, he [Billy] replied, "Please, sir, I don't know." "Don't know where you were born? Who was your father?" "God knows, sir." Struck by the straightforward simplicity of these replies, the officer next asked, "Do you know anything about your beginning?" "No, sir. But I have heard that I was found..." Yes, Billy Budd was a foundling, a presumable by-blow, and evidently, no ignoble one. Noble descent was as evident in him as in a blood horse. For the rest, with little or no sharpness of faculty or any trace of the wisdom of the serpent, nor yet quite a dove, he possessed that kind and degree of intelligence going along with the unconventional rectitude of a sound human creature, one to whom not yet has been proffered the questionable apple of knowledge....Of self-consciousness he seemed to have little or none, or about as much as we may reasonably impute to a dog of Saint Bernard's breed. (*BBS*, 51–52)

Likened to the reflexivity of a Saint Bernard dog, Billy's degree of self-consciousness might appear to betray a creature of prelapsarian innocence: an Adam whose simplicity vouches for pure, unspoiled innocence. And although the text insinuates this purity again and again, it also marks the almost imperceptible difference between the Adamic Billy and the biblical Adam: When Captain Vere congratulates "Lieutenant Ratcliffe upon his good fortune in lighting on such a fine specimen of the genus homo, who in the nude might have posed for a statue of a young Adam before the Fall" (*BBS*, 94), we are tempted to fix our eyes on "a statue of a young Adam before the Fall" and read Billy as just this representation of prelapsarian innocence and purity. But we must not overlook that Vere suggests that only "in the nude" would Billy pass for such a representation ("a statue"), only if we stripped him of all the ambiguities he presents to us, and only if we attributed—in the Radcliffean manner that echoes in the lieutenant's surname—a deeper, mysterious reason to his baffling simplicity. Although Billy does not seem to have been introduced to knowledge that comes with tasting the "questionable apple of knowledge," his innocence is neither of paradisiacal purity. Although he possessed "little or no sharpness of faculty

## Figures of Simplicity

or any trace of the wisdom of the serpent," he was neither "yet quite a dove." How do we have to account for this oxymoronic simplicity that seems to claim neither dove-white innocence, nor yet a higher form of intelligence or wisdom?

One instance in particular—the shady visit of the afterguardsman—will help here, as the incident best illustrates the peculiar character of Billy's simple ways. When sleeping one warm night with other sailors on the uppermost deck, Billy is cautiously approached by a man from the afterguard who whisperingly—and indirectly "in underhand intriguing fashion" (*BBS*, 83)—inquires if Billy would, as one of the impressed men on board, help them if needed—insinuating plans of a mutiny and offering payment. Struck by the severity of the matter, Billy's vocal defect sets in, and stuttering he sends the afterguardsman back to his own premises. The incident is almost irrelevant to the course of the plot—nothing comes of the encounter, nor does it verify any impending mutiny, as such an intent or project is never clearly stated, and Billy's abstention from reporting the incident is held neither for nor against him later in front of the court. But in regard to our present concern and the tale's sketching of Billy's character, it is highly informative as it shows nothing if not how Billy deals with the occurrence: that is how he *deals*, and although he is said to not deal in double meanings, we find him dealing here nonetheless, albeit dealing in simplicity.

The other sailors who slept on deck overheard nothing but a slight row and a stutter, and when they ask Billy upon his return what had happened, he does not mention the insinuation of mutiny, but answers "mastering the impediment, 'I found an afterguardsman in our part of the ship here, and I bid him be off where he belongs'" (*BBS*, 83). This is not really a lie, as it is precisely what Billy had told the afterguardsman: "D-d-damme, I don't know what you are d-d-driving at, or what you mean, but you had better g-g-go where you belong!" (*BBS*, 82) But Billy's answer to the sailors omits the crucial point, the suggestion of a mutiny. His explanation is sufficiently convincing for the forecastlemen, due to the fact, as the narrator tells us, that of all sections of a ship's crew they are "the most jealous in resenting territorial encroachment, especially on the part of any of the afterguard, of whom they have but a sorry opinion—chiefly landsmen, never going aloft except to reef or furl the mainsail, and in no wise competent to handle a marlin-spike or turn a deadeye, say" (*BBS*, 83). In view of the narrator's intimation of nautical custom, Billy's omission of the crucial point of the mysterious interview appears even more cunning. Being aware of the forecastlemen's disrespect for the afterguardsmen, he could not have come up with a better reply to satisfy their curiosity without saying much. For someone who suffers a vocal defect and who "does not deal in double meanings" this is a remarkable choice of words. Johnson notes in reference to this particular instance that "although he denies any discrepency [*sic*] between what is said and what is meant, ... [he] does not prove to be totally incapable of lying," and we must ask again whether Billy is "truly as 'plotless' as he appears?"[26] But we must not be misled to conclude—and this must be said before any attempt to respond to the question—that we are presented with someone who secretly understands things, clandestinely deals in double meanings and only "plays simple." Rather, he is truly puzzled by the occurrence.

> The incident sorely puzzled Billy Budd....What could it mean? And could they really be guineas, those two glittering objects that interloper had held up to his (Billy's) eyes?...The more he turned the matter over, the more he was nonplussed, and made uneasy and discomfited. In his disgustful recoil from an overture which, though he but ill comprehended, he instinctively knew must involve evil of some sort, Billy Budd was like a young horse fresh from the pasture suddenly inhaling a vile whiff from some chemical factory, and by repeated snortings trying to get it out of his nostrils and lungs. This frame of mind barred all desire of holding farther parley with the fellow, even were it but for the purpose of gaining some enlightenment as to his design in approaching him. And yet he was not without natural curiosity to see how such a visitor in the dark would look in broad day. (*BBS*, 83–84)

Billy's plotlessness is more complex than a mere coverup or playing simple. He does not quite know what the incident meant. But "though he but ill comprehended," he responds to it, and does so in a way that cannot be said to be due to a mere lack of understanding. Rather, as Johnson suggests, "Billy maintains his 'plotlessness' not spontaneously but through a complex act of filtering. Far from being simply and naturally pure, he is obsessed with maintaining his own irreproachability in the eyes of authority."[27] This resonates with Ronell's coining of a *resolute* simplicity: Both Johnson's "act of filtering" and Ronell's "resolute simplicity" stress Billy's simplicity as an acquired disposition, one that has a certain plot to it and is no innate (in)capacity of mind, and one whose maintenance—and this is the crucial point—requires a no less paradoxical passive resoluteness.

But again, in order to follow these intricate turns, we have to take it slow. Billy's initiation into life on a man-of-war was "the first formal gangway-punishment he had ever witnessed" (*BBS*, 68) a dire scene of flogging inflicted upon a young sailor for being absent from his post. "When Billy saw the culprit's naked back under the scourge,... Billy was horrified. He resolved that never through remissness would he make himself liable to such a visitation or do or omit aught that might merit even verbal reproof" (*BBS*, 68). His life on board the *Bellipotent* thus began with the resolution to maintain his own irreproachability. With that in mind, Billy's reaction to the mysterious interview in the forechains at night appears in a slightly different light. Billy's frame of mind, as we heard in that scene, "barred all desire" (*BBS*, 84) to further inquire into the matter at present, as much as his disposition bars any desire to find out what it all meant in the days to follow. The narrator anticipates that readers might find this hard to imagine, and notes that

> shrewd ones may opine that it was hardly possible for Billy to refrain from going up to the afterguardsman and bluntly demanding to know his purpose in the initial interview.... Yes, shrewd ones may so think. But something more, or rather something else than mere shrewdness is perhaps needful for the due understanding of such a character as Billy Budd's. (*BBS*, 89–90)

What readers, who are generally known for shrewdness, might find hard to imagine is that Billy is able to refrain from inquiry despite not being without natural curiosity. But although we might rather expect him to be blunt enough to simply ask, we may need to concede that Billy is not so blunt after all. He neither deliberates on whether or not to report the matter to the authorities, nor does he decide to disregard his duty as a sailor to do so. He simply refrains from clearing up the matter further, as well as from reporting it. "Refrain" in Billy Budd's case neither results from strategic deliberation, nor is it an action that has been decided upon. As we heard in the forecastle scene, it is the effect of merely recoiling from the incident, of trying to get it out of his system by figurative "repeated snortings." Quick enough to perceive the man "from something in the outline and carriage... [as] one of the afterguard" (*BBS*, 82) and to assess the danger of his insinuations, he acts on this, and wards off the approach. Yet refraining from anything further, he sticks to this mode of affectively or semiconsciously "understanding" without searching for reasons. Not the truth of the matter is relevant to Billy, but its practical consequences. Let us follow the consequences of the incident a little farther and observe how Billy goes about things here.

> A day or two afterwards, chancing in the evening promenade on a gun deck to pass Billy, he [the afterguardsman] offered a flying word of good-fellowship, as it were, which by its unexpectedness, and equivocalness under the circumstances, so embarrassed Billy that he knew not how to respond to it, and let it go unnoticed. Billy was now left more at a loss than before. The ineffectual speculations into which he was led were so disturbingly alien to him that he did his best to smother them. It never entered his mind that here was a matter, which, from its extreme dubiousness, it was his duty as a loyal bluejacket to report in the proper quarter. And, probably, had such a step been suggested to him, he would have been deterred from taking it by the thought, one of novice magnanimity, that it would savor overmuch of the dirty work of a telltale. He kept the thing to himself. Yet upon one occasion he could not forbear a little disburdening himself to the old Dansker, tempted thereto perhaps by the influence of a balmy night when the ship lay becalmed; the twain, silent for the most part, sitting together on deck, their heads propped against the bulwarks. But it was only a partial and

## Affectivity

anonymous account that Billy gave, the unfounded scruples above referred to preventing full disclosure to anybody. (*BBS*, 84–85)

Billy had been sorely puzzled, although he turned the matter over in his head. The speculations into which he is half-passively drawn ("into which he was led"), do not agree with him: They are "disturbingly alien to him." He smothers them as best he can. In her reading, Johnson opts to read the verb in its sense "to repress," implying that Billy rules out the negative implications by censorship and repression—from where they threaten to reemerge.[28] There is, however, no mention in the text of repressed speculations, or feelings that threaten to resurface: Neither when Billy is confronted with Claggart in the Captain's cabin, nor at hearing the death sentence, nor at the moment of the sacrament or the hanging. Never do we hear Billy's allegedly repressed and potentially irrepressible speculations or feelings break the surface. This might be because he smothers speculations not to "retain blank ignorance,"[29] as Johnson infers, but rather to maintain "his simple-mindedness" (*BBS*, 86) as the text explicitly tells us. Billy does not return to or retain a state of blankness, but he resolutely maintains a complex simplicity as his own breathing space by *suffocating* speculations, and I would suggest reading "to smother" in the vein of "to suffocate" here.

The maintenance of a breathing space seems to be underlined by the fact that even if an explanation of the occurrence had been offered to him, even if someone else had enlightened him about its significance, his preference to refrain from reporting it would most likely not have been altered, since he prefers to abstain from telltale. The immediately following, albeit oracular, enlightenment that the Dansker offers shows precisely this. The Dansker repeats his allegation that "Jemmy Legs is down on you" (*BBS*, 85) and must be behind the incident. But it leads Billy to nothing more—as we hear two chapters later—than thinking that "the master-at-arms acted in a manner rather queer at times. That was all. But the occasional frank air and pleasant word went for what they purported to be" (*BBS*, 88). Billy's diligent efforts to maintain the simplicity with which he takes Claggart's words for what they profess to be make him the "illiterate" he is. Resolutely, he upholds a state of mind that permits him to stick to his semi-conscious mode of assessing the situation. Even after the Dansker insinuates an explication, Billy continues to refrain from attributing ill will to Claggart. However, this refraining does not operate by repression or denial resulting in the negation of knowledge to the benefit of blank ignorance. Rather, these efforts produce a paradoxically *resolute simplicity*, which is not to be confused with innocence in the sense of a pure, unspoiled state that could be retained, ruined, or might need to be enlightened. Rather, it resolutely persists along with intelligence, it does not fade as the latter rises. We learn of this specific mindset in a brief chapter, inserted between the Dansker's insinuations and Billy's smothering of ineffectual speculations (chapter 15), and Billy's repeated affirmation of taking Claggart at his word (chapter 17). Between these, Melville inserts a brief chapter of three paragraphs (chapter 16) that reflects on the strange nature of sailors in general, and on Billy's in particular. The narrator acknowledges that the fact that Billy, even after the Dansker's hints, refrains from attributing ill will to Claggart

> is to be wondered at. Yet not so much to be wondered at. In certain matters, some sailors even in mature life remain unsophisticated enough. But a young seafarer of the disposition of our athletic foretopman is much of a child-man. And yet a child's utter innocence is but its blank ignorance, and the innocence more or less wanes as intelligence waxes. But in Billy Budd intelligence, such as it was, had advanced while yet his simple-mindedness remained for the most part unaffected. (*BBS*, 86)

We are pointed to an important difference between a child and Billy, the child-man. In a child, innocence and ignorance are said to fade proportionally with the rise of intelligence and knowledge. In our sailor's case, however, his simplemindedness persists, despite the advancement of intelligence—such as it was, or whatever it was in Billy. It does not retain Billy in a state of deficient intelligence, nor can it be accounted for as a remainder of prelapsarian innocence.[30] Billy is no innocent child, but a simple child-man, and the difference must lie in the dash. His simplicity falls neither onto the side of child nor is it advancing toward the enlightened state of man, but it resides in the dash somewhere in-between: a semiconscious and affective maintenance of simplemindedness at the threshold between ignorance and understanding. The dash Melville inserts as marker of this in-between textually resonates in the proliferating conjunction *yet*, which inscribes the structure of Billy's simplicity into the very texture of the text. Figuring as the central turning point in all descriptions of character that we have come across so far, the conjunction *yet* is the narrative's structuring principle. Unable to reread every instance that we have encountered so far, let us only recall the last one. We heard that Billy's refusal to attribute ill will to Claggart was

> to be wondered at. *Yet* not so much to be wondered at. In certain matters, some sailors even in mature life remain unsophisticated enough. But a young seafarer of the disposition of our athletic foretopman is much of a child-man. And *yet* a child's utter innocence is but its blank ignorance, and the innocence more or less wanes as intelligence waxes. But in Billy Budd intelligence, such as it was, had advanced while *yet* his simple-mindedness remained for the most part unaffected. (*BBS*, 86)

Billy is the embodiment of this "yet," the figure of a simplicity that does not mark the absence of all understanding, but the difficult subsistence of an understanding that operates in a realm of *neither* absence *nor* presence of consciousness and is resolutely maintained at their differentiating threshold. His disposition is quite operative, as the tale shows, and more so than phrasing it as "neither/nor" might suggest. Being a figure of "yet"—of "this and yet that at the same time"—Billy occupies that limit and operates at it in his affective mode of thinking. With a resolutely maintained depletion of consciousness, he parries the blows of ironic Claggart and commonsensical Vere, much like the fencing bear in Kleist's *On the Puppet Theater* parries every blow with an eye on the next, and neither trying to get to the bottom of why these blows are coming, nor strategizing with an eye to putting an end to them altogether. Much like the bear, Billy just sticks it out. When the accusation of mutiny uttered in front of Vere surpasses a critical level that makes it impossible for him to parry it by ignoring its reasons and forces Billy to speak in reaction, he does not—cannot—resort to words that might get to the bottom of this accusation and speak about their truth-value. His reaction is one with an eye on parrying the blow, not with an eye on explaining, or making amends to the ears of the law for an accusation of guilt that is unfounded. Billy does not resort to words to confess either way. He maintains the same simpleminded disposition he had shown all along, but the immensity of the publicly made accusation is such that a stutter, with which he had sent the afterguardsman back to his quarters, does not suffice. The gravity of the accusation and the circumstances of its utterance call for Billy's fist—in order to maintain his unwillingness to deal in double meanings. Nothing else could have been spoken but double meanings and they would have required endless explanations. This, I would like to suggest, is why Billy resorts to the fist. His acquiescence to be hung for his deed might make the plot even more puzzling to shrewder minds than Billy. But he—figure of the "yet," of the fold of the sensate and the intelligible, exquisite example of the affective thinking of simplicity—still bears no grudge against Claggart. There is not a moment at which we come to believe that Billy hit him out of resentment or outrage, or felt any desire to justify, explain, or amend. It was merely the "quasi-automatic" reaction to an increase in tension between Billy and Claggart, reaching a critical level when one of them intensifies his verbal ammunition, and the other is impelled to step up his "simpleminded" smothering of speculations. As we noted before, Billy resolutely maintains his complex simplicity as his own breathing space by *suffocating* speculations—and even at the moment of knocking down Claggart it is his own breathing space he is after. When Vere demands that Billy defend himself in the face of Claggart's accusation, Billy's stutter intensifies, so that Vere's "appeal caused but a strange dumb gesturing and gurgling in Billy" (*BBS*, 98). He "gave an expression to the face like that of a condemned vestal priestess in the moment of being buried alive, and in the first struggle against suffocation" (*BBS*, 99). In order not to suffocate himself, and incited by the well-intended movement of Vere who lays his hand on Billy's shoulder to signal that Billy should take his time in responding, "quick as the flame from a discharged cannon at night, his right arm shot out, and Claggart dropped to the deck" (*BBS*, 99). Billy executes literally what Kleist had considered in his essay *On the Gradual Fabrication of Thoughts While Speaking*, namely, that he who in a conversation deploys more and quicker troops will make his point. The cannons, which Billy fires for lack of words, clearly overshoot the mark and any art of conversation, and the law will have to catch up with him: "Struck dead by an angel of God! Yet the angel must hang!" (*BBS*, 101), as Vere, voice of the law, exclaims.

## Calculating Mindlessness
### *(Michael Kohlhaas)*

While Billy—a peacemaker, yet one of murderous eruptions—subsists in this semiconscious affective state of mind, Kohlhaas—a murderer yet one out of excessive righteousness—is someone unusually cunning. They are, as noted earlier, disparate yet related characters, in the sense that Kleist said of his Penthesilea and Käthchen that they "belong together, like the algebraic + and −, and are one and the same being, only thought of as inverse relations" (*SWB*, 818; translation is my own). While Billy is unable to state his intentions or speak in his own defense, Kleist's raging horse dealer from Kohlhaasenbrück is fierce and overly clear in his demands. But just like Billy, he is hard to get, and has equally puzzled readers ever since the tale's first fragment was published in *Phöbus* in June 1808.

In view of these puzzling effects, it seems surprising that Max Kommerell has called *Michael Kohlhaas* the simplest text Kleist ever wrote. And it is true that, as in the case of *Billy Budd*, its plot can be put simply: The horse dealer Michael Kohlhaas is wronged without apparent reason. Out of spite or neglect (we never quite know which) the Junker von Tronka ruins the two horses that Kohlhaas had left at von Tronka's castle, as pledge for a permit supposedly required to cross the Saxony-Brandenburg border. Stubborn and steadfast, Kohlhaas insists upon his return on his right to a full restitution for these two horses, and a punishment of the Junker. When his demand for justice is not met by the Saxon authorities, he takes matters into his own hands. Pillaging in pursuit of justice, Kohlhaas, whose "sense of justice ... was as fine as a gold-balance" (*MK*, 120/*SW II/1*, 76), turns into an incendiary and murderer. Despite many unexpected turns and contingent occurrences in the plot, he remains unyielding in his request of restitution for his two blacks. And although his demand is met in the end, he is executed for the looting committed in its pursuit. Such a brief synopsis of the plot supports Kommerell's understanding of the tale and its hero. When Kommerell calls the text the simplest Kleist ever wrote he does so because he perceives in it a certain "reduction," the reduction of the plot to an antagonism between Kohlhaas and the world: "'Kohlhaas' is the simplest of all Kleist has made: it treats of nothing but the obedience against the self becoming entangled in an antagonism to the world, and of this antagonism being carried and suffered to its end."[31] Correspondingly, he reads the tale's eponymous hero, Michael Kohlhaas, as a hero of simplicity—"einen Helden der Einfalt"[32]—suggesting a similar antagonism: the obedience vis-à-vis the self and the compliance with the exigencies of the world suddenly become antagonistic for Kohlhaas. He is a hero of simplicity because he reduces, that is simplifies, the Kleistian motif of trust to a personal relation between himself and the state. This antagonism is carried through to its end, becoming in a way an obedience *against* oneself, as Kommerell notes: "ein Gehorsam gegen das Ich."[33] Although Kohlhaas's bizarre stubbornness invites us to reduce the plot to this antagonism, I suggest the consideration that Kleist's unraveling of it does not take one hundred pages, making it his longest prose piece, for no reason. What is simple is not so much the antagonism depicted in the tale, but the mindset of its main figure, and the subsistence of this mindset is demonstrated precisely by the endless complications and turns of the plot. The tale draws its force from the dizzying abundance of physical turns taken by the protagonist and turns taken in the course of the narrative itself, which we are made to follow over one hundred pages, and which even continue beyond its end proper, when we learn in yet another turn that the house of Saxony dies out, while the house of Kohlhaas thrives, despite the fact that the former just triumphed in seeing Kohlhaas punished and the latter just perished by being executed as an outlaw. The tale can be called the simplest Kleist ever wrote precisely because of the unwavering, "simple" course of its protagonist—a course, however, in which Kohlhaas is unwavering and remains on course precisely by taking more turns than any of Kleist's other heroes.

Thus, taking off from Kommerell's suggestion, we will pursue Kohlhaas as a "hero" of simplicity, but for slightly different reasons: not so much as reduction to an antagonistic struggle, but rather as a simple position, steadfastly maintained through the whole course of the struggle by means of taking incessant turns. These turns persist throughout the tale, first and foremost literally as the ubiquitous "turning" of its hero and the turns of events. Like the poetics of proliferating prefixes that echo through *The Betrothal in Santo Domingo* and *Benito Cereno* and inscribe the point of miscognition in the very texture of the text, we find here a turn of phrase that reverberates with similar ubiquity throughout the tale. In this case, it inscribes reversals, very much like the abundant use of "yet" in *Billy Budd, Sailor*. The ubiquity of "and turned" (*und wandte sich*)—marker of bodily reversals, followed by a readjustment of perspective—inscribes the susceptibility to minute perceptions, to pressures and blows that Kohlhaas runs into and up against.[34] Incessantly entangled in new turns of events, Kohlhaas is prepared to expose himself to them and go along by making yet another turn. Instead of explicating them rationally, and instead of attempting to clear the giddiness, like Gustav von der Ried, Kohlhaas suspends conscious and rational reflection in a way that I suggest reading as simplicity. With it, he operates under the predicament of these entangled circumstances.

## Figures of Simplicity

Although one can condense the plot, as Kommerell suggests, to Kohlhaas's entanglement in an antagonism against the world, at the same time the tale present us with such a convoluted throng of events, such a web of coincidences that any attempt to summarize the plot escapes us: any summary misses the density of detail, the dizzying complexity of incidents, and is bound to omit occurrences that at first seem minor, but turn out to be of major significance and effect. Just to give one example, we can turn to the moment of Kohlhaas's chance encounter with the Elector of Saxony in Herzberg, where Kohlhaas is forced to interrupt his transport to the electoral court to Berlin, and where the Elector of Saxony happens to be stag hunting. Their chance meeting is a turning point in the narrative, after which the apparatus of the law that Kohlhaas had so far been unable to get started for his purposes is set in motion by the Elector. Ironically, once set to work, it is now in turn unstoppable for the Elector, even when he wishes to do so later for *his* own purposes. To give a comprehensive account of this scene alone would—in however compressed a manner—have to account for the curiosity of the Elector's lady, which drives her to encourage the Elector to sneak a peek at the notorious Kohlhaas, and results in Kohlhaas's version of the gypsy story, which in turn sets into motion the Elector's attempt to retrieve the locket; but it would also have to mention the sickness of Kohlhaas's child due to which his transfer to Berlin was delayed and which allows for the chance encounter in the first place. The biggest turn can be traced back to minor and even more minor incidents, without which the "chance" occurrences would not have occurred. Had Kohlhaas's child not fallen ill and had the Elector's lady not been curious, the Elector would never have realized that Kohlhaas possesses the locket. As it is, however, his realization reverses their roles in relation to the apparatus of the law, with Kohlhaas finally witnessing its action and the Elector submitted to its independent operations. Without going too far into the details of this scene, what becomes evident is that in order to do justice to these entanglements, we would have to retell them almost word by word, following every single turn.[35] This impression of a "simple" plot, which upon looking closely turns out to be composed of endless turns, corresponds to the effect of Kohlhaas himself. We are under the impression of a steadfast and relentless man, and thus enticed to read him as pursuing a set course in his relentless demand of restitution. But like the narrative's resistance to summary, this "condensed" effect of Kohlhaas, the character paradoxically escapes us the closer we look at him. When zooming in, Kohlhaas's alleged steadfastness becomes more and more fluent and pliable. Rather than propelling the action forward by his own resolute steadfastness, he seems to be blown about by coincidences and contingencies. The simplicity that is attributed to him here is, thus, not due to a reduction of complexity, but has to do with this strange pliability, hanging between the fierce activity that we attribute to him and the bizarre passivity that we perceive when looking closely. How can this be? How can a character that strikes us as relentless and obsessed with the restitution of his horses be "blown about"? How can we possibly liken him to someone like Billy Budd, who appears so submissive and inert, and call both "semiconscious"?

Let us look closely at one of the first of the narrative's intricate turns. When, one day in the middle of the sixteenth century, Kohlhaas crosses the border between Saxony and Brandenburg with a string of young horses, he unexpectedly encounters a toll bar. The warden of nearby Tronka Castle asks him for a permit, whose exigency Kohlhaas was unaware of, and which he thus does not carry. Finding the Junker, who is consulted about how to proceed, to be lenient ("let the poor wretch go" (*MK*, 117/*SW II/1*, 71)), the warden intervenes and upon his suggestion, Kohlhaas is forced to leave two of his horses as a pledge and required to present the permit upon his return. Learning at the Chancellery in Dresden that no such exigency of a permit exists, Kohlhaas sells his horses and returns to Tronka Castle to collect his two illegitimately confiscated blacks. To his surprise, he finds them worn down, and the groom, who was left behind for their care, chased off. Despite his fury at the damage done to his property, he is just about to grudgingly depart with the two nags, when the warden engages him in another argument that leads to the narrative's first momentous turn.

> Kohlhaas cursed this shameful, premeditated outrage, but suppressed his fury which he knew would be futile, and as he had no choice, was just preparing to leave this robbers' den with his horses when the warden, hearing high words, came over and asked what was going on. "What's going on?" retorted Kohlhaas. "Who gave Junker von Tronka and his men permission to take the horses I left behind here and use them for field work?"...Staring at him haughtily for a few moments, the warden exclaimed: "What a churlish fellow! A lout like you ought to thank his lucky stars that the animals are still alive!" He asked who was supposed to have looked after them when the groom had absconded, and whether it was not right that the horses should work for the fodder they had been given; and finally he said that Kohlhaas had better cause no trouble here or he would call the dogs and get peace restored in the yard that way. The horse-dealer's heart pounded against his doublet. He felt a strong impulse to hurl this pot-bellied villain into the mud and stamp on his copper-coloured face. But his sense of justice, which was as fine as a gold-balance, still wavered; the judge within his own heart could not decide whether his opponent was guilty; and as he walked over to the horses, stifling his imprecations, and combed out their manes, he asked in a subdued voice, silently weighing up the circumstances, what offence the groom had committed to be expelled from the castle. (*MK*, 119–20)[36]

When we think back to Kleist's essay *On the Gradual Fabrication of Thoughts While Speaking*, this passage appears to be the literary execution of its main contention. The warden, it seems, does not quite know at the beginning what he is getting at, but being, much like Mirabeau, "audacious enough to posit the beginning at a venture" (*SWB*, 320; translation is my own), as the essay phrases it, he fabricates his point while speaking. Incited perhaps by the hint of a feeling of powerlessness on Kohlhaas's face, the warden musters the boldness necessary to overwhelm his opponent. His increasing presumptuousness might be triggered by the still wavering sense of justice in Kohlhaas's chest. And as much as the warden increases his presumptuousness, Kohlhaas is on the downswing and suffers mental bankruptcy, as the essay calls it. His inquiry after the groom's offense, hesitatingly, in a subdued voice, is swept away by the warden's succinct retort that the groom had been insubordinate and defiant, and Kohlhaas swallows an answer. After a page of bustling noise, with the warden hurling more insults, the Junker's company galloping onto the courtyard, shouting and laughing at Kohlhaas's indignation, and the dogs howling—a commotion during which Kohlhaas remains silent—the first words he utters are the refusal to recognize these nags as his horses. Emerging from his silence, Kohlhaas exclaims: "Those are not my horses, my lord; those are not the horses that were worth thirty gold florins! I want my healthy, well-nourished horses back!" (*MK*, 121/*SW II/1*, 78) The German text significantly frames Kohlhaas's silence with two dashes. We saw that his quiet indignation at the warden's insults begins after a dash ("daß er die Hunde rufen, und sich durch sie Ruhe im Hofe zu verschaffen wissen würde. —Dem Roßhändler schlug das Herz gegen den Wams"), and here his emergence from it also ends on one ("Ich will meine wohlgenährten und gesunden Pferde wieder haben!—..."). The English translation swallows these dashes, but they are relevant since they demarcate the passage, in which Kohlhaas's disposition is set off: between them, quietly beneath the commotion of the galloping arrival of the Junker's hunting party, Kohlhaas suffers the almost imperceptible mental bankruptcy. When looking closely at this silence in the extended quote above, we find that when the warden threatens to call the dogs, Kohlhaas takes a step toward the horses, "and as he walked over to the horses, stifling his imprecations, and combed out their manes, he asked in a subdued voice... what offence the groom had committed" (*MK*, 120), in a voice that electrifies the warden into his insolent boldness. Kohlhaas swallows the insults and stands next to his horses, where he remains during the commotion in the courtyard, "reflecting"—as the English translation has it—"what was to be done in his situation" (*MK*, 120). The translators' choice to render Kohlhaas's state of mind as reflection, however, bends his comportment in a direction that the German text does not fully support. There we are told that Kohlhaas "*sann*, was in seiner Lage zu thun sey" (*SW II/1*, 77; emphasis added). Corresponding to his still wavering sense of justice, Kohlhaas muses or literally senses (*sinnen*). After he has *swallowed* the insults—"die Schimpfreden niederschluckend", as the German text notes with another depiction of more affective than reflective effects—he muses about the situation. We do not see him deliberate the pros and cons and figuratively put them on either side of his gold-scale to await the (then just or objective) result. Rather, inflicted with this musing state of mind, he jumps to the refusal of the horses, as a response to the scornful laughter, not as a result of well-weighed reflections on what an appropriate or just demand might be. This jump to refusal, I would like to suggest, is neither the outcome of thinking as rational reflection, nor of irrational or overwhelming emotion with the correspondingly assumed lack of thinking, but rather the suspension of both reflection and emotions, which results in a simplicity that glides along their divide, and continues to do so during the narrative, as we will see.

The description of how Kohlhaas approaches the horses is significant here. The minor insertion that renders the moment when "he walked over to the horses" is accompanied by the insertion that he did so "stifling his imprecations" (*MK*, 120). Much like Kohlhaas's sense of justice, this insertion itself seems to waver, as we cannot tell whether Kohlhaas stifles his own imprecations, or whether he swallows the warden's revilement. The personal pronoun is—much like the German "die Schimpfreden niederschluckend"—syntactically ambiguous and might as well refer to Kohlhaas as to the warden. Interestingly, however, this ambiguity only appears in the completed version of 1810, while in the earlier *Phöbus* version he walked over to the horses in *a dreamy mode*—"auf eine träumerische Art" (*SW II/1*, 19). If the wavering syntax of swallowed insults was preceded by a dreamy mode, what does this tell us about Kohlhaas and his disposition? László Földenyi is right to remark that the substitution in the later version is not a correction, in the sense of it being Kleist's final word, but rather unfolds an implication of Kohlhaas's swallowing the insult that allows us to read the full potential of his dreamy mode, which still underlies the later version. With reference to the *Phöbus* version, Földenyi writes:

> Instead of reflecting on his situation, Kohlhaas begins to dream; instead of weighing arguments and counter-arguments, he becomes enraptured; instead of rationally outlining, which tactic and strategy the situation requires, he switches off his consciousness. And from that moment on he moves on two levels: on the one hand, he directs the events skillfully, exceedingly well thought out, and with perfect tactical sense (much as Homburg the battle), on the other hand, he never seems to be present, as if an *automaton* were acting in his place (and in this he also anticipates Homburg). The result is a bizarre medley: everything becomes confused....[37]

Kohlhaas's dreamy mode of the *Phöbus* version gives Földenyi the hint here. The later version's ambiguity between swallowing the warden's insults and holding back his own, is—much like Kohlhaas's wavering sense of justice—not an uncertainty that, after weighing the pros and cons on a gold-scale, would reasonably be decided upon. As much as Kohlhaas's dreamy mode switches off conscious reflection, the "swallowing of insults" carries this suspension over to the later version. Kohlhaas takes the momentum for the entire course of action from these moments of falling into a dreamy mode: by suspending reflection and deliberation, he does not suffer a relapse into irrationality or an overwhelmingly strong feeling (of justice, revenge, the loss of his wife, etc.). Rather, the suspension of reflection comes to the benefit of a "simplicity" that allows him to mobilize and abide by an affectivity that yields a "perfect tactical sense" as Földenyi calls it; tacit tactics that remind us of the tactical perfection of the fencing bear in Kleist's *On the Puppet Theater*. It is, thus, not despite but rather due to his semiconscious dreamy mode—his simplicity—that he acts so tactically in his pursuit of the Junker: he is not raging out of hurt feelings, but explicitly conducts his quest like a business: a perception of, negotiation with, and susceptibility to the opponents' conduct and demands.

Although we saw Kohlhaas at the first crucial turn of events—when he encountered the warden—fall into a dreamy mode, we will have to ask if this semiconscious state of mind really holds for the whole course of the narrative. Does he not very fiercely and resolutely resolve to punish the Junker? Does he not pursue this goal undeterred, until he gains the demanded restitution of his horses in the end? That is, does he not, once he has had enough—his case dismissed, his wife killed—emerge from this dreamy mode, and calculatingly accomplish his goal of having the horses returned to him, "fattened by the Junker's men" (*MK*, 211/*SW II/1*, 156), albeit on the day of his execution? Or, on the contrary, could we not also say that Kohlhaas emerges from the dreamy mode into an irrational pursuit of personal revenge? Criticism has been very controversial on this point, and innumerable attempts have been made to decide what it is that drives Kohlhaas: rational pursuit of justice or irrational vengeance?[38] We seem to come up against the question we had encountered at the beginning: What it is that Kohlhaas really wants? On the one hand, several instances in the text suggest a reasonable pursuit of justice. When Kohlhaas's wife worries about his plan to sell their house in order to better pursue the Junker, he replies that he does "not wish to remain in a country where I and my rights are not defended. If I am to be kicked, I would rather be a dog than a man!" (*MK*, 134/*SW II/1*, 107). Appearing here as an advocate of individual rights and an emergent bourgeois individuality, Kohlhaas links this a little later to the corresponding economic rationale. These rights are necessary "if I am to go on practicing my trade" (*MK*, 135/*SW II/1*, 108), and all he demands is the freedom to assure and defend them. These moves make him appear completely rational and calculating, and Catharina Grassau's recent reading, for example, contends that Kohlhaas acts here consistently and rationally.[39] On the other hand, he pillages, with troubling brutality, in pursuit of these rights. Grassau explains this reversal from rational to irrational conduct by citing Lisbeth's death, suggesting that it was too much for Kohlhaas to bear, so that, overwhelmed by his emotions, he thereafter began to rant irrationally.[40] Her careful pursuit of the narrative's turning points concludes that a constant swinging back and forth occurs between these two poles of a rational demand for justice and an irrational rage for revenge, and her reading in this respect also epitomizes criticism's incessant oscillation between these two poles. To explain Kohlhaas's actions by either an underlying pursuit of justice (*Recht*) or a raging revenge (*Rache*) certainly attributes understandable motivation to them. However, Kleist's text makes such an attribution difficult from the start, where in the first lines of the narrative we hear that Kohlhaas was one of the most righteous, and yet at the same time one of the most terrible, men of his time—"einer der rechtschaffensten zugleich und entsetzlichsten Menschen" (*SW II/1*, 63). Taking note of this paradoxical disposition, and in view of a text that refrains from clarifying Kohlhaas's motives, I suggest—in view of the present concerns—following Kohlhaas's incessant turns, which are what the text overtly puts to the fore. These turns are conducted throughout the tale in this dreamy mode, the strangely mindless disposition that is affective without being emotional or sentimental, and tactical without being reflective or rational. What Kleist offers us with *Michael Kohlhaas*—aside from the studies of law that the narrative conducts—is a study of affective thinking. We see how Kohlhaas, much like the narrator of the essay *On the Gradual Fabrication of Thoughts While Speaking*, remains highly susceptible to the influence of his opponents' moves and maneuvers an infinitely complex web of situations, coincidences, and demands for action. Although he explicitly declares a set of demands and employs unambiguous force in pursuit of their realization, his course is not inflexible. Contrary to critical assertions that he wavers between the rational and the irrational, from the outset he conducts his work of vengeance like a business, as the German text notes when it states that, after the death of his wife Lisbeth, he "übernahm sodann das *Geschäft* der Rache" (*SW II/1*, 116; emphasis added). This is not a juncture in the narrative where Kohlhaas snaps from a rational and lawful pursuit of justice into an irrational and extralegal course of vengeance, but a confirmation of the disposition Kohlhaas drifted into right from the start with the warden, as we saw. What Kleist's tale asks us to consider is this ubiquity of turning itself, and the businesslike way in which Kohlhaas, deals with his opponents. Like Billy Budd, who maintains his resolute simplicity and deals in simplicity instead of double meanings, Kohlhaas is and remains a dealer. There is no single moment of decision or emotional breakdown on his part whereupon his course is set. Rather, his pursuit is malleable, his resolutions are never as resolute as they seem,[41] and he assesses the next turn that is to be taken by means of what we might call his *calculating mindlessness*. While we noted Billy Budd as a character who, in his peculiar ways, is much more resolute than one might think, Kohlhaas, in his own peculiar way, is much less so.

## Figures of Simplicity

In order to accurately depict the operations of Kohlhaas's *calculating mindlessness* throughout the course of the narrative, we would have to follow the dizzying turns of events as closely as we followed the onset of Kohlhaas's dreamy mode when he first encountered the warden. For the sake of conciseness of argument, let us concentrate on one exemplary instance—the visit to Erlabrunn—that demonstrates how effectively he adjusts his tacit tactics to suit whatever situation he encounters. Active and determined in his demands, he is passive at the same time, at the limit "between *automaton* and *allomaton*" (as Neumann noted in regard to the essay *On the Gradual Fabrication of Thoughts While Speaking*), suspending both emotions *and* rational calculation. The incident at Erlabrunn might strike us as a moment of particular determination and force, but we will see that it is not. After Kohlhaas fails to catch the Junker at Tronka Castle, he is certain that he will find him hiding at the convent at Erlabrunn, where the Junker's aunt holds the post of Abbess. Kohlhaas's band storms the convent and demands to see the Junker, only to learn that he has escaped again to Wittenberg.

> At this Kohlhaas, hurled back into the hellish torment of unsatisfied revenge, *turned* his horse and was about to give the order to set the convent on fire, when a huge thunderbolt struck the ground beside him. *Wheeling* his horse round again, he asked if she had received his writ. The lady answered in a weak and barely audible voice: "Only this minute!" "When?" "Two hours, as God is my judge, after my nephew the Junker had already left!" And when the groom, Waldmann, to whom Kohlhaas *turned* with menacing looks, had stuttered a confirmation of this, explaining that flood-water from the Mulde had delayed his arrival until now, Kohlhaas regained his composure. A sudden terrible deluge of rain, beating down on the cobbles of the courtyard, extinguished the torches and relieved the anguish in his tormented heart. Briefly saluting the Abbess with his hat he *turned* his horse round... and rode out of the convent. (*MK*, 142; emphases added)[42]

Although the passage seems to depict a highly determined action on Kohlhaas's part, it shows him "more as a marionette of his blind excitement and passion, than a self-determined character"[43]; a fury and passion that is, however, as Hetzner also notes, interlaced with thundering strikes from outside of Kohlhaas, whereupon he turns his horse. As he does so, a lightening bolt strikes the ground next to him, at which he turns his horse again, asking the Abbess if she did receive his first mandate that forbids anyone to give shelter to the Junker. And in a prolongation of the same movement, indicated by a dash in the German version, Kohlhaas keeps turning toward the groom Waldmann. Almost collecting himself, the pain in his chest is relieved by a deluge of rain that makes Kohlhaas turn his horse again. Although he is quite forceful during this interview, reducing the Abbess to a weak and barely audible voice, he is not altogether his own master. Susceptible to contingent blows from outside—rendered here, as in many of Kleist's texts, as thunder and lightning, much in the vein of the electrical example put forth in the essay *On the Gradual Fabrication of Thought While Speaking*—Kohlhaas is blown about. Despite this, he clearly acts strategically at this moment, collecting himself early enough to prevent an action—the sacking of the monastery—that would deprive him of any sympathy among the people. In almost every sentence of the tale we can trace an incident or a circumstance, an observation or a suddenly appearing figure, that alters the course of Kohlhaas's endeavors (variously called a *Wendung* [a twist], an *Einwand* [an objection], a *Vorwand* [a pretext]), while at the same time he will pursue his one goal of restitution of his horses undeterred. He manages to maintain this malleable yet unwavering fluid solidity by switching off his conscious reflections and entering his dreamy mode. It allows him to display a perfectly tactical sense of "battle." Without seeking his adversaries' intentions, Kohlhaas maintains until the end an assessment of the situation, which permits him to perceive closely, and, in friction with his opponents, "think" semiconsciously. Kohlhaas is at times in danger of being blinded by rage, and at times he is the calculating horse dealer, who conducts his pursuit of the Junker sober-mindedly and in a businesslike fashion. But he always manages to pull back into his calculating mindlessness—the flip side of Billy Budd's oxymoronic resolute simplicity, which managed to ward off ineffective reflections—and continue to walk this fine line between rationality and irrationality, consciousness and unconscious, albeit erupting at times toward one or the other side. The dreamy mode into which the warden's words catapulted him is neither of consciousness, nor of sentimentality, but the unplugging of both, and Kohlhaas continues to whirl in this suspension throughout his entire endeavor.

## Baroque Heroes

Circling around the strangely unbending, yet pliable characters of Michael Kohlhaas and Billy Budd, the tales by the same names oblige the reader to follow their protagonists' incessant bodily turns, twists, spasms as much as the ceaseless turns of the plot. Just like their eponymous heroes, the tales refrain from giving explications, and instead conspicuously put these turns to the fore. The present reading has therefore refrained from interpreting the heroes' motives and the tales' morals, and has instead pursued what is ostensibly exposed: the paradoxicality, with which both tales work and which prevents us from affixing to the characters one trait or motive. They are, rather, depicted as being of a baffling unaccountability, as being of a contradictory nature, which found textual expression in the chiasmic structure of the ubiquitous "yet" in *Billy Budd*, and the paradoxical "*zugleich und*" in *Michael Kohlhaas*. What both characters achieve with this—aside from baffling everyone around them—is to remain malleable enough to respond to the situations they are immersed in. Both characters, despite their apparent dissimilarities, dwell in a similarly affective, semiconscious mode of thinking that allows them to remain malleable in this sense. They are subjected to friction with encountered opponents and the minute perceptions that go into registering this friction. In the sense that we saw Kleist sketch in his essay *On the Gradual Fabrication of Thoughts While Speaking*, their semiconscious mode of thinking—which has been called their simplicity here—is their "condition that 'knows'" and they employ it not to arrest the endless turns of events in order to come to a cool-headed, final comprehension of them, but to abide by these endless turns of events and to operate under the predicament they pose. As we saw, Billy Budd's simplicity was far less ignorant than it seemed at first, and Kohlhaas's strategic considerations far less calculated than they appeared to be, but in both cases understanding was not foreclosed. Rather, a peculiarly "simple" form of it was produced, which was focused mainly on the question "What is to be done?" at each particular moment. Whereas with Gustav von der Ried and Captain Delano we had two figures who attempted to assess a situation by disentangling the giddiness of their perceptions by "reasoning" on them—a "reasoning" that we saw was framed by sentimentalities and clichés—here we have two figures who refrain from reasoning. Instead, they remain operative within the predicament posed by their perceptions and produce *with* these an assessment of their opponents; an assessment that remains immanent to the very moment it is fitted for. It does not abstract from the situation to arrive at a clear, and transferable, potentially generalizable understanding, but arrives at an understanding immanent to this situation and in view of "What is to be done?" Such an understanding is informed less by what is true than by what is remarkable, by what excites the attention and thereby compels one to act upon it. It that sense, Billy Budd and Michael Kohlhaas submit themselves to the force of minute perceptions that endlessly press upon them and surface to attention. And in that sense, they can be said to operate "in the deepest Baroque regions, and in the deepest Baroque knowledge of the world" where the "subordination of the true to what is singular and remarkable is being made manifest" (*F,* 91). Ironically, they thereby become unique and remarkable characters themselves.

Alongside the *topoi* of revolution, justice, innocence, the automaticities of bureaucratic and legal systems, and the supernatural, which are certainly all relevant to both tales, they make a genuinely *aisthetic* point, which I have foregrounded here: they expose the problem of *affective* or *sensate thinking*. Contesting the limitation of thinking to a conceptual, rational activity of the mind, these tales reclaim its affective dimension and are literary experimentations with "a certain condition...that 'knows'" (*ADE,* 222). Such a state or disposition can be called simplicity if we understand it as the depletion of consciousness to the benefit of affective thinking, and as an affective simplicity, which, far from immediacy or innocent naïveté, or the insight into deeper strata or truths of human existence, is a symptom of the fold of the sensate and the intelligible. Deleuze extracted this principle from his readings of Leibniz, and he links Kleistian characters to it insofar as they, Deleuze notes, perform it: "[A]ll of Kleist's characters are not so much Romantic as they are Baroque heroes. Prey to the giddiness of minute perceptions, they endlessly reach presence in illusion, in vanishment, in swooning, or by converting illusion into presence" (*F*, 125). Heeding the—we may call it Baroque—aesthetic principle of the fold, the heroes in these two tales do not try to grasp the fleeting giddiness of minute perceptions. They do not attempt to transform them into clear ideas and a stable understanding, as we saw Gustav von der Ried and Captain Amasa Delano try (and fail), but they draw an illusory, preliminary, relative clarity from them, only to plunge into confusion and to readjust once more. Their strange "semiconsciousness" is neither mystical clarity, nor does it achieve the "sobering up" that we saw fail in *The Betrothal in Santo Domingo* and *Benito Cereno*. Rather, the eponymous heroes of *Michael Kohlhaas* and *Billy Budd* take on the challenge of the giddiness of minute perceptions and work out for themselves a state of mind with which to operate under their predicament. But in taking on this challenge, both characters, Kohlhaas and Billy, slightly overshoot the mark. They cannot quite contain their affective assessments. Their refraining from explication propels their actions forth in a way that gets ahead of them, and makes them lose their heads too much at times. As we will see, the simplicity of Bartleby and Käthchen of Heilbronn is of a third type. We are not certain if we may call them more "successful," but in their outlandish, slightly ridiculous demeanor they seem to carry an insistence upon the inexplicit that reminds us of Kohlhaas's and Billy's refusal to explicate, yet is in contrast to the latter's affectivity, radically passive and infinitely more unsettling and forceful. They seem to handle the relation between sensation and thinking, which Kohlhaas and Billy *suspend* in an affective semiconsciousness, with great precision by subsisting at the very limit of the two.

## Chapter 4

# Insistence

Bartleby, the scrivener, and sweet little Käthchen are the flip side of the affective figures Billy Budd and Michael Kohlhaas, who overshoot their mark by hitting it too well, who respond to the resistances, obstacles, and challenges to understanding by malleably adapting and affectively assessing what is at hand. Bartleby and Käthchen pose the same problem, but upside down, or better, with Kleist, we could say: they present us with the same strange disposition as Kohlhaas and Budd, but under the opposite algebraic sign, or the opposite electric charge. While Kohlhaas and Budd are being overly rash and in their semiconscious ways incessantly busy assessing their opponents, as we saw in the last chapter, Bartleby and Käthchen hardly move at all, yet radiate a strange lucidity that seems to see right through their interlocutors and opponents. And while they stay put, their almost unbearable passivity puts everyone else around them in a flurry. Their comportment is as bewildering as Kohlhaas's and Billy Budd's, but with them the difficulty to read them resides in their stubborn immobility and the strange formulas they speak in. Their predominant trait is not so much an affectivity, which Kohlhaas and Billy Budd turn into affective thinking, but an obstinate insistence that they cannot and must not speak their reasons, preferences, motivations. And in order not to, they resort to the repetition of little formulas. The fact that they merely repeat these little formulas makes them appear straightforwardly simple, almost plainly a little dumb. But the stubbornness with which they insist on their formulas—and their strange quality of speaking broken-off utterances that insist on their absence of knowledge (Käthchen) or preferences (Bartleby)—unsettles everyone confronted with them.

Among the figures of simplicity discussed in this book, these two are the most challenging, and at the same time most obvious, types proposed by Kleist and Melville: unlike Kohlhaas and Billy Budd, whom we saw affectively assess the situations they encountered and whose semiconscious refraining from explication enabled them to stick to these assessments, and unlike Gustav von der Ried and Captain Delano who incessantly gathered sense-impressions and indulged in explication and rationalization, while failing to recognize those as sentimental projections, Käthchen and Bartleby operate by insisting upon the inexplicit. This arrests these two figures in a disarming, radical passivity, a passivity that in turn permits both to remain silent—apart from their formulas, which, as I will argue, can be read as a way of remaining silent while speaking—and to refuse to explicate. Much has been made of this passivity, most prominently in regard to Bartleby. It has been argued that his passivity cannot be accounted for as mere receptivity or inactivity, as the absence or opposite of activity, but that it is a radical passivity undercutting those very opposites. All of this is highly relevant, and will come to bear here. But what the following reading would mainly like to point to is that, beyond the ontological implications of the discussions of passivity, Käthchen and Bartleby most intriguingly delineate Kleist's "condition that knows"—perhaps most intriguingly of any of the three couples pursued in this book. Gustav and Delano were pathetically lost in the mazes of small perceptions and foreclosed any "condition that knows" because they tried to escape from these mazes by "ineffectual speculations," which we heard Billy Budd struggle to avoid. Kohlhaas and Billy Budd, in turn, pursued and achieved a sensate thinking by abiding by small perceptions, but their semiconscious *modi operandi* had to be fabricated. We saw them continuously labor to ward off the mode of speculation and to prevent being drawn out of their semiconscious states of mind. Käthchen and Bartleby seem unable to inhabit any psychic space other than this formulaic zone, which lies somewhat before consciousness. No one seems able to catapult or talk them out of it, and they just stay put. After an initial consideration of the peculiar passivity they expose, this reading will closely consider both figures with an eye on their lingering in a disposition "before-consciousness". Such a disposition does not make them harbingers of a new and better type of thinking that would be more successful in articulating knowledge. The point is that they never formulate any such knowledge—their formulaic way of speaking does not amount to what we would usually call a formulation of knowledge. In a way they are the reverse of success and undergo inhuman ordeals, of which we are not sure if they are at all undertaken in view of a successful maneuvering of a situation—if we understand it in the sense in which Kleist's essay *On the Gradual Fabrication of Thoughts While Speaking* spoke of a "successful" conversation. What they succeed to do, however, is to insist upon their preference to remain silent, to keep their enigmas until and beyond the end, as Kommerell states. And they achieve this precisely by lingering before consciousness, in a zone prior to the differentiation between sensation and thinking, as we will see. In that sense, these two simpletons might be the most successful of those we have come across so far in exposing the folded relation between sensation and thinking, by insisting on sitting at their limit.

## On Passive Resistance

*(Bartleby, the Scrivener. A Story of Wall-Street)*

Bartleby's enigma is his aggravatingly passive resistance to anything his employer demands or offers, and nothing, the lawyer himself confesses, "so aggravates an earnest person as passive resistance" (*BB*, 23). Bartleby's strange way of being— epitomized in his strange way of speaking in formulas—has been the center of attention in the recent philosophical debate about the tale.[1] This "Bartleby-debate" of the past decade largely focuses on Bartleby's formulaic utterance and its betrayal of a passivity that is no longer accountable within the common opposition of passive and active, and thus unhinges and questions this opposition. Our reading here will also take off from Bartleby's—and Käthchen's—formula, since both are hardly anything but their formulas, and look at the conditions and effects of this formulaic speech, its suspension and *disfiguration* of common logic. But what is really of more interest here is another aspect of both characters, and of Bartleby in particular: namely, his strange way of being and the kind of *figure* it invites us to sketch. Bartleby not only unsettles the opposition of passivity and activity, he offers something in its place. He is the figure of a "[c]ombat of passivity, combat which reduces itself to naught—to extreme patience—combat which the neutral does not succeed in indicating,"[2] as Blanchot was the first to note (and as Derrida and Deleuze took up, and Giorgio Agamben, Jacques Rancière, and others in turn continued). His combat is not sufficiently rendered, Blanchot notes, if we describe is as reaching the neutral (in Blanchot's sense), as laying bare and suspending the opposition of passive and active. We have to take note of the fact that Bartleby offers a combat: he *struggles* for the position of a figure that radiates or illuminates everything around it, without been accountable itself. In the poetological passages of *The Confidence-Man* (1857) Melville explains his concept of an Original in exactly these terms, to which I will come back later. For now, let us try to sketch the figure that *Bartleby, the Scrivener* invites us to read.

In response to an advertisement, Bartleby—"pallidly neat, pitiably respectable, incurably forlorn!" (*BB*, 19)—appears one morning at a law office on Wall Street and is hired as a copyist, mostly because the lawyer hoped that "a man of so singularly sedate an aspect ... might operate beneficially upon the flighty temper of Turkey and the fiery one of Nippers" (*BB*, 19), two of his other three employees. Akin to the "magnetic" aversion Claggart suffers to Billy Budd, the lawyer hopes for an energetic reaction by his dysfunctional copyists to Bartleby. Bartleby is hired for the energies he radiates, not so much for his copying skills, and his forlornness and sedateness—this singular aspect manifesting itself in his formulaic responses, soon to emerge—will indeed succeed in taking effect on everyone in the office. At first, however, he copies insatiably. But not long afterward, the lawyer's "natural expectance of instant compliance" (*BB*, 20) with his orders to copy this or that document is thwarted when Bartleby responds that he would prefer not to. From then on, Bartleby does not comply with any request and merely replies with his fixed set of words *I would prefer not to*. Increasingly immobile, he remains installed at his desk, placed behind a screen, against a window looking out onto a brick wall. Neither does he explain his behavior, nor, when fired, leave the office. Highly irritating to the lawyer, Bartleby has become entirely stationary. Unable to rid himself off his copyist who prefers not to copy, the lawyer eventually moves offices. When forced to leave by the next tenant, Bartleby merely takes a step outside the office, and remains sitting on the banister. The lawyer, as his last employer, is held accountable for him and returns to once more try and talk sense into Bartleby.

> "Bartleby," said I, "are you aware that you are the cause of great tribulation to me, by persisting in occupying the entry after being dismissed from the office?" No answer. "Now one of two things must take place. Either you must do something, or something must be done to you. Now what sort of business would you like to engage in? Would you like to re-engage in copying for some one?" "No; I would prefer not to make any change." (*BB*, 40–41)

While the lawyer assumes that, necessarily, Bartleby either must do something, or something must be done to him, Bartleby replies to all demands and questions with the repetition of a little formula that undercuts—as the growing critical debate of *Bartleby, the Scrivener* has shown—this logic of either/or and that consents neither to acting nor to being acted upon. This baffles the lawyer and unhinges his assumptions.

Let us begin by considering this method of resistance to the lawyer's logic of either/or—Bartleby's repetition of the formula—because it is not only crucial to any discussion of this tale, but it also clearly marks the connection of *Bartleby, the Scrivener* to *Das Käthchen of Heilbronn*, where Käthchen also operates by way of formula. Not long after Bartleby had been hired, the formula occurs for the first time, spoken in a "singularly mild, firm voice" (*BB*, 20). The lawyer is dumbfounded and tries at first to explain it as a harmless slip-up, or a misunderstanding. "I sat awhile in perfect silence, rallying my stunned faculties. Immediately it occurred to me that my ears had deceived me, or Bartleby had entirely misunderstood my meaning. I repeated my request in the clearest tone I could assume; but in quite as clear a one came the previous reply, 'I would prefer not to'" (*BB*, 20). Bartleby's repetition of the formula thwarts the possibility that it may have been a deception of the aural senses, and from this first repetition onward, the formula assumes a life of its own: it echoes through and spreads into the language of the other occupants of the office. We find this already at its first occurrence, when the lawyer himself repeats the words in disbelief and starts to agitatedly walk about the room.

> "Prefer not to," I echoed, rising in high excitement, and crossing the room with a stride. "What do you mean? Are you moon-struck? I want you to help me compare this sheet here—take it," and I thrust

it towards him. "I would prefer not to," said he. I looked at him steadfastly. His face was leanly composed; his gray eye dimly calm. Not a wrinkle of agitation rippled him. Had there been the least uneasiness, anger, impatience or impertinence in his manner; in other words, had there been any thing ordinarily human about him, doubtless I should have violently dismissed him from the premises. But as it was, I should have as soon thought of turning my pale plaster-of-paris bust of Cicero out of doors. I stood gazing at him awhile, as he went on with his own writing, and then reseated myself at my desk. This is very strange, thought I. What had one best do? But my business hurried me: I concluded to forget the matter for the present, reserving it for my future leisure. So calling Nippers from the other room, the paper was speedily examined. (*BB*, 20–21)

It is the inhuman calmness with which it is uttered—without any "ordinarily human" emotion—that permits no ordinary reaction to the formula. Instead, it aggravates and excites the one subjected to it. Insisting with verve on his logic of clear preferences, the lawyer demands once more what he wants: "I *want* you to help me compare this sheet here" (*BB*, 20; emphasis added). But when all is to no avail, he distracts himself from the impasse by hurrying away on business, and postpones an answer to the question what one was to do. From then on, every time a request is made upon Bartleby, he utters this formula, and we cannot quite tell whether he is compelled to use it, or whether he chooses to do so. It is repeated with a mixture of employing it in defiance, and of adhering to it submissively. In any case, Bartleby repeats it with such automaticity that the words stop being a meaningful statement, and by stepping out of the exchange of meaning, Bartleby—or the formula, which increasingly becomes the same—no longer answers to requests "made according to common usage and common sense" (*BB*, 22), as the lawyer claims his work assignments are. Faced with the formula, the lawyer is stupefied and his business logic of accountability and exchange (of meaning), his "doctrine of assumptions" (*BB*, 35) unhinged. Bartleby, on the contrary, "was more a man of preferences than assumptions" (*BB*, 34), of preferences, however, that are neither affirmed nor negated, but suspended in his formulaic phrase. In *Gift of Death*, Derrida notes the peculiar "modality of this repeated utterance that says nothing, promises nothing, neither refuses or accepts anything" and argues that "the tense of this singularly insignificant statement reminds one of a nonlanguage or a secret language."[3] It is a singularly *insignificant* statement, because it appears as harmless as mild Bartleby himself; and a *singularly* insignificant statement, because it flexes the customary use of "to prefer" to an extent that makes it unique and almost reverses its meaning. Usually, the verb precedes the affirmation of a preference. To "prefer not to," however, suspends a declaration of preferences between the expectation of their affirmation and the refusal of a disliked one. Bartleby's formula, making use of "to prefer" in this unusual way, neither affirms nor refuses or negates anything. Or, as Blanchot notes in *The Writing of Disaster*, Bartleby's "'preference not to' has none of the simplicity of a refusal."[4] It speaks not of an indecision resulting from an occasional uncertainty as to which one of two options to choose. It is no simple refusal that defies a demand by clearly refusing it. Rather, *I would prefer not to* undercuts the logic of oppositions, in which a clear choice between two determinable sides of *either/or* could be expected. It points, as Derrida notes, to a structural moment of indeterminacy. Bartleby's formula unhinges the expectation of either an affirmation or a negation by not stating the preference of either this or that, but the preference to abstain from something. While the lawyer, unable to bear or fathom this, tries to translate it back into the registers of activity and passivity, impatiently pressing Bartleby that "[e]ither you must do something, or something must be done to you" (*BB*, 41), Bartleby exposes—by retreating to his formula—a disposition that is difficult to name and insists on the right to a *neither/nor*. With explicit reference to Blanchot, Deleuze repeats that his, Bartleby's, is a "pure patient passivity, as Blanchot would say" (*BF*, 71). Much as the formula lingers between affirmation and negation, Bartleby lingers between activity and passivity, and by way of his strange modality of speaking establishes "a zone of indistinction, of indiscernibility, or of ambiguity...between two terms, as if they had reached the point immediately preceding their respective differentiation" (*BF*, 78). In this sense, Bartleby's passivity is radical: it lingers at a point immediately prior to the differentiation of active and passive. Unable to denominate this point in any other terms than the ones that are brought about by its differentiation, we are bound to call him passive—and to mark his slight, but significant, difference from regular passivity, from being inactive and acted upon, by calling it a radical passivity.

A crucial element of the radicality of Bartleby's passivity is the relentless repetition of the formula regardless of the circumstances or demands made. On the one hand, the statement would not be effective if it was a nonrecurring statement, and it would not drive Bartleby's strange passivity home to the same degree. Precisely by being repeated indifferently in response to all requests and being insisted upon relentlessly does the formula mark Bartleby's way of being as something other than mere passivity or negation. "Its repetition and its insistence render it all the more unusual, entirely so. Murmured in a soft, flat, and patient voice, it attains to the irremissible, by forming an inarticulate block, a single breath" (*BF*, 68). By being repeated in all circumstances, it is depleted of reference to the concrete situation to which it responds, and, thus condensed into an inarticulate block of utterance, it is hardened into a device that can open a little space for Bartleby in which to insist on not giving preferences, and to sit there in his passive resistance. He himself—increasingly assimilating to his formula—assumes the simplicity of this inarticulate block. On the other hand, this formulaic mode of quasi-automatic speaking—of quasi-automatic repetition of the same little phrase—is in turn part and parcel of this strange passivity. Its automaticity of utterance cannot be called a fully active use of language, nor a total passivity. Bartleby's "strange willfulness" (*BB*, 23), as the lawyer calls it, comes to bear in his strange way of speaking and is neither an accountable willfulness nor the—equally accountable—absence of a will.

Bartleby's suspension of the will in this strange manner is not, as Deleuze specifies, the sign of a nihilistic "will to nothingness, but the growth of a nothingness of the will" (*BF*, 71). Suspending his preferences and any articulation of will by way of his formula, Bartleby expands the sphere of negative preferences and of a nothingness of the will, and this suspension points—as many of the recent readings of *Bartleby* have noted—to the *constitutedness* of an opposition of active and passive, or of the intentional and unintentional on the basis of their indetermination. This is what Bartleby exposes, and from this perspective, he is a figure of *simplicity* in the sense that he exposes the point structurally immediately prior to a differentiation into the dichotomies of passive and active, intentional and unintentional, reasonable and unreasonable—the point at which these are differentiated as a result of and on the condition of their folded relationality. By lingering in this zone of indistinction, Bartleby—as well as Käthchen, as we will see momentarily—undermines and unsettles the logic of either/or, and reminds us of the fold that constitutes the two differentiated realms within which we commonly distribute our understanding, conceptualization, and thinking. But beside this structural point, his stubborn repetition of the formula also marks a growing sphere of a nothingness of the will, in which Bartleby precisely survives "by whirling in a suspense that keeps everyone at a distance" (BF, 71), in a space where his strange way of being is able to subsist. From that perspective, he is a *figure* of simplicity in that his whirling on the edges of the differentiation of dichotomies comes across as "almost stupid" and terribly simple. He marks, thus, not only the relationality and continuity permitting differentiation, but also sketches, as it were, the outlines of what could emerge from within the suspension of the assumed stability of differentiated oppositions. It is important to note that Bartleby cannot be said to be endowed with new capacities, but rather undergoes a fundamental impotency. He is "stricken with a constitutive weakness but also with a strange beauty" (*BF*, 80), and in this, he is closest to Kleist's Käthchen. Much like her, Bartleby is not, as Ronell reminds us, "a morph of the action hero, quick and present to the task, sure of aim, but...the depleted being, held back by fear or indifference (we are never sure which), a being from the start stupefied, nonpresent—'not all there.'"[5] Being the depleted figures of this fold, they are stricken with a simplicity that vouches for this very fold, for the very threshold that is neither of the two. But by presenting us with such unaccountable passivity in someone appearing fairly simple, Melville—much like Kleist with his Käthchen—has also created an immensely unsettling figure, whose unsettling effect cannot satisfactorily be explained by merely pointing to Bartleby's passivity, not even if we point to its radicality in the way of the current debates presented above. The effect Bartleby has on the lawyer—and to a similar extent on the reader—is not only due to his utter debilitation and erosion of will, nor even merely to aggravation. Bartleby is also highly captivating in that he has a strange lucidity about him; one that is in a way the same frightening—because inexplicable within our common registers of either/or—and steadfast clarity that we saw in Kohlhaas, only with the opposite algebraic sign, so to speak: while Kohlhaas whirls in endless twists around his steadfast, yet obscure goal, Bartleby stands still and insists on his unwavering and persistent repetition claiming not to phrase any goal. Whereas Kohlhaas and Billy Budd responded flexibly and affectively to their environment and the pressures it exerted upon them, twisting and turning as a result of these, Bartleby—and Käthchen, as we will see—react to everything with the same, unaltered formula. Contrary to the adaptive Kohlhaas and Billy Budd, Bartleby repeats his formula so inflexibly that it can hardly be called a response at all. It appears detached from any demand or circumstance, and uninterested in its interlocutors. Yet, as Agamben notes in his reading of the tale, it announces something. If Bartleby's formula "hovers so obstinately between acceptance and refusal, negation and position, if it predicates nothing and, in the end, even refutes itself, what is the message he has come to tell us, what does his formula announce?"[6] Precisely as an effect of the suspension of opposites, Agamben suggests, something is announced—that is, neither articulated nor presented, but merely announced. It is insistent rather than existent—and Agamben suggests, in line with Deleuze, that what shows itself with Bartleby and his formula "on the threshold between Being and non-Being, between sensible and intelligible, between word and thing, is not the colorless abyss of the Nothing but the luminous spiral of the possible."[7]

In order to perhaps see better what Agamben here merely hints at we have to recall Derrida's remark in reference to Bartleby's formula. Derrida notes that given the "modality of this repeated utterance that says nothing, promises nothing, neither refuses or accepts anything, the tense of this singularly insignificant statement reminds one of a nonlanguage or a secret language."[8] This language—which Derrida is careful not to equate with the formula, but with which the formula resonates or echoes—is secret in the sense that it cannot be uttered, yet resounds in all utterances and sets them on their course. It is secret in the sense that it "creates a tension,"[9] as Derrida writes, or in the way that Deleuze has called the formula a "kind of limit-function" (*BF,* 68): It is the differentiator which remains secret, but which secretes all other language, and the language of all others. It is not secret in the sense of *to be discovered,* but as Arsić notes, it is a secret language or "a nonlanguage... because it evokes the future without predicting it. In other words it remembers the unknown without knowing it; or it recollects the unforeseeable without foreseeing it; that is why it is a remembrance which is not, a foreseeing which is not, a language which is not. A secret language."[10] Bartleby's repeated utterance, its modality, its tense, is nothing in itself. It does not remember something that was once known, had only been forgotten, and could be brought back to mind, but it remembers what is unknown without knowing it. As a being from the start stupefied, Bartleby, the formulaic simpleton, exposes himself to this impossibility, and insists on marking, recollecting, exposing what never was: the fold "between sensible and intelligible" as Agamben said, a fold that produces the manifest dimensions of sensible and intelligible. As a figure of simplicity, Bartleby attests—much like Käthchen—to this zone between the sensible and the intelligible, without being either.

## Lingering before Consciousness
*(Das Käthchen von Heilbronn oder Die Feuerprobe)*

In order to better carve out what might be announced in this zone, I will couple Bartleby here with another strangely passive and strangely lucid figure: Kleist's Käthchen of Heilbronn. While Bartleby is—first and foremost—a man of insisted upon, yet unstated preferences, Käthchen is a woman of insisted upon, yet unstated knowledge, and they share the same method of remaining in this mode of insistence: Both speak in formulas. Their difference, however, will get us to the point of Agamben's luminous spiral, and to the claims of both texts to a superior irrationalism—which is not mere irrationalism, just as their characters' passivity is not mere passivity. Whereas Bartleby sticks to a passive immobility, Käthchen sticks to what we could call an equally bewildering passive mobility. While Bartleby is all stillness and prefers not to move or make any changes, Käthchen moves quite a bit, yet only by trailing the movement of Count Wetter vom Strahl. She follows his every step, and much like Bartleby, suspends all activity except for her insistence upon speaking in formulas. Despite trailing the count, Käthchen becomes an equally disconcerting fixture, only in this case not so much installed behind a folding screen in an office, but beneath the elder bushes ourside the count's premises. In doing so, both, I will argue, are "characters who exist in nothingness, survive only in the void, defy logic and psychology and keep their mystery until the end" (*BF,* 81).

Let us look at Käthchen, then. When one day she lays eyes upon Count Wetter vom Strahl—a knight who stopped in at her father Theobald's smithy to have a plate of his armor's breastwork fixed—she is struck by his appearance as if by the literal lightning (*Wetterstrahl*) of his name and from then on pursues him with unshakable determination. When the family sees the count off after his armor had been repaired, she jumps, as if out of her mind, from the second-floor window to run after him, breaking her loins in this fall. Forced to recover at her father's house, Käthchen refuses to speak or to explain her sudden fancy to follow the count. "There she lay... never making a move or sound. Not even delirium, that open sesame of hearts, could open hers. Nobody could get her to say a word about the secret that possessed her" (*OF,* 168/*SW I/6,* 18), reports her father Theobald. Upon recovery, she immediately tracks down the count, and installs herself at his side. During the journey to his castle, she merely asks to sleep in the stables with his horses, and upon return to his castle, quietly installs herself under the elder bushes outside its walls. From then on, she follows the count "in blind devotion, like some camp-follower, drawn by the beam from his face, like a five-strand rope about her soul ... like a dog lured by the reek of its master's sweat, she traipses after him" (*OF,* 168/*SW I/6,* 19), up until the point when her father summons a Vehmic court to charge the count with bewitching and abducting his daughter. We learn all these prior events from his testimony before the court, with which the play opens. When Käthchen is called before the court and cross-examined as to the reasons for her strange behavior, she does not give any, and they will remain unclear until the very end. The play does not allow us to conclude that Käthchen's desire was to marry Count Wetter vom Strahl; she never asserts that. Even when a marriage does come about in the end, it does not resolve any of the mysteries, as Käthchen forecloses the easy rationale of matrimonial intent once more. When the count finally asks her to marry him—"Katie! My bride! Will you accept me?"—she thwarts his and the reader's expectation of a commonsense resolution by once more avoiding an answer. Instead of the expected *I do,* she exclaims "May God and all his saints protect me!" (*OF,* 259/*SW I/6,* 198) and faints, and we are unable to tell whether she faints out of bliss, from having her prophetic dream come true, or because the assertive answer of *I do* (*Ich will*) is too much for her. What we can observe throughout the play is that she remains at the count's heels, sticks to his side, and trails him with a cringing, doggish servitude, which drives the count out of his mind. He curses her for it: "Confound your doglike readiness to serve!" (*Verflucht die hündische Dienstfertigkeit!*), when—in the scene that the title marks as her ordeal by fire (her *Feuerprobe*)—she is even prepared to run into the castle of the count's momentary fiancée Kunigunde to fetch the count's portrait for the latter—risking her life to retrieve the alleged love-token for Kunigunde, which turns out later to be of value to calculating Kunigunde because its case contains the count's gift to her of the deed to his property of Stauffen.

Käthchen survives this ordeal by fire, and miraculously emerges from underneath the debris of the collapsed castle. She is ignorant about the precise content of what she has rescued and even when handing the case to Gottschalk, the count's servant, her reply to what it contains is merely *I don't know.* Aside from her subservient behavior, this is what we get from Käthchen: the recurrent reply of *I don't know* to any inquiry—a reply as softly uttered as Bartleby's *I would prefer not to.* It is her most frequent phrase, and it works much to the same effect as Bartleby's formula. The count, much like Bartleby's employer, is unable to rid himself of Käthchen, although he tries from the first day of her pursuit and continues to try until the last act, despite the fact that he secretly admits to being enchanted by the simple girl. Käthchen, uttering her *I don't know* at all occasions, sticks to his side with incredible persistence, with an "insistingly devoted behaviour"[11] that both irritates and intrigues the count. Nevertheless, in line with his own good sense, the count woos urbane and strategic Kunigunde von Thurneck and intends to marry her. Only when Kunigunde proves three times unworthy and not the emperor's daughter the count took her to be—according to a mysteriously foreboding fever-dream that promised him a royal wife—and only after Käthchen has been declared in black and white to be of royal blood, does the count switch from Kunigunde to Käthchen and decide to marry Käthchen. We will come back to the declaration of Käthchen as the royal child. For now, we must only note that the count's demand for proof and explication—perpetuated by his inability to be absolved altogether from the power of premonition, as the count's disconcertment with the fever-dream shows—is pitched against Käthchen's insistence upon an unspeakable knowledge. Much like the collision of the logic of presupposition and the logic of preferences in *Bartleby* we have two different logics at work here: Käthchen's strange disposition, which makes her entrust herself to something she herself is unable to speak or know but upon which she bases her aggravatingly stubborn insistence on staying close to the count, and the count's will to be reasonable, in accordance with the logic of state. Although Kleist provides multiple sidelines to the plot around confusing entanglements of love relations and variously motivated feuds among the knights, the play derives its dramatic force from this confrontation between the count and Käthchen: a confrontation not merely of two lovers, but of two registers of thinking or two logics, which continue to coexist until the end. The count's reason of state remains intact as he does in the end marry the emperor's daughter as intended; and Käthchen's incapacity or refusal to give reasons remains operative as she thwarts all inquiries after her desires and intentions by recourse to her little saying *I don't know*, and does not—even before the altar—confirm a matrimonial intent, but faints. Kleist does not resolve the confrontation of these two registers of thinking in either direction. While the miraculous resolution of the count's premonition comes about by black-and-white evidence and allows the count—by unexpected detours—to adhere to his calculations and reasonable logic of state, at the same time, Käthchen's words, condensed in the sweet little formula *I don't know*, allow her to respond without giving any explanation. Kleist has neither of these two registers win out over the other, but it is certainly strangely sweet Käthchen that intrigues not only the count, but also the reader.

The suggestion that both Käthchen and Bartleby operate by way of formula takes up a hint made in passing in a footnote in Deleuze's *Bartleby; or, The Formula*, where, Deleuze, when asserting a subterranean lineage between Kleist and Melville and their strangely simple figures, states without further explanation: "Catherine Heilbronn had her own formula, close to that of Bartleby's: 'I don't know' or simply 'Don't know.'"[12] Let us first see how her formula works, before we can see what it tells us about her strange ways of being simple and the extent to which this might outline the "condition that knows" to which Kleist's essay *On the Gradual Fabrication of Thoughts While Speaking* referred.

While Käthchen certainly speaks more words than Bartleby, she nonetheless comes to acquire, much like Bartleby, a plain little formula, which she repeats incessantly and which marks her incapacity or refusal (we are never quite sure which) to state her intentions, to explain her strange conduct. Asked for her reasons, her words deny any knowledge of them—*I don't know* (*ich weiß nicht*). But their stubborn and quasi-automatic repetition, together with her obdurate pursuit of the count, insinuate something other than mere ignorance, and rather betray Käthchen as someone "who would prefer-not-to-speak" (*BF*, 80), as Deleuze remarks. Her singularly insignificant statement baffles her surroundings and results in the convening of several courts. Everyone confronted with Käthchen and her formulaic conduct is bewildered and confused. Her father cannot fathom the "secret that possessed her" (*OF*, 168/*SW I/6*, 18); Wenzel, one of the court's assessors, asks "Was ever child so stubborn seen as this?" (*OF*, 174/*SW I/6*, 30); and the count, who adheres to the registers of reason and state power, is utterly confused by her: "You wondrous maiden! What are you dreaming, what are you doing?" (*"Du wunderliche Maid! Was träumst, was treibst du?"* (*SW I/6*, 27; translation is my own)). The sweetness and mildness with which she utters these three words make this little statement at first seem to be of hardly any consequence, and to denote merely the lack of knowledge. However, her formulaic disavowal of knowing the reasons for pursuing the count is more complex than such mere absence, as well as more obscure than the mere refusal of disclosing a knowledge she might have, but would want to keep secret. In a first encounter with Käthchen, we see her sincerely trying to answer the questions posed to her. Although Wenzel calls her a stubborn child, and although her formula has already been likened to an act of resistance, a withdrawal from having to answer, we must note that Käthchen, when interrogated before the court at her first appearance on stage in Act I, Scene 2, attempts to reply truthfully to all questions posed. When Count Wetter vom Strahl cross-examines her, he insinuates charges against himself of having taken sexual advantage of her, and his false accusations provoke Käthchen's protest. Her answers produce—as the count had counted on—a narrative of past occurrences, which gives a sincere account of the count's honorable treatment of her, and in which she seems too simple and innocent to even conceive of the possibility of a sexual relation. Her narration attests that the count neither forced nor abused her, and that she follows him of her own accord.[13] However, despite her efforts to be truthful, to speak the truth with much greater verbal variety than merely her formula, all of her words are to no other avail than the one basic claim that she does not know. While this claim, coupled with her honest and sweet comportment, seems to vouch for an immense simplicity of mind, it is not altogether ignorance that prevents her from explaining herself, as we learn already in this scene. When asked by the court to speak her mind, her reply to the count strongly suggests that she *would rather not* speak the reasons for her pursuit, rather than being entirely ignorant of them. This opening sets the tone for the subsequent use of her little formula.

> KATIE: Speak, your honours! What do you want to know?
>
> COUNT OTTO: Why, on the day the Count vom Strahl appeared
> In your father's house, did you prostrate yourself—
> And why did you, as he rode off, then fling
> Yourself as though demented from the window
> Into the street and why, before your legs
> Were healed, pursue him everywhere he rode
> Come fog or fearsome dark by dead of night?
>
> KATIE: (*Blushing deeply, to* VOM STRAHL) What am I supposed to tell these men?
>
> VOM STRAHL: The foolish child's bewitched, her wits confused!
> Why ask me? Is it not enough that you're
> Commanded by those men to speak the truth!
>
> KATIE: (*Falling to the ground; to* VOM STRAHL) My lord, if I've done wrong, then take my life!
> What happens in the spirit's silent realm—
> If God has sanctioned it—no man need know.
> And cruel is he who questions me about it!
> But if you wish to know, you've but to ask:
> For you, my soul's an ever-open book. (*OF*, 175)[14]

Although she invites the court to ask her about the deeds the count is charged with, willing to exonerate him with her answers, she defies an answer to the questions after her own reasons: no man needs to know them, and she resists the cruelty of him who asks them to be spoken. Despite being called demented, and her wits confused, she will continue to insist on not having to speak them. Even when she seems prepared, while refusing an answer to the court, to tell her secret motivations for this strange behavior to Count Wetter vom Strahl (*But if you wish to know, you've but to* ask), what she in fact says, is that if he wants to know, he himself may speak (*Wenn du es wissen willst, wohlan, so rede*). The count, however, misreads her words and, thinking that she will tell him, asks for her secret reasons.

> VOM STRAHL: (*To* KATIE, *still on her knees*)
> Katie, pay heed, are you prepared to share

> The deepest of those secret thoughts with me,
> That slumber in the cavern of your heart?
> KATIE: My heart entire, my lord, if that's your wish—
> That you may know for sure what dwells inside. (OF, 176)[15]

Her reply only repeats the earlier injunction that he, if he desires, may read her heart, which she is willing to give him entirely. But, although pressed hard for her secret thoughts, her deepest feelings, her reasons, even to the point of torture in the subsequent examination, she defies the count's (and the court's) assumption that she possesses a knowledge that could be extracted from her inner depth and reveal hidden truths. Rather, Käthchen hints at a different procedure: For the count to know he would have to take her whole heart and read it; what it implies is not up to her to speak. This does not necessarily suggest Käthchen's ignorance of the reasons, as we remember from the end of the first extended quote (*What happens in the spirit's silent realm—/ If God has sanctioned it—no man need know./ And cruel is he who questions me about it!*). What it rather notes is the cruelty of the attempt to extract them; it resists the inquisitive search, much akin to the passive resistance with which Bartleby's formula defied the lawyer's demands. In the scene quoted above, the count however misreads her again, and when he presses her on behalf of the court for a third time to give her reasons for trailing him, she retreats to her formula for the first time.

> VOM STRAHL: What was it then, quite simply—tell me straight—
> That drove you to desert your father's house?
> What forced you slavishly to dog my steps?
> KATIE: My noble lord! You ask too much of me.
> Were I to lie—as now before you—
> Prone in the dust before my conscious mind,
> Upon a golden judgement seat, with all
> The instruments of torture close at hand
> And blazing furnaces in readiness,
> I still could utter only one reply
> In answer to your question: I don't know! (OF, 176)[16]

By closing her declaration with her first *I don't know*, she complies with the count's request to tell him her reasons "quite simply" or—as the German text has it—"with one rounded word." Although her answer of eight lines is longer than one rounded word, it accounts with few words for the very thing that her condensed formula insists on: the impossibility of answering. She condenses this impossibility into the formula, which she uses from then on—the rounded word that answers for the impossibility of answering.

In order to see how it functions, we need to look at the composition of her formula, which has several variants to it. Its fullest version *I don't know it* (*Ich weiß es nicht*) occurs only twice: At the very first moment of its utterance, just mentioned (Act I, Scene 2) (cf. German version in notes), and toward the end of the play (Act V, Scene 10), when Käthchen receives the emperor's decree that makes her his daughter. This extended version is mostly shortened to *I don't know* (*Ich weiß nicht*), which omits the pronoun indicating the referent that is supposedly known or not known ("it"). Comparable to Bartleby's omission of the object of negative preference, Käthchen here omits the object of knowledge. And in a final step, the bearer of knowledge is removed, when the still shorter version *don't know* (*weiß nit*) even drops the personal pronoun—and in fact, it does so entirely, as it erases not only the personal pronoun ("I" or *ich*), but in the German text even its anagrammatic marker: removing the letters *ch* from the German *nicht*, this becomes *nit* and the I as a speaker also graphically disappears. It is as if Kleist were pointing again to the thought of his earlier essay *On the Gradual Fabrication of Thoughts While Speaking*—finished a year before he began working on *Das Käthchen von Heilbronn* in 1807—that "it is not *we* who 'know'; it is rather a certain condition, in which we happen to be, that 'knows'" (*ADE*, 222/*SWB*, 323; emphasis added). With Käthchen, this seems to be the case, and her method of insisting on this state is the repetition of a formula that also literally omits the "I" from knowledge and replaces it with an adherence to a formula. On the one hand, then, the knowledge is not possessed by the speaker, "I" does not know. On the other hand, although the "I" disappears in this disavowed knowledge, Käthchen, or her formula (we could say, adapting the title of Deleuze's essay on Bartleby), persists and stubbornly repeats itself, betraying that the increasingly vanishing speaker acts upon something she does "not know" with remarkable determination. It is true that we have a grammatically carefully designed statement—like Bartleby's carving out "a kind of foreign language within language" (*BF*, 72). But it is the insistence on it, its repetition that makes it as effective and that signals Käthchen as other than plainly dull-witted. The brief little statement is not effective as an isolated phrase, but it allows Käthchen to claim something other than mere ignorance precisely by being relentlessly repeated in various circumstances. Rather than just helplessly confirming that she simply has no idea, or that it is a knowledge she does not yet have access to, but might in the future, the formula insists on the right to remain silent, or better: implicit. It is a procedure—Käthchen's method for keeping things implicit, not because she is ashamed or afraid to explicate, or because she, despite being able to say it, chooses to keep things hidden, but rather because *she* does not know it, and yet does not not know it. It provides her, much like Bartleby, with a space in which her insistence on not giving reasons can survive, and by means of her formula, Käthchen seems to sketch the condition that knows, to which Kleist was alluding with his essay, a condition to which she hands herself over with an entrustment that would be ruined if she were forced to explicate.

In order for her formula to operate in this way, she combines it with a second, even more frequent turn of phrase—*my noble lord* (*mein hoher Herr*)—which already accompanied her formula at its first exemplary moment of utterance.

## Insistence

As an expression of reverence, she exclaims these words with a variety of undertones—at times surprise, or confusion, at other times slight irritation. Sometimes they ask for clarification, or appeal to her addressee's clemency and kindness. They are the very first words she utters when initially entering the stage, and during the ensuing interrogation, she retreats to them again and again. During the initial court scene, they are spoken both in reverence for the count, and in indignation at his suggestions of indecency. As substitutes for a more definite response, they are an intermediary between answer and address, between reverence and reproach. The following sequence from Act I, Scene 2 shows the wide spectrum that the repetition of her *my noble lord* covers.

> COUNT OTTO: (*To VOM STRAHL*)
> Then ask her what transpired five days ago
> In the stable at Strahl Castle in the dusk,
> When you instructed Gottschalk to withdraw.
>
> VOM STRAHL: That evening, five days past, what happened in
> The stable at my castle as dusk fell
> And I instructed Gottschalk to withdraw?
>
> KATIE: *My lord*, forgive me if I failed you—I
> Will now recount the incident in full.
>
> VOM STRAHL: Good, So I touched you—didn't I? Of course!
> That you've admitted?
>
> KATIE: Yes, *my noble lord!*
>
> VOM STRAHL: Well?
>
> KATIE: *My lord?*
>
> VOM STRAHL: What do I want to know?
>
> KATIE: What do you want to know?
>
> VOM STRAHL: Yes, out with it!
> I then caressed and kissed you, did I not?
> And put my arm around you—
>
> KATIE: No, *my lord!*
>
> VOM STRAHL: What then?
>
> KATIE: You thrust me from you with your foot!
>
> VOM STRAHL: A kick? Not that! I wouldn't kick a dog!
> For what? Why should I? What was it you did?
>
> KATIE: Because I turned my back upon my father—
> Who'd kindly come to fetch me home with horses—
> And, terror-stricken, begged you to protect me,
> Before collapsing senseless at your feet.

VOM STRAHL: You say I thrust you from me with a kick?

KATIE: You did, *my noble lord!*

VOM STRAHL: A knavish trick!
Designed to fool your father, that was all.
You went on living in my castle, didn't you?

KATIE: No, *my noble lord!*

VOM STRAHL: If not, then where?

KATIE: When you, with fiery cheeks, took down the whip
That hung upon a beam, I ran outside
Beyond the mossy gate and there lay down
Among the ruins of the rampart wall,
Close by the fragrant elder bushes where
A twittering finch had built itself a nest.

VOM STRAHL: Then did I loose my hounds to drive you off?

KATIE: Why no, *my lord!* (*OF,* 180–81; emphases added)[17]

This wide spectrum of *my noble lord,* covering anything from reverence to indignation, epitomizes the unaccountable amalgamation of her "doglike readiness to serve" (*OF,* 225/*SW I/6,* 132) with her stubborn insistence not to be deterred from her path—this strange will that makes Käthchen's conduct so hard to fathom and her *I don't know* more than a statement of mere ignorance. Her *my noble lord* complements the *I don't know* and prevents her disavowal of knowledge from being read as a pure negation of knowledge. If she were merely to say *I don't know,* we could read it as plain refusal of an answer vis-à-vis the inquirer, or as stating the fact that she is simply unaware. Retranslated into Bartleby's vocabulary, it is as if Bartleby had said: "I don't want to". But like him, she never plainly refuses to explain herself. Instead, while her *I don't know* signals that she "would prefer-not-to speak" (*BF,* 80) her mind or her reasons, it does maintain, in conjunction with her inquisitive or surprised, sometimes pained, *my noble lord* an openness to the inquirer. She does not solipsistically draw in on herself, but continues to address her interlocutor; she does so with a determinate indeterminacy, however, that oscillates between reverence and reproach, question and exclamation, asking her opponent for a little patience—for the patience to merely suffer her presence under the elder bushes, as if she were nothing but a finch.

At first sight, Käthchen might seem to speak in a more decided manner than Bartleby, using the negative indicative *I don't know.* But as we saw, supplemented and assisted by her *my noble lord,* this *I don't know* does not outright refuse to answer. Nor does Käthchen unambiguously deny knowledge. She rather cannot say a knowledge, which she nevertheless hints at, both by way of her comportment—where else could she draw her determination to pursue the count from?—and even verbally at one time. During the initial court session, the count reports to the court that "I accosted her one day at the stable-door and asked her straight out what she was doing in Strasburg. 'Good master,' she said, blushing fit to set fire to her apron, 'why do you ask? You already know!'" (*OF*, 170).[18] Surprised at his question she returns it, and as if it were too evident to be spoken about, merely points out that he knows. What the surprised *ja!* at the end of her response (*Ihr wißts ja!*) insinuates is that she also knows that he knows, but that this is not something to be spoken about, something that could be done justice by speaking. After this we do not hear Käthchen give any other piece of knowledge until she sleep-talks to reveal her dream to the count. Until then, whenever asked anything directly, she replies with her *I don't know*. Thus, despite being in the negative indicative, the modality of her formula suspends the clear distinction between "knowing" and "not knowing" and marks a zone of indeterminacy comparable to that of Bartleby's strange willfulness, as expressed in his formula. By preferring not to give reasons, yet without clearly denying them, Käthchen's formula suspends our common registers of knowing/not knowing and, thereby much like Bartleby, unsettles everyone around her who does take recourse to these clear and common distinctions. This takes effect on the count already at the very beginning, when, after the Vehmic court has dismissed the case, the count wonders sadly: "Dearest one, what am I to call you? Katie! But why can I not call you mine?" (*OF*, 184/*SW* I/6, 51). Although stricken by her, he is confused because he lacks a name or a concept for her, and that makes it impossible for him to desire her as wife. In the monologue that follows, he affirms his manly power, reassuring himself that he will get a grip (*sich fassen*) and return to (geneaological) reason. "For I intend to join your [the forefathers'] noble ranks. That was a foregone conclusion, even before you appeared.... I know I must control myself and this wound will heal; what wound was ever beyond man's power to heal?" (*OF.* 185/*SW* I/6, 51–2). Although she haunts him, he is being reasonable and goes for wealthy and urbane Kunigunde as a wife. Accordingly, he also asks Käthchen to be a little reasonable and leave off following him. Much as Bartleby dashed the lawyer's hopes for this—"'Bartleby,... let me entreat you, as a friend, to comply as far as may be with the usages of this office. Say now, you will help to examine papers tomorrow or next day: in short, say now, that in a day or two you will begin to be a little reasonable:—say so, Bartleby.' 'At present I would prefer not to be a little reasonable,' was his mildly cadaverous reply" (*BB*, 30)—Käthchen thwarts the count's hopes to get her back to her good senses. Instead, as we saw earlier, all she asks is to be suffered as indifferently as the finch in the elder bushes.

> KATIE: On the third day, you sent Gottschalk to me,
> To tell me: that I am your dear Katie;
> But should like to be reasonable and leave.
> VOM STRAHL: And what did you reply to this?

KATIE: I said that as you suffered the twittering finch
In the sweet-smelling elder bushes;
You should then also like to suffer Katie of Heilbronn. (*OF,* 181)[19]

Both Kätchen and Bartleby refuse to be a little reasonable, and just as Ginger Nut, one of the lawyer's assistants, is mistaken when he reduces Bartleby to being merely "a little *luny*" (*BB*, 22), Käthchen is not simply insane. Although her father Theobald describes her "like some poor wretched woman who's lost her wits" (*OF,* 167/*SW I/6,* 18), he himself doubts this retreat to madness as an explication, when recounting her recovery after she fell from the window. Insinuating that one would generally assume this state of hers to be madness ("delirium" in the English translation) he notes that it is not quite appropriately understood thus. Madness or delirium would produce their own discourses, talk of hidden narratives, while Käthchen just lay there, "never making a move or sound. Not even delirium, that open sesame of hearts, could open hers. Nobody could get her to say a word about the secret that possessed her" (*OF,* 168/*SW I/6,* 18). We would, thus, be too rash if we assumed her disposition to be madness—something other than reason, irrationally or unreasonably following a sentimental, sudden fancy for the count. She does not reveal her secret in either register, but rather—neither mad nor a little reasonable—insists on retaining it until the end, if not beyond it.[20] She is a "depleted being, ... a being from the start stupefied, nonpresent" as we heard Ronell say in relation to Billy Budd. But even more than Billy's maintaining a semiconscious state of mind, affectively responding to the tasks put to him, Käthchen's formula makes the "I" vanish. It increasingly suspends any possible bearer of knowledge, becoming a mere *don't know* (*weiß nit*). We might call this state of mind a "before consciousness," much as Käthchen herself does before the cross-examination starts in Act I, Scene 2. When the count asks her to tell him her reasons for behaving so strangely, Käthchen answers that even if she were "to lie—as now before you—/ Prone in the dust before my conscious mind" she still could only give one reply: *I don't know!* Her conscious mind is as threatening an instance as the imminent torturous cross-examination that is to follow before the court. She likens it it to "golden judgement ... with all instruments of torture close at hand," and even faced with "blazing furnaces in readiness" (all *OF,* 176/*SW I/6,* 32), she has no way to access it. This is her predicament, her disposition, and she shares it with Bartleby. Both are lying, as Deleuze notes in his text on Bartleby, *en deça de la conscience*: "Achab et Bartleby, comme pour Kleist la terrible Penthésilée et la douce petite Catherine, l'au-delà et l'en deça de la conscience ...."[21] Recourse to the original French version of Deleuze's essay allows us to read the specificity of Käthchen's and Bartleby's relations to consciousness here. Firstly, the French *conscience* means both consciousness and conscience, and the English translation resolves this ambiguity in one direction by opting to translate *en deça de la conscience* as "before conscience" (*BF*, 80).[22] Given this ambiguity of the French version, and the fact that the essay develops its argument along figures that are derived from Kleist's and Melville's writings, it seems safe to assume that Deleuze's *en deçà de la conscience* echoes with Käthchen's response to the count's interrogation cited above that she lies "before consciousness" (*vor meinem eigenen Bewusstsein*), and that it allows us to consider the peculiar forms of consciousness these figures (Bartleby, Käthchen, but also Ahab and Penthesilea, another frequent couple in the essay) expose, rather than the questions of conscience the English translation of the essay suggests. Secondly, the French version alerts us to not misread this "before" teleologically or temporally as a lack or deficiency of consciousness, an innate innocence or ignorance to be overcome, and subsequently reaching or developing consciousness. It is rather, as the French notes, an *en-deçà* of consciousness, and thereby not consciousness's other (madness, delirium, unconscious), but undercutting this distinction by remaining "before" it: *en-deçà* or "*diesseits* des Bewusstseins,"[23] as in turn the German translation of the essay brings out. It is as if Käthchen's and Bartleby's formulas—this quasi-automaticity of speaking that epitomizes their bizarre passivity—allow them to establish a "zone of indistinction, of indiscernibility, or of ambiguity ... between two terms, as if they had reached the point immediately preceding their respective differentiation: not a similitude, but a slippage" (*BF*, 78); as if their formulas allowed them to lay claim to a state of mind that marks a zone prior to the differentiation between conscious and unconscious, or rationality and irrationality. As inhabitants of this zone, they are bound to come across as a little stupid, unaccountable within the registers of either of the two sides. But they are certainly only "almost stupid," as Deleuze remarks, and to mark the difference from what we usually call stupidity, they are read here as figures of *simplicity*. Their simplicity exposes the fold that differentiates the two registers, and at the same time dashes any hope for a clear-cut separation between sensation and thinking, irrational and rational. Lying before consciousness in this sense, Käthchen is depleted of it, and with that she is depleted of knowledge that a conscious "I" could have or articulate. Unable to explicate, explain, and unravel what she does not (not) know, her stubborn repetitions of a defiant *I don't know* and a reverent *my noble lord* rather claim the right to implication. This is, I would argue, why Kommerell calls Käthchen one of Kleist's unspeakable or inexpressible (*unaussprechliche*)[24] characters: She displays a simplicity that claims a zone "before consciousness" that cannot be spoken, yet can be adhered to, and if done so, impels one to retain the secret until the end. In line with his entire reading of Kleist's figures as resting on a constitutive obscurity of the secret or riddle, Kommerell stresses that Käthchen does not know or have access to her secret. Käthchen's "will to open herself can not what it might want. She lives the enigma, she does not know it. Asked what ties her to the count, she answers him with a terribly holy formula of sincerity ...: 'I don't know!'"[25] Kommerell builds his reading of Kleist, in particular of *Das Käthchen von Heilbronn* and *Michael Kohlhaas*, around the observation that the Kleistian characters become riddles to themselves, riddles that obscure the characters to themselves and challenge them to endure themselves. The mysterious fact of Kleist's drama—the fact that Käthchen is bound to follow the count—"is both the enigma of a character, and of an obscure connection between two people."[26] We are given an unraveling of the riddle, a purported solution to the mystery of Käthchen's strange comportment, when her enigma is illuminated by three prehistories, which together form, as Kommerell states, "a Kleistian novella within the drama"[27]: The first is supplied by Käthchen's father Theobald (Act I, Scene 2), who narrates the encounter between Käthchen and the count at his smithy; the second by Brigitte, housekeeper at the count's castle (Act II, Scene 9), who tells Kunigunde of the count's fever dream, in which a wife of royal blood was promised to him; and the third by Käthchen (Act IV, Scene 2), when, sleep-talking, she tells the count of her own New Year's Eve dream, mysteriously matching his own. This last one is the key that explicates the earlier two, and in retrograde fashion, from the chronologically youngest to the chronologically oldest piece of information, they purport to explain what Käthchen has formulaically insisted upon not knowing. According to Kommerell, this novella within the drama unfolds the background and provides a narration that permits us to make sense of the occurrences on stage.[28] However, these explanations remain partial, and the Kleistian tale within the drama only furnishes inconclusive explanations that continue to require further narrations. After Käthchen has revealed her dream in her sleep, the emperor is in turn required to provide the background for the dream by explaining his liaison with Käthchen's mother (in Act V, Scene 2). The emperor recalls a meeting with Käthchen's mother Gertrude some sixteen years before, and as a result of this recollection he decrees that Käthchen is in fact his daughter, which makes Käthchen the royal wife the count was waiting for. Marking the performativity of this royal speech act, Kleist has the emperor call the recalled meeting a *conversation*: "Gertrud, as far as I remember, was her name, who I *conversed* with in a part of the garden less frequented by the people."[29] Although Kleist underlines Käthchen's parentage as the product of a conversation, and makes her royal by another verbal declaration, the emperor, the father, and the count take this statement to be the truth. It allows an explication of the meaning of the matching dreams, and allows the count to articulate his desire, that is to marry—very much in line with his reason of state—the emperor's daughter. Despite this resolution, however, Käthchen's persistence in not-knowing does not waver, and she escapes any resolution or explication by fainting in the last scene.

    Kleist plays here with the performative quality of language, as much as with its potential to enfold and unfold endlessly, something that writers like Roussel or Blanchot will later perfect.[30] However, interesting for our reading are the figures of simplicity around which these narrative unravelings garrulously unfold, something we also saw occur in *Billy Budd*, where Claggart's search for double meanings and tales behind what meets the eye was set in motion by Billy's simple ways. In the cases of Bartleby and Käthchen, we see the people around them sent flying, confused, challenged or summoned to explain, while they themselves prefer not to speak and insist on not being explicit, on not stating their preferences. In being figures "that exceed ... any explicable form" (*BF*, 82) they call forth explication, something we see at work in the different prehistories that need to be provided in *Das Käthchen von Heilbronn* to make sense of Käthchen. Bartleby and Käthchen themselves, however, are solitary figures—figures of simplicity, because they appear simple according to our common registers of thinking, set our explanatory apparatuses into motion, and insist themselves on the zone before the differentiated registers of conscious and unconscious, rational and irrational, on their *pli*. Deleuze notes that they

> project ... flamboyant traits of expression that mark the stubbornness of a thought without image, a question without response, an extreme and nonrational logic. Figures of life and knowledge, they know something inexpressible, live something unfathomable. They have nothing general about them, and are not particular— they escape knowledge, defy psychology. Even the words they utter surpass the general law of language (presuppositions) as well as the simple particularities of speech, since they are like the vestiges or projections of a unique, original language [*langue*], and bring all of language [*language*] to the limit of silence and music. (*BF*, 82–83)

Whirling in the zone of indistinction—a zone that permits the production of expressible, graspable, eventually conceptual knowledge—these figures do not "possess" speakable, discursive knowledge. Theirs is a nonrational logic, perhaps one of formulaic simpletons: of Bartleby's "logic of negative preference, a negativism beyond all negation" (*BF*, 71), and Käthchen's logic of implications, which prefers not to speak, yet bears the implications of a knowledge that is not hers to have. What they lay claim to—and in this they entertain a subterranean and prestigious lineage, we might say, with literature itself—are "the rights of a superior irrationalism" (*BF*, 81).

## Supersensible Figures of the Fold

Operating by means of their respective formulas, both Bartleby and Käthchen display a passivity that we have called formulaic—formulaic, because with their strange little statements they carved out little forms that allow them to reduce their actions to hardly anything but the automatic repetition of these statements. This almost automatic way of speaking is neither adequately described as active nor as passive, neither as willful nor as being without a will, and both figures occupy a zone that lies, as we saw, prior to this division between active and passive. In order to mark this state "before consciousness," and its difference from a passivity commonly opposed to activity, their passivity has been called radical and formulaic. What interested me here was the suspension of the opposition between active and passive as well as this peculiar passivity that arises from it. Their passive speaking runs parallel, we could say in reference to Kleist's essay *On the Gradual Formation of Thoughts While Speaking*, to a certain passivity of thinking that is situated before consciousness, *en-deçà de la conscience*, and where we have to understand *before* not in the temporal sense of progressively being on the path to consciousness, but in a more topological sense of standing perpetually as its limit. Corresponding to the Leibnizian observation that all consciousness, as Deleuze remarked in *The Fold*, is "a matter of threshold" (*F*, 88), both Kleist and Melville literally mark these insistent figures as sitting at this threshold. As such a figure of the threshold, we saw Käthchen not only sit on the figurative threshold to consciousness, but also on the stable's literal threshold, when the count asks after her reasons for following him (cf. *SW I/6*, 22). And Bartleby makes his appearance "upon the office threshold" and even after crossing it to become a copyist, he remains a limit-figure who sits enfolded between two screens in the lawyer's office, in a peculiar position between a folding door and a folding screen. The lawyer delineates this carefully in his account of Bartleby's installation in the office.

> In answer to my advertisement, a motionless young man one morning stood upon the office threshold, the door being open, for it was summer. I can see that figure now—pallidly neat, pitiably respectable, incurably forlorn! It was Bartleby. After a few words touching his qualifications, I engaged him, glad to have among my corps of copyists a man of so singularly sedate an aspect, which I thought might operate beneficially upon the flighty temper of Turkey, and the fiery one of Nippers. I should have stated before that ground glass folding-doors divided my premises into two parts, one of which was occupied by my scriveners, the other by myself. According to my humor, I threw open these doors, or closed them. I resolved to assign Bartleby a corner by the folding-doors, but on my side of them, so as to have this quiet man within easy call, in case a trifling thing was to be done. I placed his desk close up to a small side window in that part of the room, a window which originally had afforded a lateral view of certain grimy backyards and brick, but which, owing to subsequent erections, commanded at present no view at all, though it gave some light. Within three feet of the panes was a wall, and the light came down from far above, between two lofty buildings, as from a very small opening in a dome. Still further to a satisfactory arrangement, I procured a high green folding screen, which might entirely isolate Bartleby from

my sight, though not remove him from my voice. And thus, in a manner, privacy and society were conjoined. (*BB*, 19)

The lawyer's satisfactory arrangement enfolds Bartleby within a space that places him between two screens, where he sits motionlessly and becomes a figure at the limit of the two realms of privacy and society that these screens delimit, without belonging to either. His motionless unbelonging is epitomized in the formula that propels the plot forward from Bartleby's arrival at the office to the lawyer's departure from it. And when the lawyer moves office and removes all furniture including the green screen, Bartleby is forced to stand, and we see that nothing remains of him. He has become a pallid sheet of paper, flat and folded, much like the papers on which he used to copy, before the formula eroded this activity.

> On the appointed day I engaged carts and men, proceeded to my chambers, and, having but little furniture, everything was removed in a few hours. Throughout, the scrivener remained standing behind the screen, which I directed to be removed the last thing. It was withdrawn; and, being folded up like a huge folio, left him the motionless occupant of a naked room. I stood in the entry watching him a moment, while something from within me upbraided me. I re-entered, with my hand in my pocket—and—and my heart in my mouth. "Good-by, Bartleby; I am going—good-by, and God some way bless you; and take that" slipping something in his hand. But it dropped upon the floor, and then—strange to say—I tore myself from him whom I had so longed to be rid of. (*BB*, 39)

When the lawyer wants to slip a token of parting into Bartleby's hand, the latter does not grasp it, and it falls to the ground. He seems to have become as flat as a sheet of paper to which nothing sticks, and from which all glides off. The text marks this by a syntactically ambiguous sentence: "It was withdrawn"—referring to the green screen behind which Bartleby had been sitting—"and, being folded up like a huge folio, left him the motionless occupant of a naked room." We cannot tell who is "being folded up like a huge folio": Does this refer to the screen being folded up like a huge folio, or to "him," Bartleby, who, folded up like a huge folio, is left motionless in the room? What we are left with is a character, who—as an effect of this syntactical fold of the text itself—might have become a folio: a sheet of paper folded once; and whose passivity is such that he does not even passively receive what the lawyer attempts to slip into his hand.

Revolving around these stubborn figures and their ways of being simple, my reading has traced their state as one *before consciousness*: their ways of suspending the claims to a logic of reason, to explicable reason and graspable knowledge.

Faced with advocates of reason and law—Bartleby with the lawyer; Käthchen with urbane and calculating Count Wetter vom Strahl—they thwart the expectations of both to be a little reasonable. Their unsettling formulas do not oppose, or aim to reverse their counterparts' logic, but they suspend it. By means of their formulas, they sit *before consciousness*, and with that state of mind defy the reason their counterparts wish them to return to. Until the end, Käthchen and Bartleby refuse to be held accountable according to those registers. Käthchen does not in the end subscribe to a resolution of her mysterious attachment to the count as having been the understandable wish to marry the count: she faints in front of the altar, when marriage and the count's reason of state seem to prevail. And Bartleby even dies after once stating his will, of having been in the least accountable vis-à-vis the lawyer. In prison, he surprises the lawyer (and the reader) by confessing a preference for the first (and last) time. To get rid of the lawyer, he snarls at him: "I know you, and I want nothing to say to you" (*BB*, 43). After this, he will say precisely nothing, not even any longer his formula, and instead lies down and dies, as if the determination of *I want* has left no space for him to breathe in. Both figures not only unhinge the lawyer's and the count's reasoning by becoming the very suspension of the differences that those reasonings rest on, but they expose the moment of differentiating and unfolding the two series—series we may call on different levels conscious and unconscious, intelligible and sensual, passive and active. In view of this suspension of opposites we may call them supersensibles that are beyond feeling as much as they are before consciousness. These "angels or saintly hypochondriacs, almost stupid," as Deleuze remarks, "can only survive by becoming stone, by denying the will and sanctifying themselves in this suspension" (*BF*, 79). They are not overly sensitive, but rather supersensible—becoming stone. With all the weakness and ridiculousness that result from that, they powerfully claim their right to a superior (a super-sensible) irrationalism that is superior not because it transcends the differentiation between rational and irrational, reaching an alleged synthesis, but because they deterritorialize, erode, thwart all the fixations and presuppositions of reason, point us to its structure and its differential processes of formation. They allude to a—perhaps unlivable—position just before the differentiation into conscious and unconscious.

## Chapter 5
# Conclusion

The preceding chapters have pursued a subterranean lineage between the texts of Heinrich von Kleist and Herman Melville. The hypothesis that a remarkable alliance exists between their texts is not only based upon the strikingly similar characters that both writers devised and that we have examined, but it also finds support in the repeated references to such an alliance in Gilles Deleuze's writings on literature, frequently those written together with Félix Guattari. In a number of these texts, Deleuze (and Guattari) elaborate their points by connecting literary figures from Kleist's and Melville's writings, and Deleuze develops many of his own concepts with their help.[1] Mostly, Deleuze's references to these Kleistian and Melvillean figures merely place them adjacent to each other, and incorporate them in passing within the discussion of his own concepts. The suggestions of similarity that such a textual arrangement makes are rarely unfolded with reference to the literary texts themselves. Deleuze's essay *Bartleby; or, The Formula* is a little different in that respect, as it is, on the one hand, his most explicit confrontation with Melville, and, on the other hand, also contains the most elaborate and productive passages on Melville's connection to Kleist. A footnote in this text asserts their proximity in procedure, when, as was said before, it states in reference to Bartleby's formula that "Catherine Heilbronn had her own formula, close to that of Bartleby's: 'I don't know' or simply 'Don't know.'"[2] This was the point of departure for my pursuit of Kleist's and Melville's figures of simplicity in this book. From Bartleby's and Käthchen's speaking in formulas and their baffling passivity, which their speech expresses, I was able to also trace the alliances between Michael Kohlhaas and Billy Budd, and between Captain Delano and Gustav von der Ried—all of whom can be regarded as, among other things, *études* in simplicity as a relation between sensation and thinking. Certainly, Deleuze never limits the connection between Kleist and Melville to the two formulaic characters of *Bartleby, the Scrivener* and *Das Käthchen von Heilbronn*. He also connects Ahab to Penthesilea, and is quite interested in Melville's Pierre and Kleist's Prince of Homburg.[3] And Deleuze certainly does not limit his examination of the subterranean alliances he sees, or his interest in literature in general, merely to the works of Kleist and Melville. At the beginning of *Bartleby; or, The Formula* we immediately find other writers who share these affinities to each other. We are told that "'Bartleby' ... is like the tales of Kleist, Dostoyevsky, Kafka, or Beckett, with which it forms a subterranean and prestigious lineage" (*BF,* 68). But from among this initial list of four, the essay returns repeatedly to Melville and Kleist, finding Kleist's narratives to operate "in the same way" (*BF,* 78) and "like" (*BF,* 80) those of Melville, and the two supply a particular force to some of Deleuze's central concepts, and, as I would argue, to a delineation of *affective thinking.*

The figures of simplicity were treated here as a *problematic* which Kleist's and Melville's texts share. They cannot be explained as resulting from a particular Kleistian influence upon Melville. As stated in the introduction, Melville, as far as literary scholarship has established, never read Kleist. But what the two writers share is their approach to the same problem, very much in line with Deleuze's remark—following Sacher-Masoch, another literary source from which his work draws conceptual inspiration—that writers "must go from the 'figure' to the 'problem': one must start from the obsessive phantasy in order to rise to the problem, to the theoretical structure where the problem is posed."[4] Obsessed with these simpletons, we suggest, Kleist and Melville tackled a problem through their use of the figures they invented. Starting from the recurring figures of simplicity in their work, this book has attempted to expose the underlying problem the authors were addressing with them—the theoretical point at which the problem is posed. With regard to their concrete literary and philosophical milieus—which I have unwound here in light of the questions of *aisthetics*, perception, and the debates of sensation and thinking in the wake of Kant in both Kleist's and Melville's philosophical and literary habitats—these two share the same concerns, and come up with analogous answers: they engage, this book suggests, in a critique of the strict separation between sensation and thinking, and they offer analyses of their folded relationality.

And it is precisely with these eccentric characters that their texts implicitly critique this separation of sensation and thinking and expose their folded relationality. Leaving aside Gustav von der Ried and Amaso Delano—whom we saw as studies, in which small perceptions were shown to be at the basis of the characters' assessments, but were overcoded by all-too-human explanatory devices bound to miss what was before their eyes—we have seen that Michael Kohlhaas, Billy Budd, Bartleby, and Käthchen operate in affective, inexplicable, eccentric ways that disturb the order their opponents are determined to uphold. They are what Melville called in his novel *The Confidence-Man* (1857) "original." The novel's famous chapter 44 outlines much of Melville's poetological position, and depicts these original characters as shedding light onto their surroundings, as being constitutive for the narrative, in short, as being more than merely the exception that confirms the rule.

## Conclusion

[W]hat is popularly held to entitle characters in fiction being deemed original, is but something personal—confined to itself. The character sheds not its characteristics on its surrounding, whereas, the original character, essentially such, is like a revolving Drummond light, raying away from itself all round it—everything is lit by it, everything starts up to it (mark how it is with Hamlet), so that, in certain minds, there follows upon the adequate conception of such a character, an effect, in its way, akin to that which in Genesis attends upon the beginning of things.[5]

Deleuze takes up this notion of a radiating original, and it becomes crucial to his consideration of the subterranean lineage between Kleist and Melville in *Bartleby; or, The Formula*. After paying close attention to Bartleby's formula and how it operates in the tale, the essay moves in the second half from Melville's textual operations to the bizarre figures invented in his tales. The "Bartleby-debate" that was referenced in chapter 4 mostly focuses on Bartleby's formula, and foregrounds the differentiating structure and the constitutive zone of indifference upon which the structure is based. In Deleuze's essay—a particularly influential one within this debate, as Agamben, Rancière, Arsić, and others draw on it—this point is made only in the first half. In a second step, the essay turns to the strange figures and takes up Melville's poetological concept of originals. It seems, in a way, that we must then move from figure to problem, as Deleuze stated in relation to Sacher-Masoch, and affirm at the same time that the problem is epitomized in the figure—in our case the *problem* of a relation between sensation and thinking in the *figures* of simplicity. These figures are not figurative, they are not allied to figuration and representation. They are, rather, distilled forms of the problem, we might say; much as Deleuze notes that Bacon's paintings oppose "the 'figural' to the figurative.... the figurative (representation) implies the relationship of an image to an object that this common logic is supposed to illustrate."[6] With reference to Melville's originals in contrast, Deleuze notes that these are not representations of living beings, they do not portray anything or anyone, but they epitomize the problem—in our specific case that of a zone from which our common logic and law may be derived, but which itself does not pertain to. These originals, Deleuze adds to Melville's observation, are divided between two equally solitary, inhuman poles.

> At one pole, there are those monomaniacs or demons who, driven by the will to nothingness, make a monstrous choice: Ahab, Claggart, Babo...But at the other pole are those angels or saintly hypochondriacs, almost stupid,...denying the will and sanctifying themselves in this suspension. Such are Cereno, Billy Budd, and above all Bartleby. And although the two types are opposed

> in every way—the former innate traitors and the latter betrayed in their very essence; the former monstrous fathers who devour their children, the latter abandoned sons without fathers—they haunt one and the same world, forming alternations within it, just as Melville's writing, like Kleist's, alternates between stationary, fixed processes and mad-paced procedures: *style*, with its succession of catatonias and accelerations. (*BF*, 79)

What distinguishes these two poles is their handling of this "one and the same world," of the zones of indistinction in which they exist: their composure, or style. One pole makes a monstrous choice, wills where it should let go and where it should substitute: for example, where it should chase whales and not fixate on the White Whale (Ahab), or where it should mate with all prisoners of war and not fixate on Achilles (Penthesilea). The other pole suspends choices, acts almost stupid, is "stricken with a constitutive weakness but also with a strange beauty" (*BF*, 79). None of these figures operate in accordance with the law, or by way of explicable reasons, or all-too-human rationale and calculation. Returning to Melville's concept of the "original," Deleuze continues that, rather,

> both types of characters, Ahab and Bartleby, *belong to this Primary Nature*, they inhabit it, they constitute it. Everything sets them in opposition, and yet they are perhaps the same creature—primary, original, stubborn, seized from both sides, marked merely with a "plus" or "minus" sign: Ahab and Bartleby. Or in Kleist, the terrible Penthesilea and the sweet little Catherine, the first beyond conscience, the second before conscience: she who chooses and she who does not choose, she who howls like a she-wolf and she who would prefer-not-to-speak. (*BF*, 79–80)

Such *primary nature* is not to be misunderstood as a return to a—eventually corruptible—state of innocence. It is, to again remind us of our discussion in chapter 1, as little primary in a temporal sense as Baumgarten's sensate thinking was lower in a hierarchical sense. Their *primary nature*, rather, marks a zone—as chapter 4 has stressed—that our figures inhabit, "a terrible supersensible Primary Nature, original and oceanic,... knowing no Law" making them "creatures of the abyss" (*BF*, 78), but "inseparable from the world or from secondary nature, where they exert their effect" (*BF*, 83).

With respect to our context, we have to note that Deleuze, by dividing Melville's original characters between two poles, implicitly short-circuits Melville's with Kleist's poetology—a connection that results in what we might call a Deleuzian theory of the literary, of literature as a form of thinking. Such a theory of the literary would need to be considered in more detail, with reference

## Conclusion

to Deleuze's and Guattari's Kafka, to Carroll and *The Logic of Sense*, as well as to D. H. Lawrence and the concept of life, but for the limited context of this book, suffice it to note that in the above quote, Deleuze takes the idea of the original from Melville's *The Confidence-Man* and connects it with Kleist's imagery of (electric) force, whose aesthetic potential Kleist sounded out in his essay *On the Gradual Fabrication of Thoughts While Speaking*. The footnote on Bartleby's and Käthchen's shared formulaic conduct that stood at the beginning of this project confirms this connection Deleuze makes, when we follow its laconic reference to Kleist's letter to Heinrich von Collin of 8 December 1808. In this letter, Kleist explains the connection between Käthchen and Penthesilea as one of a similarly "inhuman" nature, merely thought from opposite poles: therefore, "to whomever loves Käthchen, Penthesilea cannot remain entirely unfathomable, since they belong together like + and − in algebra, and are one and the same being, only thought under opposite relations."[7] Taking this idea from Kleist in conjunction with Melville's idea of "originals" we thus have, at one pole, the "almost stupid" ones (Käthchen, Billy Budd, Michael Kohlhaas, Bartleby), and at the opposite pole the monomaniacs with their monstrous choices (Penthesilea, Claggart, Nicolo [of Kleist's *The Foundling*] or Ahab), none of whom were pursued here in his or her own right. Both poles, however are of a relentlessly indifferent, almost inhuman, disposition, and whether they turn out to be terrible or terribly sweet is merely a question of their electric charge, we might say with Kleist thinking back to the example of Mirabeau.

What interested me in this book were the "almost stupid" characters, the ones struck by a simplicity that is neither mere lack of knowledge nor unspoiled innocence. By calling them *almost* stupid, Deleuze situates them within the realm that lies *before* the differentiation of ignorance and knowledge, sensibility and reason; the realm that can be rendered as the fold of sensation and thinking, inscribed as a *pli* in the simplicity of these simpletons who defy the claims to a logic of reason, to explicable reasons and graspable knowledge. Theirs is a "superior irrationalism." Melville coined the term in *The Confidence-Man* in refutation of "certain psychological novelists"[8] who believe that any inconsistency or incomprehensibility of character can be satisfactorily unraveled, "in this way throwing open, sometimes to the understanding even of school misses, the last complications of that spirit which is affirmed by its Creator to be fearfully and wonderfully made."[9] Deleuze supplants this with his own words by asking, "Why should the novelist believe he is obliged to explain the behavior of his characters, and to supply them with reasons, whereas life for its part never explains anything and leaves in its creatures so many indeterminate, obscure, indiscernible zones that defy any attempt at clarification?" (*BF*, 81) As figures of simplicity, they epitomize the insistence of Melville's tales on not unraveling, but exposing, the complications of spirit of these "powerful, solitary Figure[s] that exceed...any explicable form" (*BF*, 82). They mark "the stubbornness of a thought without image, a question without response, an extreme and nonrational logic" (BF, 82–83), which, we could say, is not only the case for Bartleby or Käthchen, but also for the tales themselves.

One of the cornerstones of this book has been the aesthetic principle of the fold. With a focus on the fold, we have been able to see the continuity between philosophical debates that were, predominately, held during the first half of the eighteenth century and concerned the relation between sensibility and reason, and literary writings from the first half of the nineteenth century that exposed the crucial dimension of these aesthetic debates in a literary manner. While the former debates discussed the fold as a principle, inviting consideration of the paradoxical relation between the senses and reason, and sketching the parameters of a *sensate thinking* that would take this relation into account, the latter exposed the operations of this "logic" and performed what such a thinking might look like, if the affective dimensions of thinking are taken into account. What is at stake in both—although expressed differently—is the question of a certain mode of thinking that does not fully coincide with demands for conceptual clarity and rational thinking. In this sense, Kleist and Melville were shown to engage with a concern that in the discipline of philosophy had been forestalled by the Copernican divide, which Kantian transcendental philosophy and its idealist receptions and transformations introduced into the debates about manners and forms of understanding. Kleist's and Melville's texts echo the same questions that Leibniz and Baumgarten were asking, and the figures of simplicity they invented pose the question anew, responding to a dissatisfaction with the Kantian framework. By echoing the Leibnizian and Baumgartian problem Kleist's and Melville's texts become "a kind of repetition, an echo of the voice of philosophy,"[10] which they express in a different manner and with the incalculable results for philosophy and literature that we found in them, ultimately contesting disciplinary boundaries.

Such an emphasis on the different expressions of the same problem is by no means intended to conflate them. Quite the contrary. In line with the principle of the fold such an emphasis asserts that things can be continuous and yet different. One of the crucial advantages of Leibniz's principle of the fold is, as Deleuze shows, that it claims that "two things can be thought as being really distinct without being separable" (F, 55). The point is, thus, not to show that literary texts do *the same as* philosophico-aesthetic debates on the relation between sensibility and reason, but much rather to show the potential of the literary to expose, and thereby also pose, a question, or, to say it differently: to think. In line with Deleuze's and Guattari's remark in *What is Philosophy?* the point is to confirm that both

> [a]rt and philosophy crosscut the chaos and confront it, but it is not the same sectional plane; it is not populated in the same way. In the one there is a constellation of a universe of affects and percepts; and in the other, constellations of immanence or concepts.

## Conclusion

Art thinks no less than philosophy, but it thinks through affects and percepts.... There is such force in those unhinged works of Hölderlin, Kleist, Rimbaud, Mallarmé, Kafka, Michaux, Pessoa, Artaud, and many English and American novelists, from Melville to Lawrence or Miller, [but...] to be sure, they do not produce a synthesis of art and philosophy. They branch out and do not stop branching out. They are hybrid geniuses who neither erase nor cover over differences in kind but, on the contrary, use all the resources of their "athleticism" to install themselves within this very difference.[11]

Seeing art, and more specifically, literature in this way radically breaks with the assumption of its mimetic task, just as Kleist's and Melville's texts do. The texts we have considered closely here conduct experiments in perception and affective thinking by sketching figures of simplicity that are not representations of possible living figures, but rather depict a problem—the paradoxical implication of the sensate in thinking—in the form of a Figure: in the form of these figures of simplicity. What these figures expose and produce at the same time is a superior irrationalism, or nonrational logic, a "logic" that shines through them, without becoming explicit, rendered in the modality of insistence, and that is also, as we saw, the logic of the literary texts themselves. Despite being always drawn back into narration and figuration, we might adapt Deleuze's statement on the strange creatures he finds in Melville and Kleist—these figures of "life and knowledge" who "know something inexpressible, live something unfathomable" (*BF,* 83)—to literature itself: it also is a creature between life and knowledge, and much like Käthchen, literature lives the enigma without knowing it.

# Notes

## Introduction

1. For Kleist, cf. most recently Anselm Haverkamp, "Schwarz/Weiß. Kleists Moral der Verkennung," in *Latenzzeit. Wissen im Nachkrieg* (Berlin: Kadmos, 2004); for Melville, cf. most prominently Charles Olson, *Call me Ishmael* (Baltimore: Johns Hopkins University Press, 1997).
2. For the difficulty in ascertaining the influence of these wider familiarities upon their works, cf. exemplarily and respectively Carol Jacobs, "The Style of Kleist," *diacritics* (1979): 47–61; and Merton M. Sealts Jr., "Melville and Emerson's Rainbow," in *Pursuing Melville 1940–1980* (Madison: University of Wisconsin Press, 1982).
3. Martin Greenberg, "The Difficult Justice of Melville and Kleist," *The New Criterion* 3 (2005); Niels Werber, *Die Geopolitik der Literatur. Eine Vermessung der medialen Weltraumordnung* (Munich: Hanser, 2007).
4. D. H. Lawrence, "Melville's *Typee* and *Omoo*," Studies in Classic American Literature (New York: Seltzer, 1923), quoted in Gilles Deleuze and Félix Guattari, *A Thousand Plateaus. Capitalism and Schizophrenia* (Minneapolis: University of Minnesota Press, 1987), 186.
5. Gilles Deleuze and Félix Guattari, *Kafka. Toward a Minor Literature* (Minneapolis: University of Minnesota Press, 1986), 55.
6. Ibid., 17.
7. Ronald Bogue, "Minor Writing and Minor Literature," *Symploke* 5, no. 1 (1997): 116; cf. also exemplarily for the concepts fruitful translation into cultural studies: Shu-mei Shih and Françoise Lionnet, eds. *Minor Transnationalism* (Durham: Duke University Press, 2005).
8. Cf. the studies of Proust in Gilles Deleuze, *Proust and Signs* (Minneapolis: University of Minnesota Press, 2000); of Carroll in Gilles Deleuze, *The Logic of Sense* (New York: Columbia University Press, 1990); of Sacher-Masoch in Gilles Deleuze, *Masochism. Coldness and Cruelty* by Gilles Deleuze and *Venus in Fur* by Leopold Sacher-Masoch (New York: Zone Books, 1991); of Artaud, Whitman,

Melville, Jarry, D. H. Lawrence in the essays collected in Gilles Deleuze, *Essays Critical and Clinical* (Minneapolis: University of Minnesota Press, 1997).

9. Gilles Deleuze and Félix Guattari, *What is Philosophy?* (London: Verso Books, 1994), 65.
10. Sensation is a term used by Deleuze to describe the question of Bacon's paintings, and accordingly employed here in the sense of "a 'logic of the senses'... which is neither rational nor cerebral" (Gilles Deleuze, *Francis Bacon. The Logic of Sensation* (Minneapolis: University of Minnesota Press, 2002), 37), and which attests to a "spirituality of the body" (ibid., 41). It surpasses the phenomenological notion of sensation as a perception of "the world of 'lived experience'" (Daniel W. Smith, Introduction to Deleuze, *Francis Bacon*, xiv), and is in line with Leibniz's notion of minute perceptions and their contribution to apperception. What Leibniz captures are the forces implied in apperception, rather than the minute perceptions themselves. In the same vein, sensation is used by Deleuze as a concept of a "non-rational logic" (ibid., xxvii) that considers the affective dimensions of thinking, and is not to be reduced to a derivation of thoughts from sense impressions. This notion of sensation will also be linked in this book to Alexander G. Baumgarten's term *cognitio sensitiva*, one of the earliest, decidedly aesthetic discussions of the relation of sensibility and thinking (cf. chapter 1).
11. On Deleuze's notion of the fold (discussed later in chapter 1), cf. Sjoerd van Tuinen and Niamh McDonnell, eds., *Deleuze's* The Fold. *A Critical Reader* (London: Palgrave, 2010); on Baumgarten's adaptation of Leibniz's thinking to the field of aesthetics, cf. Birgit M. Kaiser, "Two Floors of Thinking—or, Deleuze's Aesthetics of Folds," in *Deleuze's* The Fold. *A Critical Reader*, ed. Sjoerd van Tuinen and Niamh McDonnell (London: Palgrave, 2010).
12. For the debates on aesthetics as aisthetics, cf. Hans Adler, ed., *Aesthetics and Aisthetics. New Perspectives and (Re)Discoveries* (Oxford/New York: Peter Lang, 2002); Karlheinz Barck et al., *Aisthesis. Wahrnehmung heute oder Perspektiven einer anderen Ästhetik* (Leipzig: Reclam, 2002).
13. Brian Massumi, *Parables for the Virtual. Movement, Affect, Sensation* (Durham: Duke University Press, 2002), 27.
14. Cf. exemplarily for Kleist, Gerhard Fricke, *Gefühl und Schicksal bei Heinrich von Kleist* (New York: AMS Press, 1971); and for debates around Melville's assertion to Hawthorne that "I stand for the heart. To the dogs with the head!" (letter of 1 June 1851 in Herman Melville, *Tales, Poems, and other Writings*, ed. John Bryant [New York: The Modern Library, 2001], 38), cf. S. Ross Beharriell, *The Head and the Heart in the Mind and Art of Herman Melville* (Madison: University of Wisconsin Press, 1954); and Aaron Kramer, *Melville's Poetry. Toward the Enlarged Heart* (Madison: Fairleigh Dickinson University Press, 1971) with an eye on Melville's poetry.
15. Gilles Deleuze, "Bartleby; or, The Formula," in *Essays critical and clinical* (Minneapolis: University of Minnesota Press, 1997), 80, hereafter cited as *BF*.

## Chapter 1. Aesthetics

1. Heinrich von Kleist, *An Abyss Deep Enough: The Life of Heinrich von Kleist in His Parables, Essays and Letters*, ed. and trans. Philip B. Miller (Boston: Dutton Books, 1982), 95, hereafter cited as *ADE*. German original in Heinrich von Kleist, *Sämtliche Werke*, Vol. IV/1, Briefe I (März 1793-April 1801), ed. Peter Staengle in cooperation with Roland Reuß (Basel/Frankfurt/M: Stroemfeld/Roter Stern, 1996), 505, hereafter cited as *SW IV/1*.
2. Different plausible suggestions have been made, but the question remains unresolved. For a comprehensive summary of the debate, cf. Urs Strässle, *Heinrich von Kleist. Die keilförmige Vernunft* (Würzburg: Königshausen & Neumann, 2002), 97ff.
3. The ubiquitous metaphors of both the Fall and falling are significant, and critics have rightly pointed this out; cf. Cathy Caruth, "The Falling Body and the Impact of Reference (de Man, Kant, Kleist)," in *Unclaimed Experience. Trauma, Narrative, and History* (Baltimore: Johns Hopkins University Press, 1993), 73–90; Werner Hamacher, "Das Beben der Darstellung," in *Positionen der Literaturwissenschaft. Acht Modellanalysen am Beispiel von Kleists Das Erdbeben in Chili*, ed. David Wellbery (Munich: Beck, 1993), 149–73; Gerhard Neumann, ed., *Heinrich von Kleist. Kriegsfall—Rechtsfall—Sündenfall* (Freiburg: Rombach, 1994). Following Carrière, I consider Kleist's obsession with falling as *one* direction of the movement vital to Kleist's texts, and therefore less as a lamentation of loss than an experiment with instabilities (cf. Mathieu Carrière, *Pour une littérature de guerre, Kleist* [Arles: Actes Sudes, 1993]).
4. Friedrich Cramer, "Vorwort," in Christian-Paul Berger, *Bewegungsbilder. Kleists Marionettentheater zwischen Poesie und Physik* (Paderborn: Ferdinand Schöningh, 2000), IX. Both read Leibniz as Enlightenment rationalist.
5. The entire passage reads in German: "Ich hatte schon als Knabe (mich dünkt am Rhein durch eine Schrift von Wieland) mir den Gedanken angeeignet, daß die Vervollkomnung der Zweck der Schöpfung wäre. Ich glaubte, daß wir einst nach dem Tode von der Stufe der Vervollkomnung, die wir auf diesem Sterne erreichten, auf einen andern weiter fortschreiten würden, u. daß wir den Schatz von Wahrheiten, den wir hier sammelten, auch dort einst brauchen könnten" (*SW IV/1*, 505).
6. "Wenn alle Menschen statt der Augen grüne Gläser hätten, so würden sie urtheilen müssen, die Gegenstände, welche sie dadurch erblicken, sind grün—und nie würden sie entscheiden können, ob ihr Auge ihnen die Dinge zeigt, wie sie sind, oder ob es nicht etwas zu ihnen hinzuthut, was nicht ihnen, sondern dem Auge gehört. So ist es mit dem Verstande. Wir können nicht entscheiden, ob das, was wir Wahrheit nennen, wahrhaft Wahrheit ist, oder ob es uns nur so scheint. Ist das letzte, so ist die Wahrheit, die wir hier sammeln, nach dem Tode nicht mehr—u. alles Bestreben, ein Eigenthum sich zu erwerben, das uns auch in das Grab folgt, ist vergeblich…Mein einziges, mein höchstes Ziel ist gesunken, und ich habe nun keines mehr" (*SW IV/1*, 505).

## Notes

7. Jacobs, "The Style of Kleist," 55. The assumption of a *sudden* crisis becomes problematic, when we consider that Kleist made critical references to Kant and other philosophers earlier in *Über die Aufklärung des Weibes*, an essay written on September 16, 1800, during his stay in Würzburg six months before the so-called crisis-letters (cf. *SWB 2*, 315). Ironizing the efforts of enlightenment, this essay demonstrates Kleist's long-standing differences with philosophy, and we thus have no abrupt end to a hitherto naïve belief in rationalism, but an ongoing debate with philosophy.
8. Ibid.
9. Howard Caygill, *A Kant Dictionary* (Oxford: Blackwell, 1995), 55–56.
10. Melville's waning success was largely blamed on his increasing interest in philosophical questions, and the growing complications in style that went along with it. While his early sea-novels *Typee* (1846) and *Omoo* (1847) were a great success with readers, *Mardi* (1849), formally and philosophically more complex, lost readership. Melville tried to win readers back with *Redburn* (1849) and *White-Jacket* (1850), narratives with straightforward plots and autobiographical references, but never again matched his early success. *Moby-Dick; or, The Whale* (1851), written after his invigorating trip to Europe, frustrated his readers again, and he lost them for good with *Pierre; or, The Ambiguities* (1852). In June 1851, Melville writes to Hawthorne: "Dollars damn me....What I feel most moved to write, that is banned,—it will not pay. Yet, altogether, write the other way I cannot. So the product is a final hash, and all my books are botches" (Melville, *Tales, Poems, and other Writings*, 38). His writing of tales (1853–56) will not seriously change this. Only with the posthumous publication of *Billy Budd, Sailor* in 1924 did readers begin to appreciate his complexities in style and *sujet*.
11. Herman Melville, *The Writings of Herman Melville. Journals*, ed. Howard C. Horsford with Lynn Horth (Evanston/Chicago: Northwestern University Press, 1989), 4, hereafter cited as *J*.
12. For comprehensive summaries of Melville's philosophical readings, cf. John Wenke, "'Ontological Heroics': Melville's philosophical art," in *A Companion to Melville Studies*, ed. John Bryant (Greenwood: Westport, 1986); Merton M. Sealts Jr., *Melville's Reading. A Check-List of Books Owned and Borrowed* (Madison: University of Wisconsin Press, 1966); Laurie Robertson-Lorant, *Melville. A Biography* (Amherst: University of Massachusetts Press, 1996), 172; Andrew Delbanco, *Melville. His World and Work* (London: Picador, 2005), 116.
13. Cf. Elizabeth S. Foster, "Introduction," reprinted in Herman Melville, *The Confidence-Man: His Masquerade* (New York: Norton, 1971).
14. Herman Melville, *Moby-Dick or, The Whale*, ed. Harrison Hayford, Hershel Parker, and G. Thomas Tanselle (Evanston/Chicago: Northwestern University Press, 1988), 323.
15. Ibid., 327.
16. Ralph Waldo Emerson, "The Transcendentalist," in *Emerson on Transcendentalism*, ed. Edward L. Ericson (New York: Continuum, 1994).

17. Melville, *Moby-Dick*, 335.
18. Anselm Haverkamp, "Wie die Morgenröte zwischen Nacht und Tag. Alexander Gottlieb Baumgartens Begründung der Kulturwissenschaft," in *Latenzzeit. Wissen im Nachkrieg* (Berlin: Kadmos, 2004), 93. All translations are my own.
19. E.g., Jean-François Lyotard, "God and the Puppet," in *The Inhuman. Reflections on Time* (Stanford: Stanford University Press, 1991), 153–64.
20. Despite the early and crucial revision of Kant by Hegel's encyclopedic philosophy and his *Lectures on Aesthetics* and the tremendous influence they had upon subsequent aesthetic debates, the framework of aesthetic judgment has been set by Kant and continues to be our frame of reference. Recent aesthetic debates have reassessed the potential of Kant's aesthetic beyond its Schillerian reception or Hegelian transformations. For the most intriguing among these, cf. Rodolphe Gasché, *The Idea of Form* (Stanford: Stanford University Press, 2002); Jean-François Lyotard, *Lessons on the Analytic and the Sublime* (Stanford: Stanford University Press, 1994); the section on Kant's Anthropology in Ronell, *Stupidity* (Urbana/Chicago: University of Illinois Press, 2003), 278–310; and Paul de Man, "Kant's Materialism," in *Aesthetic Ideology* (Minneapolis: University of Minnesota Press, 1996), 119–28.
21. Calling Kant's aesthetics "subjective" might seem to resonate with Hegel's critique of Kant's aesthetics as remaining with the "subjective" assessment of and interest in art. While honoring Kant as the turning point of modern philosophy by introducing self-reflective rationality as the basis of philosophy, Kant, according to Hegel, did not go far enough. Transcendental philosophy only found an abstract resolution of the oppositions between concept and reality, reason and sensibility, by looking at art and aesthetic judgment as "merely subjective in respect of our appreciation as in respect of our production," which is only an "apparently complete reconciliation" and not a "naturally and completely true and real" one (G. W. F. Hegel, *Introductory Lectures on Aesthetics*, ed. Michael Inwood [London: Penguin, 1993], 66). Although Hegel is hard to escape, the term *subjective* is not used in his sense here, but rather to note that reflective judgment remains relevant to the reasoning, transcendental subject, and is thus, *per definitionem*, of no relevance to the understanding.
22. Howard Caygill, "Die Erfindung und Neuerfindung der Ästhetik," *Deutsche Zeitschrift für Philosophie* 49 (2001): 233. All translations are my own.
23. Baumgarten's main critics and recipients were Moses Mendelssohn, J. G. Herder, and of course Kant. Despite Mendelssohn's enthusiastic review of Baumgarten ("A.G. Baumgarten, *Aestheticorum Pars altera*" [1759]), his own work on aesthetics (esp. *Über die Empfindung* [1755]) diminished the cognitive dimension Baumgarten had ascribed to sensation. Cf. Groß, *Felix Aestheticus, Die Ästhetik als Lehre vom Menschen. Zum 250. Jahrestag des Erscheinens von Alexander Gottlieb Baumgartens 'Aesthetica'* (Würzburg: Königshausen & Neumann, 2001), 115f; and Naumann-Beyer, "Sinnlichkeit," *Ästhetische Grundbegriffe* 5 (2003): 545. Herder in turn criticized Baumgarten for not going far enough in his stress on feeling in

aesthetics. Although his *Begründung einer Ästhetik in der Auseinandersetzung mit Alexander Gottlieb Baumgarten* (1767) valued Baumgarten as "writer of my finest hours" (in *Werke*, Vol. 1, by Johann Gottfried Herder [Frankfurt/M: Deutsche Klassiker Verlag, 1985], 677; all translations my own) and a "philosopher of feeling" (ibid., 685), and despite the fact that Herder's own outline of aesthetics from 1769 onward in *Viertes Kritisches Wäldchen* critically continued Baumgarten's project (cf. Solms, *Disciplina Aesthetica. Zur Frühgeschichte der ästhetischen Theorie bei Baumgarten und Herder* [Stuttgart: Klett, 1990]; Jeffrey Barnouw, "The Cognitive Value of Confusion and Obscurity in the German Enlightenment: Leibniz, Baumgarten, Herder," *Studies in Eighteenth-Century Culture* 24 [1995]: 29–50), Herder still viewed Baumgarten as adhering too closely to a logical model; cf. Karl-Heinz Barck, Dieter Kliche, and Jörg Heininger, "Ästhetik/ästhetisch," *Ästhetische Grundbegriffe* 1 (2000): 332; Solms, *Disciplina Aesthetica*, 79; Menke, *Kraft. Ein Grundbegriff ästhetischer Anthropologie* (Frankfurt/Main: Suhrkamp, 2008), 46–51. Although intrigued by Baumgarten's early *Meditationes*, Herder thought him too faithful to Wolff, attempting to transplant Wolffian philosophy onto poetry and applying a "precision and rigor" (Herder, *Begründung einer Ästhetik*, 683) inappropriate to it. Until recently, this reception consolidated Baumgarten as indebted to Wolffian rationalism.

24. Although *Sinnlichkeit* is translated here as "sense," in §1 the same term is given as "sensibility" (cf. Immanuel Kant, *Critique of Pure Reason* [Amherst: Prometheus Books, 1990], 21, hereafter cited as *CPR*) and will throughout be used as "sensibility."
25. For the notion of "mereness," cf. Gasché, *Idea of Form*, 60–88.
26. Jacques Derrida, "Parergon," in *The Truth in Paining* (Chicago: University of Chicago Press, 1987), 37. For the architecture of Kant's three Critiques, cf. Gilles Deleuze, *Kant's Critical Philosophy* (Minneapolis: University of Minnesota Press, 1984).
27. Caygill, "Neuerfindung," 240.
28. Cf. the sections "Analytic of the Beautiful" and "Analytic of the Sublime" in Immanuel Kant, *The Critique of Judgment* (Amherst: Prometheus Books, 2000), 45–94 and 101–31 respectively, hereafter cited as *CJ*.
29. Derrida, "Parergon," 38.
30. Ibid.; cf. also preface to *CJ*.
31. Caygill, *Kant Dictionary*, 55.
32. Ibid., 364.
33. Ibid., 363.
34. Cf. Kai Hammermeister, *The German Aesthetic Tradition* (Cambridge: Cambridge University Press, 2002); Barck et al., "Ästhetik."
35. Haverkamp, "Morgenröte," 93. Reconsiderations of Baumgarten's potential for the reformulation of aesthetics in view of its epistemological import include the recent German translation of the *Aesthetica*, for the first time in its entirety, by Dagmar Mirbach, the special Baumgarten issue of the *Deutsche Zeitschrift für*

*Philosophie* (49/2001), ed. Christoph Menke, and a growing body of publications on his aesthetics: cf. Adler, *Aesthetics and Aisthetics*; Barnouw, "Cognitive Value"; Rüdiger Campe, "Der Effekt der Form. Baumgartens Ästhetik am Rande der Metaphysik," in *Literatur als Philosophie/Philosophie als Literatur*, ed. Eva Horn, Bettine Menke, and Christoph Menke (Munich: Fink, 2005), 17–34; Groß, *Felix Aestheticus*; Haverkamp, "Morgenröte"; Christoph Menke, *Kraft*; Solms, *Disciplina Aesthetica*.

36. Haverkamp, "Morgenröte," 95; cf. also Caygill, "Neuerfindung," 235.
37. Alexander Gottlieb Baumgarten, *Ästhetik*, vol. 1, ed. and trans. Dagmar Mirbach (Hamburg: Felix Meiner, 2007), §13, hereafter cited as *Ä*. All translations are my own.
38. For Descartes' redistribution of sensibility and reason, cf. René Descartes, *Meditations on First Philosophy: In Which the Existence of God and the Distinction of the Soul from the Body Are Demonstrated* (Indianapolis: Hackett, 1993), 24–35; for Baumgarten's claim of analyzability, cf. Menke, *Kraft*, 25f.
39. Haverkamp, "Morgenröte," 95.
40. Alexander Gottlieb Baumgarten, *Philosophische Briefe von Aletheophilus* (Frankfurt/Leipzig: Universität zu Halle, 1741), 6, hereafter cited as *PB*. All translations are my own.
41. Alexander Gottlieb Baumgarten, *Reflections on Poetry. Meditationes philosophicae de nonnullis ad poema pertinentibus*, ed. and trans. Karl Aschenbrenner and William Holther (Berkeley: University of California Press, 1954), 77; emphasis added.
42. Wolff's work provided a foil not only for Baumgarten, but also for many of Baumgarten's critics and recipients. Wolff's scholastically inspired and rationalist treatises *Psychologia empirica* (1732) and *Psychologia rationis* (1734) take recourse to Leibniz's categories of perception (clear, obscure, confused, and distinct ideas) and were instructive texts for Baumgarten, who studied with Wolff. But Wolff revised one crucial aspect of Leibniz's philosophy: he introduced a distinction between inferior and superior faculties, and consolidated a hierarchical relation between them. Only distinct ideas can be clear and only those belong to the superior faculties of the intellect. All other categories of ideas are subsumed under the fairly vast *facultatis cognoscendi parte inferior*, which Wolff lists as *sensus, imaginatio, memoria, oblivio*, and *reminiscentia*. Inscribing himself in the tradition of Leibniz, Wolff contributed to the interpretation of the latter as a stern rationalist. Baumgarten remains within Wolff's terminological framework of inferior/superior, but with Haverkamp we may see it as a bad metaphoric choice, as it suggests a hierarchy that does not correspond to the complex relation of inferior/superior faculties Baumgarten's theory otherwise works with (cf. Haverkamp, "Morgenröte," 100). For the departure from Wolff's philosophical framework, but the continuation of his terminology, cf. also Solms, *Disciplina aesthetica*, 25.
43. Baumgarten, *Reflections on Poetry*, 78; the Latin original calls aesthetics also επιστήμης αισθητικης, or aesthetic epistemologies.
44. For these transformations, cf. Caygill, "Neuerfindung," 239.

45. René Descartes, *Discours de la méthode/Discourse on the Method. A Bilingual Edition*, ed. and trans. George Heffernan (Notre Dame: University of Notre Dame Press, 1994), 59.
46. Gottfried Wilhelm Leibniz, "Meditations on Knowledge, Truth, and Ideas," in *Philosophical Papers and Letters*, vol. 1, ed. Leroy E. Loemker (Chicago: University of Chicago Press, 1956), 448–49.
47. Ibid.
48. Quoted after Robert McRae, *Leibniz: Perception, Apperception, and Thought* (Toronto: University of Toronto Press, 1976), 68; also in Leibniz, *Philosophical Papers and Letters*, 636ff.
49. Barnouw, "Cognitive Value," 31.
50. Gottfried Wilhelm Leibniz, "The Monadology," in *The Monadology and Other Philosophical Writings* (Oxford: Oxford University Press, 1965), 224.
51. Ibid.
52. Ulrich Johannes Schneider, introduction to *Monadologie und andere metaphysische Schriften*, by Gottfried Wilhelm Leibniz (Hamburg: Felix Meiner, 2002), VII; translation is my own.
53. Gilles Deleuze, *The Fold: Leibniz and the Baroque* (Minneapolis: University of Minnesota Press, 1988), 32, hereafter cited as *F*.
54. Baumgarten's indebtedness to Leibniz has been established in Baumgarten-research, but it was mostly a Leibniz according to Wolff. With Deleuze's rereading of Leibniz, but also Barnouw's work on sensation, and Menke's recent consideration of force as an aesthetic concept, the connection can be fruitfully reevaluated; cf. Jeffrey Barnouw, "The Beginnings of 'Aesthetics' and the Leibnizian Conception of Sensation," in *Eighteenth-century Aesthetics and the Reconstruction of Art*, ed. Paul Mattick (Cambridge: Cambridge University Press, 1993), 52–95; Menke, *Kraft*, 11–45; also Kaiser, "Two Floors of Thinking."
55. Gottfried Wilhelm Leibniz, "Discourse on Metaphysics," in *Philosophical Papers and Letters*, 501.
56. Barnouw, "The Beginnings of 'Aesthetics,'" 76; emphasis added.
57. Caygill, "Neuerfindung," 240.
58. Ibid., 239.
59. E.g., Schweizer speaks of Baumgarten's "double approach...combining an epistemological point of view with a poetic-rhetorical one" (Hans Rudolf Schweizer, "Begründung der Ästhetik als Wissenschaft der sinnlichen Erkenntnis," introduction to Alexander Gottlieb Baumgarten, *Theoretische Ästhetik* (Hamburg: Felix Meiner, 1988), X; translation is my own.
60. Hannes Böhringer, "Attention im Clair-obscur: Die Avantgarde," in Barck et al., *Aisthesis*, 14; translation is my own.
61. Ibid.
62. Solms, *Disciplina Aesthetica*, 40.
63. Alexander Gottlieb Baumgarten, *Texte zur Grundlegung der Ästhetik*, ed. Hans Rudolf Schweizer (Hamburg: Felix Meiner, 1983), 8.

64. Menke, *Kraft*, 18; all translations are my own.
65. Solms, *Disciplina Aesthetica*, 40.
66. Derrida, *Truth in Painting*, 51.
67. Menke, *Kraft*, 29.
68. Groß calls it an "Erkenntnishaltung", *Felix Aestheticus*, 48.
69. The contemporary reviews of the dense, nonsequential, at times self-contradictory narrative of *Pierre* were devastating; cf. Sacvan Bercovitch, "How to Read Melville's Pierre," in *Herman Melville. A Collection of Critical Essays*, ed. Myra Jehlen (Englewood Cliffs: Prentice-Hall, 1994), 117. Appreciation for the novel grew only in the mid-1980s, Bercovitch being one of the first to point to its poetic potential.
70. Herman Melville, *Pierre; or, The Ambiguities*, ed. Harrison Hayford, Hershel Parker, and G. Thomas Tanselle (Evanston/Chicago: Northwestern University Press, 1971), 267, hereafter cited as P.

## Chapter 2. Sentimentalities

1. Cf. Caygill, *Kant Dictionary*, 55–56; also for other, significant literary instances; cf. Karl Heinz Bohrer, *Kritik der Romantik. Der Verdacht der Philosophie gegen die literarische Moderne* (Frankfurt/M: Suhrkamp, 1989); Ronell, *Stupidity*; Joseph Vogl, ed., *Poetologien des Wissens um 1800* (Munich: Fink, 1999).
2. These readings are indebted to the debates on affect and thought stimulated largely by Deleuze's philosophy and wish to consider what, e.g., Brian Massumi calls—as title to the section on art in his *A Shock to Thought. Expressions after Deleuze and Guattari*, (London: Routledge, 2002)—"that thinking feeling." Melissa McMahon shows in her essay in this section that such "thinking feeling" amounts to a "'total conversion of thought.' Thought would no longer rely on a pre-existing determined order which it would stand back and 'reflect,' but remains indeterminate until an encounter at a contingent moment (an interception) obliges it to *make* a difference" (6). For the debate, cf. also Claire Colebrook, "The Sense of Space: On the Specificity of Affect in Deleuze and Guattari," *Postmodern Culture* 15, no. 1 (2004); Massumi, *Parables for the Virtual*; Charles Stivale, "From Zigzag to Affect, and Back," *Angelaki* 11 (2006): 25–33.
3. For a comprehensive historical account, cf. Hans Christoph Buch, *Die Scheidung von San Domingo. Wie die Negersklaven von Haiti Robespierre beim Wort nahmen* (Berlin: Klaus Wagenbach, 1976).
4. For reasons of readability, all quotes from Kleist are given in English, and for reasons of textual economy, the German is not quoted parallel to the English except for extended quotes, which are given in German in the notes. For interested readers, however, the corresponding German passages are indicated with the abbreviations listed in the front of the book.
5. For Kleist, cf. Peter Horn, "Hatte Kleist Rassenvorurteile?" in *Heinrich von Kleists Erzählungen. Eine Einführung* (Königstein: Scriptor, 1978); Hans Peter Herrmann, "Die Verlobung in St. Domingo," in *Interpretationen. Kleists Erzählungen*, ed.

## Notes

Walter Hinderer (Stuttgart: Reclam, 1998); Gerhard Neumann, "Die Verlobung in St. Domingo. Zum Problem literarischer Mimesis im Werk Heinrich von Kleists," in *Gewagte Experimente und kühne Konstellationen. Kleists Werk zwischen Klassizismus und Romantik*, ed. Christine Lubkoll and Günter Oesterle (Würzburg: Königshausen & Neumann, 2001); Haverkamp, "Schwarz/Weiß"; for Melville, cf. Robert Burkholder, introduction to *Critical Essays on Herman Melville's "Benito Cereno"* (New York: G. K Hall, 1992).

6. Christine Lubkoll, "Soziale Experimente und ästhetische Ordnung. Kleists Literaturkonzept im Spannungsfeld von Klassizismus und Romantik ('Die Verlobung in St. Domingo')," in *Gewagte Experimente und kühne Konstellationen*, 124.
7. Cf. Eric J. Sundquist, "'Benito Cereno' and New World Slavery," in *Critical Essays on Herman Melville's "Benito Cereno"*; Carolyn L. Karcher, "The Riddle of the Sphinx: Melville's 'Benito Cereno' and the Amistad Case," in *Critical Essays on Melville's "Benito Cereno."*
8. "[E]r forderte, in seiner unmenschlichen Rachsucht, sogar die alte Babekan mit ihrer Tocher, einer jungen funfzehnjährigen Mestize, Namens Toni, auf, an diesem grimmigen Kriege...Antheil zu nehmen" (*SW II/4*, 9).
9. Haverkamp, "Schwarz/Weiß," 124.
10. Ibid.
11. "Babekan, welche in Folge einer grausamen Strafe, die sie in ihrer Jugend erhalten hatte, an der Schwindsucht litt, pflegte in solchen Fällen die junge Toni, die wegen ihrer ins Gelbliche gehenden Gesichtsfarbe, zu dieser gräßlichen List besonders brauchbar war, mit ihren besten Kleidern auszuputzen; sie ermunterte dieselbe, den Fremden keine Liebkosung zu versagen, bis auf die letzte, die ihr bei Todesstrafe verboten war: und wenn Congo Hoango mit seinem Negertrupp von den Streifereien, die er in der Gegend gemacht hatte, wiederkehrte, war unmittelbarer Tod das Loos der Armen, die sich durch diese Künste hatten täuschen lassen" (*SW II/4*, 9–10).
12. "Es war ihm unmöglich zu glauben, daß alle diese Bewegungen, die er an ihr wahrnahm, der bloße elende Ausdruck einer kalten und gräßlichen Verrätherei seyn sollten. Die Gedanken, die ihn beunruhigt hatten, wichen, wie ein Heer schauerlicher Vögel, von ihm; er schalt sich, ihr Herz nur einen Augenblick verkannt zu haben, und während er sie auf den Knieen schaukelte, und den süßen Athem einsog, den sie ihm heraufsandte, drückte er, gleichsam zum Zeichen der Aussöhnung und Vergebung, einen Kuß auf ihre Stirn" (*SW II/4*, 38–39).
13. Christian Moser, *Verfehlte Gefühle. Wissen—Begehren—Darstellen bei Kleist und Rousseau* (Würzburg: Königshausen & Neumann, 1993), 20.
14. "[W]ie sie die Laterne so gehalten, daß ihr der volle Strahl davon ins Gesicht gefallen wäre. Aber seine Einbildung, sprach sie, war ganz von *Mohren und Negern* erfüllt; und wenn ihm *eine Dame von Paris oder Marseille* die Thüre geöffnet hätte, er würde sie für eine Negerin gehalten haben" (*SW II/4*, 26; emphases added).
15. Babekan relates that she "conceived...*in* Paris" (*BSD*, 240; emphasis added; in German accordingly *Schwangerschaft* zu *Paris*), which is a prelude to Toni's

betrothal *in* Santo Domingo. Mother and daughter share a similar fate of being betrayed by white men. Kleist draws attention to this by the idiosyncratic use of both adverbs ("zu" and "in"), which stress the locations of the occurrences, whereas usually a pregnancy is *with* a child, and a betrothal *with* a lover. The love and bonding implied by "with" are foreclosed in these constellations, Kleist seems to suggest, by a persistent reinscription of Babekan and Toni into racial categories that even efface any however much highlighted place of birth.

16. "Der Fremde, der nicht *begriff*, was diese Anstalten zu bedeuten hatten, fragte den Knaben, den er mit Entsetzen, als er ihm nahe stand, für einen Negerknaben erkannte: wer in dieser Niederlassung wohne? und schon war er auf die Antwort desselben: 'dass die Besitzung, seit dem Tode Hrn. Villeneuves dem Neger Hoango anheim gefallen,' *im Begriff*, den Jungen *niederzuwerfen*, ihm den Schlüssel der Hofpforte, den er *in der Hand* hielt, zu *entreißen* und das weite Feld zu suchen, als Toni, die Laterne *in der Hand*, vor das Haus hinaus trat. "Geschwind!" sprach sie, indem sie *seine Hand ergriff* und ihn nach der Thür *zog*: 'hier hinein!' Sie *trug* Sorge, indem sie dies sagte, das Licht so zu stellen, daß der volle Strahl davon auf ihr Gesicht fiel.—Wer bist du? rief der Fremde sträubend, indem er, um mehr als einer Ursache willen betroffen, ihre liebliche Gestalt betrachtete. Wer wohnt in diesem Hause, in welchem ich, wie Du vorgibst, meine Rettung finden soll?— 'Niemand, bei dem Licht der Sonne,' sprach das Mädchen, 'als meine Mutter und ich!' und bestrebte und beeiferte sich, ihn mit sich *fortzureißen*. Was, niemand! rief der Fremde, indem er, mit einem Schritt rückwärts, *seine Hand losriß*: hat mir dieser Knabe nicht eben gesagt, daß ein Neger, Namens Hoango, darin befindlich sey?—'Ich sage, nein!' sprach das Mädchen, indem sie, mit einem Ausdruck von Unwillen, mit dem Fuß stampfte; 'und wenn gleich einem Wütherich, der diesen Namen führt, das Haus gehört: abwesend ist er in diesem Augenblick und auf zehn Meilen davon entfernt!' Und damit *zog* sie den Fremden mit ihren *beiden Händen* in das Haus hinein, befahl dem Knaben, keinem Menschen zu sagen, wer angekommen sei, *ergriff*, nachdem sie die Thür erreicht, des Fremden *Hand* und führte ihn die Treppe hinauf, nach dem Zimmer ihrer Mutter" (*SW II/4*, 15–16; emphases added, not all identical to emphases in translation).

17. "Bei diesen Worten trat der Fremde, indem er das Mädchen losließ, an das Fenster; und da diese sah, daß er sein Gesicht sehr gerührt in ein Tuch drückte: so übernahm sie, von manchen Seiten geweckt, ein menschliches Gefühl; sie folgte ihm mit einer plötzlichen Bewegung, fiel ihm um den Hals, und mischte ihre Thränen mit den seinigen. Was weiter erfolgte, brauchen wir nicht zu melden, weil es jeder, der an diese Stelle kommt, von selbst lies't.

 Der Fremde, als er sich wieder gesammelt hatte, wußte nicht, wohin ihn die That, die er begangen, führen würde; inzwischen sah er so viel ein, daß er gerettet, und in dem Hause, in welchem er sich befand, für ihn nichts von dem Mädchen zu befürchten war. Er versuchte, da er sie mit verschränkten Armen auf dem Bett weinen sah, alles nur Mögliche, um sie zu beruhigen" (*SW II/4*, 42–43).

18. For these different options, cf. Neumann, "Verlobung," 106; Herrmann, "Verlobung in Santo Domingo," 118 (love); Lubkoll, "Soziale Experimente und ästhetische Ordnung" (love); Moser, *Verfehlte Gefühle* (seduction); Haverkamp, "Schwarz/Weiß" (rape).
19. Neumann, "Verlobung," 105.
20. Phillipe Jaworski, "Desert and Empire: From 'Bartleby' to 'Benito Cereno,'" in *Herman Melville: A Collection of Critical Essays*, 154.
21. Peter Coviello, "The American in Charity: 'Benito Cereno' and Gothic Anti-Sentimentality," *Studies in American Fiction* 30, no. 2 (2002): 157.
22. Ibid., 158.
23. Ibid., 157.
24. Cf. Neumann, "Verlobung," 107. For Melville, cf. Hermann Josef Schnackertz, "Wahrnehmungsperspektiven als Medium kultureller Exposition in Herman Melvilles 'Typee' und 'Benito Cereno,'" in *Vergessen. Entdecken. Erhellen. Literaturwissenschaftliche Aufsätze*, ed. Jörg Drews (Bielefeld: Aisthesis, 1993).
25. Haverkamp, "Schwarz/Weiß," 125.
26. The anagrammatical variation of Gustav as "August" at four significant moments in the text created much confusion and was, until the Berlin/Brandenburg edition by Reuß/Staengle, seen as a misspelling and thus corrected. Its potential significance as an anagram has been noted since Reuß/Staengle (cf. Neumann, "Verlobung"), which in the context of this reading makes sense as a pun on *dummer August*, the clown becoming popular at the beginning of the nineteenth century as the clumsy counterpart to the intelligent "white clown" (a popular version of *Harlekin*).
27. Cf. Deleuze and Guattari, *A Thousand Plateaus*, 62ff. and 200ff.
28. Ibid., 201.

# Chapter 3. Affectivity

1. Dirk Grathoff asks this question in "Michael Kohlhaas," in *Interpretationen. Kleists Erzählungen*, ed. Walter Hinderer (Stuttgart: Reclam, 1998).
2. Martin Greenberg, "The Difficult Justice of Melville and Kleist," 25.
3. Barbara Johnson, "Melville's Fist: The Execution of Billy Budd," in *The Critical Difference* (Baltimore: Johns Hopkins University Press, 1980), 88.
4. "Dabei ist mir nichts heilsamer, als eine Bewegung meiner Schwester, als ob sie mich unterbrechen wollte; denn mein ohnehin schon angestrengtes Gemüt wird durch diesen Versuch von außen, ihm die Rede, in deren Besitz es sich befindet, zu entreißen, nur noch mehr erregt, und in seiner Fähigkeit, wie ein großer General, wenn die Umstände drängen, noch um einen Grad höher gespannt" (*SWB*, 320; translation is my own).
5. Gerhard Neumann, "Das Stocken der Sprache und das Straucheln des Körpers," in *Heinrich von Kleist: Kriegsfall—Rechtsfall—Sündenfall*, 23.
6. "'Ja', antwortete Mirabeau [dem Zeremonienmeister], 'wir haben des Königs Befehl vernommen'—ich bin gewiß, daß er bei diesem humanen Anfang, noch

nicht an die Bajonette dachte, mit welchen er schloß: 'ja, mein Herr', wiederholte er, 'wir haben ihn vernommen'—man sieht, daß er noch gar nicht recht weiß, was er will. 'Doch was berechtigt Sie'—fuhr er fort, und nun plötzlich geht ihm ein Quell ungeheurer Vorstellungen auf—'uns hier Befehle anzudeuten? Wir sind die Repräsentaten der Nation.'—Das war es was er brauchte! (etc.)" (*SWB*, 320).

7. "Wenn man an den Zeremonienmeister denkt, so kann man sich ihn bei diesem Auftritt nicht anders, als in einem völligen Geistesbankerott vorstellen; nach einem ähnlichen Gesetz, nach welchem in einem Körper, der von dem elektrischen Zustand Null ist, wenn er in eines elektrisierten Körpers Atmosphäre kommt, plötzlich die entgegengesetzte Elektrizität erweckt wird" (*SWB*, 321).

8. On Kleist's knowledge of experimental physics, cf. Roland Borgards, "'Allerneuester Erziehungsplan' Ein Beitrag Heinrich von Kleists zur Experimentalkultur um 1800 (Literatur, Physik)," in *Literarische Experimentalkulturen. Poetologien des Experiments im 19. Jahrhundert*, ed. Marcus Krause and Nicolas Pethes (Würzburg: Königshausen & Neumann, 2005), 75–102; also Kleist's corresponding text "Allerneuester Erziehungsplan" (*SWB*, 329–35), translated as "The Very Last Word in Modern Educational Theory" (*ADE*, 223–28).

9. The electrical condenser also known as the Leyden jar, invented in Germany in 1745 by Ewald Georg von Kleist.

10. Cf. Neumann, "Stocken der Sprache," 15.

11. Sembdner gives 1805–06 (Helmut Sembdner, "Anmerkungen zu Heinrich von Kleist," in *SWB*, 925), Neumann 1804 as year of composition (Neumann, "Stocken der Sprache," 13).

12. Cf. Denis Dyer, *The Stories of Kleist* (New York: Holmes and Meier, 1977), 109; Sembdner, "Anmerkungen," 925.

13. Cf. Erika Fischer-Lichte, *Heinrich von Kleist: Michael Kohlhaas* (Frankfurt/Main: Diesterweg, 1991).

14. Paul de Man, "Aesthetic Formalization: Kleist's Über das Marionettentheater," in *The Rhetoric of Romanticism* (New York: Columbia University Press, 1984), 269.

15. All ibid., 267f.

16. Both ibid., 287.

17. Cf. Deleuze and Guattari, *Kafka. Toward a Minor Literature*, 13; cf. also Gilles Deleuze, "On the Superiority of Anglo-American Literature," in Gilles Deleuze and Claire Parnet, *Dialogues II* (London: Continuum, 2002).

18. For the concept and turn of phrase "What is to be done next?" I am indebted to Kathrin Thiele, *The Thought of Becoming. Gilles Deleuze's Poetics of Life* (Zurich/Berlin: diaphanes, 2008), 26.

19. Ronell, *Stupidity*, 100–101.

20. Ibid.

21. Ibid.

22. It thus falls outside of Melville's phase of tale writing and marks his late return to prose after writing poetry (most prominently the collections *Battle Pieces and Aspects of the War* (1866), *Clarel* (1876), and *John Marr and Other Sailors* (1888)).

## Notes

23. Many explanations for Claggart's aversion have been proposed, an influential one being the suggestion of a homosexual subtext, as in many others of Melville's narratives; cf. most prominently Eve Kosofsky Sedgwick, "Billy Budd: After the Homosexual," in *Herman Melville. A Collection of Critical Essays*. Sedgwick's reading gave rise to a whole strand of Melville criticism, examining the homoerotic undertones of his fiction. Without disputing the homoeroticism at work in *Billy Budd, Sailor* and in Melville at large, we must note, however, that the text literally operates with an unexplained "immediate dislike." The reading of homosexual undertones is much like Claggart's desire for double entendres driven by a desire for explanation, a desire the text—indispensably—evokes and sets in motion. Instead of searching for the reasons behind Claggart's and Billy's conduct, however, I suggest—taking off from Johnson's observation that the reception of *Billy Budd, Sailor* has opted either for "metaphysical" readings (seeing the text as symbolizing the struggle between good and evil), or "psychoanalytic" readings (arguing for Claggart's repressed homosexuality, his hatred of Billy as a repressed form of love, and Billy's slippage with and spilling of the soup as signs of Billy's own secret desires), cf. Johnson, "Melville's Fist," 88–89—focusing on the figure of Billy as Melville's experiment with a "condition that knows."'
24. Johnson, "Melville's Fist," 88.
25. Ronell, *Stupidity*, 100; emphasis added.
26. Johnson, "Melville's Fist," 88.
27. Ibid.
28. Ibid., 88–89.
29. Ibid., 89.
30. Andrew Delbanco argues, that Billy Budd is "Melville's version of the sacred idea of beforeness: what man had been before the acquired the sense of boundary between himself and others (between what Emerson called the 'Me' and the 'Not-Me')" (Delbanco, *Melville*, 301). As my reading demonstrates, however, Melville's literary and aesthetic experiments not only differ from Emersonian transcendentalism (most explicitly noted in Melville, *Tales, Poems, and Other Writings*, 32), but Billy's problematic murder of Claggart also prevents Billy from being "the Romantic dream personified—the dream of man restored to the integrity he had possessed before (again in Emerson's phrase) man 'became… disunited with himself'" (Delbanco, *Melville*, 301).
31. Max Kommerell, "Die Sprache und das Unaussprechliche. Eine Betrachtung über Heinrich von Kleist," in *Geist und Buchstabe der Dichtung: Goethe, Schiller, Kleist, Hölderlin* (Frankfurt/Main: Klostermann, 1991), 259. All translations are my own.
32. Ibid., 294.
33. Ibid. Kommerell builds his whole argument around the observation that Kohlhaas's "ego" is not self-presence, but an obedience against itself despite itself. Kleist's resistance to Enlightenment aspirations of a transparency of thought and language, Kommerell argues, manifests itself in his characters, in the fact that they become characters precisely by becoming riddles to themselves and to the world: riddles

that obscure the characters to themselves and that challenge them to endure themselves. The question of subjectivity—a relation to an "I"—has been a focus in much of the tale's criticism; cf. Helga Gallas, *Das Textbegehren des 'Michael Kohlhaas'. Die Sprache des Unbewußten und der Sinn der Literatur* (Reinbek: Rowohlt, 1981); Michael Hetzner, "Der Kaufmann als Held. Das Problem der Bürgerlichen Identität in Kleists Michael Kohlhaas," *Beiträge zur Kleist-Forschung* (2001).

34. To give evidence of this ubiquity we could go through the entire text and find this turn of phrase inscribed on almost every page. For an exemplary succession of it, cf. quote 42 on page 135.

35. Accordingly, Hillis Miller remarks that in order to do justice to *Michael Kohlhaas*—and Kleist's stories in general—"to talk about it, 'read' it, analyze it, evaluate it, it seems necessary to tell the story again" ("Laying Down the Law in Literature," in *Topographies* [Stanford: Stanford University Press, 1995], 90), something to which much of Kleist criticism unduly limits itself, as Miller laments.

36. "Kohlhaas fluchte über diese schändliche und abgekartete Gewalttätigkeit, verbiß jedoch, im Gefühl seiner Ohnmacht, seinen Ingrimm, und machte schon, da doch nichts anders übrig blieb, Anstalten, das Raubnest mit den Pferden nur wieder zu verlassen, als der Schloßvogt, von dem Wortwechsel herbeigerufen, erschien, und fragte, was es hier gäbe? Was es gibt? antwortete Kohlhaas. Wer hat dem Junker von Tronka und dessen Leuten die Erlaubnis gegeben, sich meiner bei ihm zurückgelassenen Rappen zur Feldarbeit zu bedienen?...Der Schloßvogt, nachdem er ihn eine Weile trotzig angesehen hatte, versetzte: seht den Grobian! Ob der Flegel nicht Gott danken sollte, daß die Mähren überhaupt noch leben? Er fragte, wer sie, da der Knecht weggelaufen, hätte pflegen sollen? Ob es nicht billig gewesen wäre, daß die Pferde das Futter, das man ihnen gereicht habe, auf den Feldern abverdient hätten? Er schloß, daß er hier keine Flausen machen möchte, oder daß er die Hunde rufen, und sich durch sie Ruhe im Hofe zu verschaffen wissen würde.—Dem Roßhändler schlug das Herz gegen den Wams. Es drängte ihn, den nichtswürdigen Dickwanst in den Kot zu werfen, und den Fuß auf sein kupfernes Antlitz zu setzen. Doch sein Rechtsgefühl, das einer Goldwaage glich, wankte noch; er war, vor der Schranke seiner eigenen Brust, noch nicht gewiß, ob eine Schuld den Gegner drückte; und während er, die Schimpfreden niederschluckend, zu den Pferden trat, und ihnen, in stiller Erwägung der Umstände, die Mähnen zurecht legte, fragte er mit gesenkter Stimme: um welchen Versehens halber der Knecht denn aus der Burg entfernt worden sei?" (*SW II/1*, 77).

37. László Földenyi, *Heinrich von Kleist. Im Netz der Wörter* (Munich: Matthes und Seitz, 1999), 415. Translation is my own.

38. This has been a predominant concern of many critics, cf. e.g. Catharina Grassau, "Recht und Rache. Eine Betrachtung der inneren Wendepunkte in Kleists Michael Kohlhaas," *Beiträge zur Kleist-Forschung* (2002): 245; Wolfgang Wittkowski, "Rechtspflicht, Rache und Noblesse: Der Kohlhaas-Charakter," *Beiträge zur Kleist-Forschung* (1998): 92–113.

39. Cf. Grassau, "Recht und Rache," 247.

40. Ibid.
41. Carol Jacobs has convincingly made this point in "Soothsaying and Rebellion," in *Uncontainable Romanticism* (Baltimore: Johns Hopkins University Press, 1989).
42. "—so *wandte* Kohlhaas, in die Hölle unbefriedigter Rache zurückgeschleudert, das Pferd, und war im Begriff: steckt an! zu rufen, als ein ungeheurer Wetterschlag, dicht neben ihm, zur Erde niederfiel. Kohlhaas, indem er sein Pferd zu ihr *zurückwandte*, fragte sie: ob sie sein Mandat erhalten? und da die Dame mit schwacher, kaum hörbarer Stimme antwortete: eben jetzt!—'Wann?'—Zwei Stunden, so wahr mit Gott helfe, nach des Junkers, meines Vetters, bereits vollzogener Abreise!—und Waldmann, der Knecht, zu dem Kohlhaas sich, unter finsteren Blicken, *umkehrte*, stotternd diesen Umstand bestätigte, indem er sagte, daß die Gewässer der Mulde, vom Regen geschwellt, ihn verhindert hätten, früher, als eben jetzt, einzutreffen: so sammelte sich Kohlhaas; ein plötzlich furchtbarer Regenguß, der die Fackeln verlöschend, auf das Pflaster des Platzes niederrauschte, löste den Schmerz in seiner unglücklichen Brust; er *wandte* sein Pferd und verließ das Stift" (*SW II/1*, 127–28; emphases added).
43. Hetzner, "Der Kaufmann als Held," 72.

## Chapter 4. Insistence

1. Cf. Giorgio Agamben, "Bartleby, or On Contingency," in *Potentialities* (Stanford: Stanford University Press, 1999); Branca Arsić, "Active Habits and Passive Events or Bartleby," in *Between Deleuze and Derrida*, ed. Paul Patton and John Protevi (London/New York: Continuum, 2003); Maurice Blanchot, *The Writing of Disaster* (Lincoln: University of Nebraska Press, 1995); Alexander Cooke, "Resistance, Potentiality, and the Law. Deleuze and Agamben on 'Bartleby,'" *Angelaki* 10, no. 3 (2005); Gilles Deleuze, "Bartleby; or, The Formula," in *Essays Critical and Clinical*; Jacques Derrida, *The Gift of Death* (Chicago: University of Chicago Press, 1996); Jacques Rancière, "Deleuze, Bartleby, and the Literary Formula," in *The Flesh of Words. The Politics of Writing* (Stanford: Stanford University Press, 2004); Ann Smock, *What Is There to Say? Blanchot, Melville, des Forêts, Beckett* (Lincoln: University of Nebraska Press, 2003).
2. Blanchot, *Writing of Disaster*, 140.
3. Derrida, *Gift of Death*, 75.
4. Blanchot, *Writing of Disaster*, 141.
5. Ronell, *Stupidity*, 9.
6. Giorgio Agamben, "Bartleby, or On Contingency," 257.
7. Ibid.
8. Derrida, *Gift of Death*, 75.
9. Ibid.
10. Arsić, "Active Habits and Passive Events," 154.
11. Günter Oesterle, "Vision und Verhör," in *Gewagte Experimente und kühne Konstellationen*, 314. Translation is my own.

12. Deleuze, *Essays Critical and Clinical*, 193.
13. For Kleist's frequent use of court scenes, legal testimonies, and interrogations, as well as his general obsession with questions of law and truth, cf. Manfred Schneider, "Die Inquisition der Oberfläche. Kleist und die juristische Kodifikation des Unbewußten," in *Heinrich von Kleist: Kriegsfall—Rechtsfall—Sündenfall*.
14. "Käthchen. Sprecht ihr verehrten Herrn; was wollt ihr wissen? / Graf Otto. Warum, als Friedrich Graf vom Strahl erschien, / In deines Vaters Haus, bist du zu Füßen, / Wie man vor Gott thut, nieder ihm gestürzt? / Warum warfst du, als er von dannen ritt, / Dich aus dem Fenster sinnlos auf die Straße, / Und folgtest ihm, da kaum dein Bein vernarbt, / Von Ort zu Ort, durch Nacht und Graus und Nebel, / Wohin sein Roß den Fußtritt wendete? / Käthchen (*hochrot zum Grafen*). Das soll ich hier vor diesen Männern sagen? / Der Graf vom Strahl. Die Närrin, die verwünschte, sinnverwirrte, / Was fragt sie m i c h? Ists nicht an jener Männer / Gebot, die Sache darzuthun, genug? / Käthchen (*in Staub niederfallend*). Nimm mir, o Herr, das Leben, wenn ich fehlte! / Was in des Busen stillem Reich geschehn, / Und Gott nicht straft, das braucht kein Mensch zu wissen; / Den nenn' ich grausam, der mich darum fragt! / Wenn d u es wissen willst, wohlan, so rede, / Denn dir liegt meine Seele offen da!" (*SW I/6*, 30–31).
15. "Der Graf vom Strahl (*wendet sich zu Käthchen, die noch immer auf Knien liegt*). Willst den geheimsten der Gedanken mir, / Kathrina, der dir irgend, fass mich wohl, / Im Winkel wo des Herzens schlummert, geben? / Käthchen. Das ganze Herz, o Herr, dir, willt du es, / So bist du sicher deß, was darin wohnt" (*SW I/6*, 31–32).
16. "Der Graf vom Strahl. Was ists, mit einem Wort, mir rund gesagt, / Das dich aus deines Vaters Hause trieb? / Was fesselt dich an meine Schritte an? / Käthchen. Mein hoher Herr! Da fragst du mich zuviel. / Und läg ich so, wie ich vor dir jetzt liege, / Vor meinem eigenen Bewusstsein da: / Auf einem goldnen Richtstuhl laß es thronen, / Und alle Schrecken des Gewissens ihm, / In Flammenrüstungen, zur Seite stehn; / So spräche jeglicher Gedanke noch, / Auf das, was du gefragt: ich weiß es nicht" (*SW I/6*, 32).
17. "Graf Otto (*zum Grafen vom Strahl*). Befragt sie, was geschehn, fünf Tag' von hier / Im Stall zu Strahl, als es schon dunkelte, / Und Ihr den Gottschalk hießt, sich zu entfernen? / Der Graf vom Strahl (*zum Käthchen*). Was ist geschehn, fünf Tage von hier, am Abend, / Im Stall zu Strahl, als es schon dunkelte, / Und ich den Gottschalk hieß, sich zu entfernen?/ Käthchen. *Mein hoher Herr!* Vergib mir, wenn ich fehlte; / Jetzt leg ich alles, Punkt für Punkt, dir dar. / Der Graf vom Strahl. Gut. —Da berührt ich dich und zwar—nicht? Freilich! / Das schon gestand'st du? / Käthchen. Ja, *mein verehrter Herr*. / Der Graf vom Strahl. Nun? / Käthchen. *Mein verehrter Herr?* / Der Graf vom Strahl. Was will ich wissen? / Käthchen. Was du willst wissen? / Der Graf vom Strahl. Heraus damit! Was stockst du? / Ich nahm, und herzte dich, und küßte dich, / Und schlug den Arm dir—? / Käthchen. Nein, *mein hoher Herr*. / Der Graf vom Strahl. Was sonst? /

KÄTHCHEN. Du stießest mich mit Füßen von dir. / DER GRAF VOM STRAHL. Mit Füßen? Nein! Das thu' ich keinem Hund. / Warum? Weshalb? Was hatt'st du mir gethan? / KÄTHCHEN. Weil ich dem Vater, der voll Huld und Güte, / Gekommen war, mit Pferden, mich zu holen, / Den Rücken, voller Schrecken, wendete, / Und mit der Bitte, mich vor ihm zu schützen, / Im Staub vor dir bewustlos nieder sank. / DER GRAF VOM STRAHL. Da hätt' ich dich mit Füßen weggestoßen? / KÄTHCHEN. Ja, *mein verehrter Herr.* / DER GRAF VOM STRAHL. Ei, Possen, was! / Das war nur Schelmerei, des Vaters wegen. / Du bliebst doch nach wie vor im Schloß zu Strahl. / KÄTHCHEN. Nein, *mein verehrter Herr.* / DER GRAF VOM STRAHL. Nicht? Wo auch sonst? / KÄTHCHEN. Als du die Peitsche, flammenden Gesichts, / Herab vom Riegel nahmst, ging ich hinaus, / Vor das bemoos'te Thor, und lagerte / Mich draußen, am zerfallnen Mauernring / Wo in süßduftenden Hollunderbüschen / Ein Zeisig zwitschernd sich das Nest gebaut. / DER GRAF VOM STRAHL. Hier aber jagt' ich dich mit Hunden weg? / KÄTHCHEN. Nein, *mein verehrter Herr!*" (*SW* I/6, 41–44, emphases added).

18. "[S]o trete ich [Graf Wetter vom Strahl] eines Tages, da ich sie auf der Stallschwelle finde, zu ihr und frage: was für ein Geschäft sie in Straßburg betreibe? Ei, spricht sie gestrenger Herr, und eine Röthe, daß ich denke, ihre Schürze wird angehn, flammt über ihr Antlitz empor: 'was fragt Ihr doch? Ihr wißts ja!'" (*SW* I/6, 22).
19. KÄTHCHEN: "Du sandtest Gottschalk mir am dritten Tage, / Daß er mit sagt: dein liebes Käthchen wär' ich; / Vernünftig aber mögt' ich sein, und geht." / GRAF VOM STRAHL: "Und was entgegnetest du dem?" / KÄTHCHEN: "Ich sagte, / Den Zeisig littest du, den Zwitschernden, / In den süßduftenden Hollunderbüschen: / Mögt'st denn das Käthchen von Heilbronn auch leiden" (*SW* I/6, 44).
20. Even in front of the altar at the moment of attaining the alleged goal of her pursuit, Käthchen prefers not to speak, and seems rather to *side*step the opposition reason/madness, in the sense that Sedgwick speaks of *beside* as a preposition that has "nothing very dualistic about it…permit[ting] a spacious agnosticism about several of the linear logics that enforce dualistic thinking…."(Eve K. Sedgwick, *Touching Feeling* (Durham: Duke University Press, 2003), 8).
21. Gilles Deleuze, "Bartleby, ou la formule," in *Critique et Clinique* (Paris: Minuit, 1993), 103.
22. We find this ambiguity spelled out in the other direction, for example, in the essay's German translation ("vor dem Bewusstsein" [*consciousness*], Gilles Deleuze, "Bartleby oder die Formel," in *Kritik und Klinik*, trans. Joseph Vogl [Frankfurt/Main: Suhrkamp, 2000], 110).
23. Deleuze, "Bartleby oder die Formel," 110; emphasis added.
24. Cf. Kommerell, "Sprache," 244.
25. Ibid., 247.
26. Ibid.
27. Ibid., 248.
28. Ibid., 249.

29. "Gertrud, so viel ich mich erinnere, hieß sie, mit der ich mich in einem, von dem Volk minder besuchten, Teil des Gartens...*unterhielt*" (*SW* I/6, 177; translation is my own, emphasis added).
30. For the use of folds in Roussel, cf. Michel Foucault, *Death and the Labyrinth: The World of Raymond Roussel* (London: Continuum, 2007); Birgit M. Kaiser, "Falte. Die Implikation des Literarischen," in *Latenz. 40 Annäherungen an einen Begriff*, ed. Stefanie Diekmann and Thomas Khurana (Berlin: Kadmos, 2007), 67–72.

## Conclusion

1. Most prominently perhaps the *War Machine* (with reference to Kleist in Deleuze and Guattari, *A Thousand Plateaus*. 351–421), *becoming* (with reference to Kleist and Melville in Deleuze, "On the Superiority of Anglo-American Literature"; and Deleuze and Guattari, *What is Philosophy?*, 171–78); and *superior irrationalism* (with reference to Melville in Deleuze, "Bartleby; or, the Formula").
2. Deleuze, *Essays Critical and Clinical*, 193.
3. Cf. *BF,* 80; Deleuze and Guattari, *What Is Philosophy?*, 173.
4. Deleuze, *Masochism*, 47–48, 53.
5. Herman Melville, *The Confidence-Man: His Masquerade*, ed. Hershel Parker (New York/London: Norton, 1971).
6. Gilles Deleuze, *Francis Bacon*, 6. For Deleuze's challenging notion of the figure, challenging especially in regard to its literary uses, cf. Rancière, "Deleuze, Bartleby, and the Literary Formula."
7. "Denn wer das Käthchen liebt, dem kann die Penthesilea nicht ganz unbegreiflich sein, sie gehören ja wie das + und – in der Algebra zusammen, und sind ein und dasselbe Wesen, nur unter entgegengesetzten Beziehungen gedacht" (*SWB*, 818; translation is my own).
8. Melville, *The Confidence-Man*, 59.
9. Ibid.
10. Jacobs, "Style of Kleist," 55.
11. Deleuze and Guattari, *What Is Philosophy?*, 65–66.

# Bibliography

Adler, Hans, ed. *Aesthetics and Aisthetics. New Perspectives and (Re)Discoveries.* Oxford/New York: Peter Lang, 2002.

Agamben, Giorgio. "Bartleby, or On Contingency." In *Potentialities*, 243–71. Stanford: Stanford University Press, 1999.

Arsić, Branca. "Active Habits and Passive Events or Bartleby." In *Between Deleuze and Derrida*, ed. Paul Patton and John Protevi, 135–57. London/New York: Continuum, 2003.

Barck, Karlheinz, Dieter Kliche, and Jörg Heininger. "Ästhetik/ästhetisch." *Ästhetische Grundbegriffe* 1 (2000): 308–17.

Barnouw, Jeffrey. "The Beginnings of 'Aesthetics' and the Leibnizian Conception of Sensation." In *Eighteenth-Century Aesthetics and the Reconstruction of Art*, ed. Paul Mattick, 52–95. Cambridge, Cambridge University Press, 1993.

———. "The Cognitive Value of Confusion and Obscurity in the German Enlightenment: Leibniz, Baumgarten, Herder." *Studies in Eighteenth-Century Culture* 24 (1995): 29–50.

Baumgarten, Alexander Gottlieb. *Ästhetik*, ed. and trans. Dagmar Mirbach. Hamburg: Felix Meiner, 2007.

———. *Philosophische Briefe von Aletheophilus.* Frankfurt/Leipzig: Universität zu Halle, 1741.

———. *Reflections on Poetry. Meditationes philosophicae de nonnullis ad poema pertinentibus*, ed. and trans. Karl Aschenbrenner and William Holther. Berkeley: University of California Press, 1954.

———. *Texte zur Grundlegung der Ästhetik*, ed. Hans Rudolf Schweizer. Hamburg: Felix Meiner, 1983.

Beharriell, S. Ross. *The Head and the Heart in the Mind and Art of Herman Melville.* Madison: University of Wisconsin Press, 1954.

Bercovitch, Sacvan. "How to Read Melville's *Pierre*." In *Herman Melville. A Collection of Critical Essays*, ed. Myra Jehlen, 116–25. Englewood Cliffs: Prentice-Hall, 1994.

Blanchot, Maurice. *The Writing of Disaster.* Lincoln: University of Nebraska Press, 1995.

Böhringer, Hannes. "Attention im Clair-obscur: Die Avantgarde." In *Aisthesis. Wahrnehmung heute oder Perspektiven einer anderen Ästhetik*, ed. Karlheinz Barck et al., 14–32. Leipzig: Reclam, 1990.
Bogue, Ronald. "Minor Writing and Minor Literature." *Symploke* 5, no. 1 (1997): 99–118.
Buch, Hans Christoph. *Die Scheidung von San Domingo. Wie die Negersklaven von Haiti Robespierre beim Wort nahmen*. Berlin: Klaus Wagenbach, 1976.
Burkholder, Robert. "Introduction." In *Critical Essays on Herman Melville's "Benito Cereno,"* ed. Robert Burkholder, 1–18. New York: G. K. Hall, 1992.
Busch, Frederick. "Introduction." In Herman Melville, *Billy Budd and Other Stories*, vii–xxiv. New York: Penguin, 1986.
Campe, Rüdiger. "Der Effekt der Form. Baumgartens Ästhetik am Rande der Metaphysik." In *Literatur als Philosophie/Philosophie als Literatur*, ed. Eva Horn, Bettine Menke, and Christoph Menke, 17–34. Munich: Fink, 2005.
Carrière, Mathieu. *Pour une littérature de guerre, Kleist*. Arles: Actes Sudes, 1993.
Caruth, Cathy. "The Falling Body and the Impact of Reference (de Man, Kant, Kleist)." In *Unclaimed Experience. Trauma, Narrative, and History*, 73–90. Baltimore: Johns Hopkins University Press, 1993.
Caygill, Howard. *A Kant Dictionary*. Oxford: Blackwell, 1995.
———. "Die Erfindung und Neuerfindung der Ästhetik." *Deutsche Zeitschrift für Philosophie* 49 (2001): 233–41.
Colebrook, Claire. "The Sense of Space: on the Specificity of Affect in Deleuze and Guattari." *Postmodern Culture* 15, no. 1 (2004).
Cooke, Alexander. "Resistance, Potentiality, and the Law. Deleuze and Agamben on 'Bartleby.'" *Angelaki* 10, no. 3 (2005): 79–89.
Coviello, Peter. "The American in Charity: 'Benito Cereno' and Gothic Anti-Sentimentality." *Studies in American Fiction* 30, no. 2 (2002): 155–80.
Cramer, Friedrich. "Vorwort." In Christian-Paul Berger, *Bewegungsbilder. Kleists Marionettentheater zwischen Poesie und Physik*, I–XIV. Paderborn: Ferdinand Schöningh, 2000.
Delbanco, Andrew. *Melville. His World and Work*. London: Picador, 2005.
Deleuze, Gilles. "Bartleby oder die Formel." In *Kritik und Klinik*, 94–123. Frankfurt/Main: Suhrkamp, 2000.
———. "Bartleby; or, The Formula." In *Essays Critical and Clinical*, 68–90. Minneapolis: University of Minnesota Press, 1997.
———. "Bartleby, ou la formule." In *Critique et Clinique*, 89—114. Paris: Minuit, 1993.
———. *Difference and Repetition*. New York: Columbia University Press, 1994.
———. Deleuze, Gilles. *Francis Bacon. The Logic of Sensation*. Minneapolis: University of Minnesota Press, 2002.
———. Deleuze, Gilles. *Kant's Critical Philosophy*. Minneapolis: University of Minnesota Press, 1984.

# Bibliography

———. *Masochism. Coldness and Cruelty and (by Leopold Sacher-Masoch) Venus in Fur*. New York: Zone Books, 1991.
———. "On the Superiority of Anglo-American Literature." In Gilles Deleuze and Claire Parnet, *Dialogues II*, 27–56. London: Continuum, 2002.
———. *Proust and Signs*. Minneapolis: University of Minnesota Press, 2000.
———. *The Fold: Leibniz and the Baroque*. Minneapolis: University of Minnesota Press, 1988.
———. *The Logic of Sense*. New York: Columbia University Press, 1990.
Deleuze, Gilles, and Félix Guattari. *A Thousand Plateaus. Capitalism and Schizophrenia*. Minneapolis: University of Minnesota Press, 1987.
———. *Kafka. Toward a Minor Literature*. Minneapolis: University of Minnesota Press, 1986.
———. *What is Philosophy?* London: Verso Books, 1994.
Derrida, Jacques. "Parergon." In *The Truth in Paining*, 15–147. Chicago: University of Chicago Press, 1987.
———. *The Gift of Death*. Chicago: The University of Chicago Press, 1996.
Descartes, René. *Discours de la méthode/Discourse on the Method. A Bilingual Edition*. Notre Dame: University of Notre Dame Press, 1994.
———. *Meditations on First Philosophy: In which the Existence of God and the Distinction of the Soul from the Body Are Demonstrated*. Indianapolis: Hackett, 1993.
Dyer, Denis. *The Stories of Kleist*. New York: Holmes and Meier, 1977.
Emerson, Ralph Waldo. "The Transcendentalist." In *Emerson on Transcendentalism*, ed. Edward L. Ericson, 91–109. New York: Continuum, 1994.
Fischer-Lichte, Erika. *Heinrich von Kleist: Michael Kohlhaas*. Frankfurt/Main: Diesterweg, 1991.
Földenyi, László. *Heinrich von Kleist. Im Netz der Wörter*. Munich: Matthes und Seitz, 1999.
Foucault, Michel. *Death and the Labyrinth: The World of Raymond Roussel*. London: Continuum, 2007.
Foster, Elizabeth S. "Introduction." In *The Confidence-Man: His Masquerade*, reprinted in Herman Melville, *The Confidence-Man: His Masquerade*, 333–39. New York: Norton, 1971.
Fricke, Gerhard. *Gefühl und Schicksal bei Heinrich von Kleist*. New York: AMS Press, 1971.
Gallas, Helga. *Das Textbegehren des 'Michael Kohlhaas'. Die Sprache des Unbewußten und der Sinn der Literatur*. Reinbek: Rowohlt, 1981.
Gasché, Rodolphe. *The Idea of Form*. Stanford: Stanford University Press, 2002.
Grassau, Catharina Silke. "Recht und Rache. Eine Betrachtung der inneren Wendepunkte in Kleists Michael Kohlhaas." *Beiträge zur Kleist-Forschung* (2002): 239–58.
Grathoff, Dirk. "Michael Kohlhaas." In *Interpretationen. Kleists Erzählungen*, ed. Walter Hinderer, 43–66. Stuttgart: Reclam, 1998.
Greenberg, Martin. "The Difficult Justice of Melville and Kleist." *The New Criterion* 3 (2005): 24–32.

Groß, Steffen. *Felix Aestheticus. Die Ästhetik als Lehre vom Menschen. Zum 250. Jahrestag des Erscheinens von Alexander Gottlieb Baumgartens 'Aesthetica'*. Würzburg: Königshausen & Neumann, 2001.

Hamacher, Werner. "Das Beben der Darstellung." In *Positionen der Literaturwissenschaft. Acht Modellanalysen am Beispiel von Kleists Das Erdbeben in Chili*, ed. David Wellbery, 149–73. Munich: Beck, 1993.

Hammermeister, Kai. *The German Aesthetic Tradition*. Cambridge: Cambridge University Press, 2002.

Haverkamp, Anselm. "Schwarz/Weiß. Kleists Moral der Verkennung." In *Latenzzeit. Wissen im Nachkrieg*, 121–38. Berlin: Kadmos, 2004.

———. "Wie die Morgenröte zwischen Nacht und Tag. Alexander Gottlieb Baumgartens Begründung der Kulturwissenschaft." In *Latenzzeit. Wissen im Nachkrieg*, 91–119. Berlin: Kadmos, 2004.

Hegel, G. W. F. *Introductory Lectures on Aesthetics*. ed. Michael Inwood. London: Penguin, 1993.

Herder, Johann Gottfried. "Begründung einer Ästhetik in der Auseinandersetzung mit Alexander Gottlieb Baumgarten." In *Werke*, vol. 1, 653–94. Frankfurt/Main: Deutsche Klassiker Verlag, 1985.

Herrmann, Hans Peter. "Die Verlobung in St. Domingo." In *Interpretationen. Kleists Erzählungen*, ed. Walter Hinderer, 111–40. Stuttgart: Reclam, 1998.

Hetzner, Michael. "Der Kaufmann als Held. Das Problem der Bürgerlichen Identität in Kleists Michael Kohlhaas." *Beiträge zur Kleist-Forschung* (2001): 69–98.

Horn, Peter. "Hatte Kleist Rassenvorurteile?" In *Heinrich von Kleists Erzählungen. Eine Einführung*, 134–47. Königstein: Scriptor, 1978.

Jacobs, Carol. "Soothsaying and Rebellion." In *Uncontainable Romanticism*, 138–58. Baltimore: Johns Hopkins University Press, 1989.

———. "The Style of Kleist." *diacritics* (1979): 47–61.

Jaworski, Phillipe. "Desert and Empire: From 'Bartleby' to 'Benito Cereno.'" In *Herman Melville: A Collection of Critical Essays*, ed. Myra Jehlen, 151–59. Englewood Cliffs: Prentice-Hall, 1994.

Johnson, Barbara. "Melville's Fist: The Execution of Billy Budd." In *The Critical Difference*, 79–109. Baltimore: Johns Hopkins University Press, 1980.

Kaiser, Birgit M. "Falte. Die Implikation des Literarischen." In *Latenz. 40 Annäherungen an einen Begriff*, ed. Stefanie Diekmann and Thomas Khurana, 67–72. Berlin: Kadmos, 2007.

———. "Two Floors of Thinking: Deleuze's Aesthetics of Folds" In *Deleuze and The Fold: A Critical Reader*, ed. Sjoerd van Tuinen and Niamh O'Donnell. London: Palgrave MacMillan, 2010.

Kant, Immanuel. *The Critique of Judgment*. Amherst: Prometheus Books, 2000.

———. *Critique of Pure Reason*. Amherst: Prometheus Books, 1990.

Karcher, Carolyn L. "The Riddle of the Sphinx: Melville's 'Benito Cereno' and the Amistad Case." In *Critical Essays on Herman Melville's "Benito Cereno,"* ed. Robert Burkholder, 196–229. New York: G. K. Hall, 1992.

## Bibliography

Kleist, Heinrich von. *An Abyss Deep Enough: The Life of Heinrich von Kleist in his Parables, Essays and Letters*, ed. and trans. Philip B. Miller. Boston: Dutton Books, 1982.

———. "Ordeal by Fire." In *Three Plays. Prince Friedrich von Homberg, The Broken Pitcher, Ordeal by Fire*, trans. Noel Clark, 159–259. London: Oberon Books, 2000.

———. *Sämtliche Werke*. Berliner Ausgabe. Vol. II/1, ed. Roland Reuß and Peter Staengle. Basel, Frankfurt/Main: Stroemfeld/Roter Stern, 1997.

———. *Sämtliche Werke und Briefe*. Vol. 1 and 2, ed. Helmut Sembdner. Munich: Deutscher Taschenbuch Verlag, 2001.

———. *The Marquise of O— and Other Stories*, trans. David Luke and Nigel Reeves. London: Penguin, 2004.

Kommerell, Max. "Die Sprache und das Unaussprechliche. Eine Betrachtung über Heinrich von Kleist." In *Geist und Buchstabe der Dichtung: Goethe, Schiller, Kleist, Hölderlin*, 243–317. Frankfurt/Main: Klostermann, 1991.

Kramer, Aaron. *Melville's Poetry. Toward the Enlarged Heart*. Madison: Fairleigh Dickinson University Press, 1971.

Leibniz, Gottfried Wilhelm. "Discourse on Metaphysics." In *Philosophical Papers and Letters*, vol. 1, ed. Leroy E. Loemker, 464–506. Chicago: University of Chicago Press, 1956.

———. "Meditations on Knowledge, Truth, and Ideas." In *Philosophical Papers and Letters*, vol. 1, ed. Leroy E. Loemker, 448–54. Chicago: University of Chicago Press, 1956.

———. "The Monadology." In *The Monadology and Other Philosophical Writings*. Oxford: Oxford University Press, 1965.

Lubkoll, Christine. "Soziale Experimente und ästhetische Ordnung. Kleists Literaturkonzept im Spannungsfeld von Klassizismus und Romantik ('Die Verlobung in St. Domingo')." In *Gewagte Experimente und kühne Konstellationen. Kleists Werk zwischen Klassizismus und Romantik*, ed. Christine Lubkoll and Günter Oesterle, 119–36. Würzburg: Königshausen & Neumann, 2001.

Lyotard, Jean-François. *Lessons on the Analytic and the Sublime*. Stanford: Stanford University Press, 1994.

———. "God and the Puppet." In *The Inhuman. Reflections on Time*, 153–64. Stanford: Stanford University Press, 1991.

de Man, Paul. "Aesthetic Formalization: Kleist's *Über das Marionettentheater*." In *The Rhetoric of Romanticism*, 263–90. New York: Columbia University Press, 1984.

———. "Kant's Materialism." In *Aesthetic Ideology*, 119–28. Minneapolis: University of Minnesota Press, 1996.

Marx, Stefanie. *Beispiele des Beispiellosen. Heinrich von Kleists Erzählungen ohne Moral*. Würzburg: Königshausen & Neumann, 1994.

Massumi, Brian. *Parables for the Virtual. Movement, Affect, Sensation*. Durham: Duke University Press, 2002.

———, ed. *A Shock to Thought. Expressions after Deleuze and Guattari*. London: Routledge, 2002.

McMahon, Melissa. "Beauty: Machinic Repetition in the Age of Art." In *A Shock to Thought. Expressions after Deleuze and Guattari*, ed. Brian Massumi, 3–8. London: Routledge, 2002.

McRae, Robert. *Leibniz: Perception, Apperception, and Thought*. Toronto: University of Toronto Press, 1976.

Melville, Herman. *Billy Budd, Sailor (An Inside Narrative)*, ed. Harrison Hayford and Merton M. Sealts Jr. Chicago: University of Chicago Press, 1962.

———. *Moby-Dick or, The Whale*, ed. Harrison Hayford, Hershel Parker, and G. Thomas Tanselle. Evanston/Chicago: Northwestern University Press, 1988.

———. *Pierre; or, The Ambiguities*, ed. Harrison Hayford, Hershel Parker, and G. Thomas Tanselle. Evanston/Chicago: Northwestern University Press, 1971.

———. *Tales, Poems, and other Writings*, ed. John Bryant. New York: The Modern Library, 2001.

———. *The Confidence-Man: His Masquerade*, ed. Hershel Parker. New York/London: Norton, 1971.

———. *The Writings of Herman Melville. Journals*, ed. Howard C. Horsford with Lynn Horth. Evanston/Chicago: Northwestern University Press, 1989.

Menke, Christoph. *Kraft. Ein Grundbegriff ästhetischer Anthropologie*. Frankfurt/Main: Suhrkamp, 2008.

Miller, Hillis. "Laying down the Law in Literature." In *Topographies*. Stanford: Stanford University Press, 1995.

Moser, Christian. *Verfehlte Gefühle. Wissen—Begehren—Darstellen bei Kleist und Rousseau*. Würzburg: Königshausen & Neumann, 1993.

Naumann-Beyer, Waltraud. "Sinnlichkeit." *Ästhetische Grundbegriffe* 5 (2003): 534–77.

Neumann, Gerhard. "Das Stocken der Sprache und das Straucheln des Körpers." In *Heinrich von Kleist: Kriegsfall—Rechtsfall—Sündenfall*, ed. Gerhard Neumann, 13–29. Freiburg: Rombach, 1994.

———. "Die Verlobung in St. Domingo. Zum Problem literarischer Mimesis im Werk Heinrich von Kleists." In *Gewagte Experimente und kühne Konstellationen. Kleists Werk zwischen Klassizismus und Romantik*, ed. Christine Lubkoll and Günter Oesterle, 93–118. Würzburg: Königshausen & Neumann, 2001.

Oesterle, Günter. "Vision und Verhör." In *Gewagte Experimente und kühne Konstellationen. Kleists Werk zwischen Klassizismus und Romantik*, ed. Christine Lubkoll and Günter Oesterle, 303–28. Würzburg: Königshausen & Neumann, 2001.

Olson, Charles. *Call me Ishmael*. Baltimore: Johns Hopkins University Press, 1997.

Rancière, Jacques. "Deleuze, Bartleby, and the Literary Formula." In *The Flesh of Words. The Politics of Writing*, 146–64. Stanford: Stanford University Press, 2004.

Robertson-Lorant, Laurie. *Melville. A Biography*. Amherst: University of Massachusetts Press, 1996.

Ronell, Avital. *Stupidity*. Urbana/Chicago: University of Illinois Press, 2003.

Schnackertz, Hermann Josef. "Wahrnehmungsperspektiven als Medium kultureller Exposition in Herman Melvilles 'Typee' und 'Benito Cereno.'" In *Vergessen. Entdecken. Erhellen. Literaturwissenschaftliche Aufsätze*, ed. Jörg Drews. Bielefeld: Aisthesis, 1993.

# Bibliography

Schneider, Manfred. "Die Inquisition der Oberfläche. Kleist und die juristische Kodifikation des Unbewußten." In *Heinrich von Kleist. Kriegsfall—Rechtsfall—Sündenfall*, ed. Gerhard Neumann, 107–26. Freiburg: Rombach, 1994.

Schneider, Ulrich Johannes. "Introduction." In Gottfried Wilhelm Leibniz, *Monadologie und andere metaphysische Schriften*, VII–XXXII. Hamburg: Felix Meiner, 2002.

Schweizer, Hans Rudolf. "Begründung der Ästhetik als Wissenschaft der sinnlichen Erkenntnis." Introduction to Alexander Gottlieb Baumgarten, *Theoretische Ästhetik*, VII–XVI. Hamburg: Felix Meiner, 1988.

Sealts, Merton M., Jr. "Melville and Emerson's Rainbow." In *Pursuing Melville 1940–1980*, 250–77. Madison: University of Wisconsin Press, 1982.

———. *Melville's Reading. A Check-List of Books Owned and Borrowed*. Madison: University of Wisconsin Press, 1966.

Sedgwick, Eve Kosofsky. "Billy Budd: After the Homosexual." In *Herman Melville. A Collection of Critical Essays*, ed. Myra Jehlen, 217–34. Englewood Cliffs: Prentice-Hall, 1994.

———. *Touching Feeling*. Durham: Duke University Press, 2003.

Shih, Shu-mei, and Françoise Lionnet. *Minor Transnationalism*. Durham: Duke University Press, 2005.

Smith, Daniel W. "Introduction." In Gilles Deleuze, *Francis Bacon. The Logic of Sensation*. Minneapolis: University of Minnesota Press, 2002.

Smock, Ann. *What Is There to Say? Blanchot, Melville, des Forêts, Beckett*. Lincoln: University of Nebraska Press, 2003.

Solms, Friedrich. *Disciplina aesthtica. Zur Frühgeschichte der ästhetischen Theorie bei Baumgarten und Herder*. Stuttgart: Klett, 1990.

Stivale, Charles. "From Zigzag to Affect, and Back." *Angelaki* 11 (2006): 25–33.

Strässle, Urs. *Heinrich von Kleist. Die keilförmige Vernunft*. Würzburg: Königshausen & Neumann, 2002.

Sundquist, Eric J. "'Benito Cereno' and New World Slavery." In *Critical Essays on Herman Melville's "Benito Cereno*," ed. Robert Burkholder, 146–67. New York: G. K. Hall, 1992.

Thiele, Kathrin. *The Thought of Becoming. Gilles Deleuze's Poetics of Life*. Zurich/Berlin: diaphanes, 2008.

van Tuinen, Sjoerd, and Niamh McDonnell, eds. *Deleuze and The Fold: A Critical Reader*. London: Palgrave MacMillan, forthcoming 2010.

Vogl, Joseph ed. *Poetologien des Wissens um 1800*. Munich: Fink, 1999.

Wenke, John. "'Ontological Heroics': Melville's Philosophical Art." In *A Companion to Melville Studies*, ed. John Bryant, 567–601. Westport: Greenwood, 1986.

Werber, Niels. *Die Geopolitik der Literatur. Eine Vermessung der medialen Weltraumordnung*. Munich: Hanser, 2007.

Wittkowski, Wolfgang. "Rechtspflicht, Rache und Noblesse: Der Kohlhaas-Charakter." *Beiträge zur Kleist-Forschung* (1998): 92–113.

# Index

Aesthetics, xx–xxi, **1–22**, 31, 68, 123n11, 123n12, 124–125n23, 125–126n35, 126n43, 127n54, 127n56
   and aesthetic judgment, **7–9**, 21, 124n20, 124n21
   as *aisthetics*, xx–xxi, **13–14**, 61, 114, 121n12
   Kantian turn in aesthetics, xx–xxi, **7–12**, 20–21, 124n20, 124n21
Affect, xiii–xxii, 9, 55, **57–87**, 95, 106, 121n10, 121n13, 128n2
Affective (sensate) thinking, xvi–xxii, 4, **11–22**, 25–26, 28–29, 57–58, 62, 75, 83–87, 88–89, 114, 116, 118–119, 121n10, 128n2
Agamben, Giorgio, 90, 95–96, 115, 135n1, 135n6
Arsic, Branca, 95, 115, 135n1, 135n10

Bacon, Francis, v, 22, 115, 121n10, 138n6
Barnouw, Jeffrey, 17, 125n23, 126n35, 127n49, 127n54, 127n56
Baumgarten, Alexander Gottlieb, xx–xxi, 3, 7, 9–10, **11–19**, 20–22, 116, 124n18, 126n37, 126n38, 126n42, 126n43, 127n59, 127n63
   *Aesthetica*, **11–13**, 17–18, 21–22, 124–125n23, 125–126n35
   on *analogon rationis*, 12–13, 18–19
   on *felix aestheticus*, 22
   and Leibniz, xx, **12–19**, 20, 118, 121n10, 121n11, 127n54
   *Meditationes*, 13, 125n23, 126n41
   *Metaphysica*, 20
   *Philosophische Briefe von Aletheophilus*, 12–13, 126n40
   on *scientia cognitionis sensitivae*, **11–14**, 17, 121n10
   on *ubertas aesthetica*, 20
Blanchot, Maurice, 90, 93, 108, 135n1, 135n2, 135n4
Böhringer, Hannes, 19, 21, 127n60

Carrière, Matthieu, 122n3
Caygill, Howard, 4, 9–10, 27, 123n9, 124n22, 125n27, 125n31, 126n36, 126n44, 127n57, 128n1
   on Baumgarten, 7, 18
chiaroscuro, 16, 18–19, 42
Coleridge, Samuel Taylor, xv
confusion [confused ideas], xxi, 10, **14–18**, 20–21, 125n23, 126n42

Deleuze, Gilles, v, xviii, 4, 7, 15, **113–119**, 120–121n8, 125n26, 128n2, 132n17, 132n18, 136n12, 138n1, 138n2

# Index

on Bartleby, 90, **93–95**, 98, 102, 106–107, 109–110, 112–119, 121n15, 135n1, 137n21, 137n22, 137n23, 138n6
on Carroll, 117, 120n8
*Fold. Leibniz and the Baroque, The,* xx, 16, 87, 110, 121n11, 127n53, 127n54
on Käthchen von Heilbronn, 98–99, 102, **106–107**, 109–110, 112–115, 117–119
on Proust, 120n8
on Sacher-Masoch, 114–115, 120n8, 138n4
on sensation, v, 114, **117–118**, 121n10
Deleuze, Gilles and Félix Guattari, xv–xvi, **xviii–xix**, 113, 117–118, 128n2
*Kafka. Toward a Minor Literature,* xviii–xix, 62, 117, 120n5, 132n17
*Thousand Plateaus, A,* xv–xvi, 54, 120n4, 131n27, 138n1
*What is Philosophy?,* xix, 118, 121n9, 138n1, 138n3, 138n11
de Man, Paul, 61–62, 122n3, 124n20, 132n14
Derrida, Jacques, 8–10, 21, 125n26, 125n29, 128n66, 135n1, 135n3, 135n8
on Bartleby's formula, 92–93, 95–96
Descartes, Réné, **13–16**, 20–21, 126n38, 127n45

Emerson, Ralph Waldo, xxi, 5–6, 120n2, 123n16, 133n30

Földenyi, László, 81–82, 134n37

Gasché, Rodolphe, 124n20, 125n25
Goethe, Johann Wolfgang von, xiv, 133n31
Greenberg, Martin, xv, 57, 120n3, 131n2

Haverkamp, Anselm, 6, 11, 120n1, 124n18, 126n36, 126n39, 129n5, 129n9, 131n18, 131n25

on Baumgarten, 11, 125–126n35, 126n42
Hawthorne, Nathaniel, xv, 121n14, 123n10
Hegel, Georg Wilhelm Friedrich, 4–5, 10, 124n20, 124n21
Herder, J.G., 124–125n23

Jacobs, Carol, 3, 120n2, 123n7, 135n41, 138n10
Johnson, Barbara, 57, 63, 67, 70–71, 73, 131n3, 133n23, 133n24, 133n26

Kafka, Franz, xviii–xix, 22, 56, 62, 114, 117, 119, 120n5, 132n17
Kant, Immanuel, xx–xxi, **1–11**, 23, 25, 118, 122n3, 123n7, 124n20, 124n21, 125n26
on Baumgarten, 7, **9–11**, 20–21, 124n23
*Critique of Judgment, The* 9–10, 125n28
*Critique of Pure Reason, The* 7–9, 125n24
Kleist, Heinrich von, **xiii–xxii**, 3–6, 19, 22, 27–31, 55, 57–61, 77, 88, 98, 107–108, 110, **113–119**, 120n1, 120n2, 120n3, 121n14, 122n1, 122n2, 122n3, 123n7, 128–129n5, 129n6, 129n13, 130n15, 131n5, 132n11, 132n12, 132n14, 133n31, 133–134n33, 134n37, 136n13, 138n1, 138n10
*Battle of Herrmann, The* xiv–xv
*Betrothal in Santo Domingo, The,* xvi, **29–39**
*Das Käthchen von Heilbronn,* xvii–xviii, 25, 76, 88–89, 91, 94–95, **96–109**, 110–112, 136n14, 136n15, 136n16, 136–137n17, 137n19, 137n20, 138n7
*Die Marquise von O…,* xvii
letters, xiv, 1–2, 28
and literature of war, xvi, xix

147

# Index

Michael Kohlhaas, xv, xvii–xviii, 21, 25, 27, 55, 56–62, **76–85**, 86–87, 88–89, 95, 107, 131n1, 132n13, 134n33, 134n35, 134n36, 134n38, 135n42
   *On the Gradual Fabrication of Thoughts While Speaking,* **58–60**, 76, 80, 83–85, 86, 89, 99, 102, 117
   *On the Puppet Theater,* 1, 58, **60–62**, 75, 82
   Penthesilea, 76, 106–107, 113, **116–117**, 138n7
   Prince of Homburg, 113
   and realism, 21, 30–31
   and sense data (haptic), 32, **36–38**, 40
   and sense data (visual), **32–36**, 40, 43, 45, 50
   on theories of electricity, **60**, 85, 88, 132n8, 132n9
Kommerell, Max, **76–78**, 89, 107–108, 133n31, 133n32, 133n33, 137n24

Lawrence, D.H., xvi, 117, 119, 120n4, 121n8
Leibniz, Gottfried Wilhelm, xx–xxi, 1–4, **12–19**, 87, 110, 118, 121n11, 122n4, 127n46, 127n48, 147n50, 147n52, 147n54, 147n55
   on confused ideas, 10, 14–15, **17–18**, 20, 125n23, 126n42
   *Discourse on Metaphysics,* 16, 127n55
   *Meditations on Knowledge,* 14
   *Monadology, The,* 15, 127n50
   on perceptions/apperceptions, 10, 15–18, 20, 22, 121n10
   *Principles of Nature and of Grace, The,* 15
Locke, John, 5–6, 10

Melville, Herman, **xiii–xxii**, 3–6, 19, 22, 25, 27–31, 55, 57, 88, 98, 107, 110, **113–119**, 120n1, 120n2, 120n3, 120n4, 121n8, 121n14, 123n10, 123n11, 123n12, 123n13, 123n14, 124n17, 128n69, 128n70, 129n5, 131n24, 131n2, 132n22, 133n23, 138n1
   Bartleby, the Scrivener, xvii–xviii, 23, 25, 88–89, **90–96**, 97–98, 104–112, 121n15, 131n20, 135n1, 135n6, 137n21, 137n22, 137n23, 138n6
   Benito Cereno, xvi, 25, 29–31, **41–53**, 54, 57, 77, 87, 129n5, 129n7, 131n20, 131n21, 131n24
   *Billy Budd, Sailor,* xv, xvii–xviii, 21, 23–25, 27, 55, 56–57, 59, 61, **62–76**, 77, 83, 85–87, 88–90, 95, 106, 108, 113–115, 123n10, 131n3, 133n23, 133n30
   *Confidence-Man, The,* 5, **25**, 90, 114, 117, 123n13, 138n5, 138n8
   *Moby-Dick,* xv, 5, 22, 24, 123n10, 123n14, 124n17
   *Pierre; or, the Ambiguities,* 5, **22–26**, 123n10, 128n69, 128n70
   and realism, 21, **30–31**, 65–66
   and rhizomatic space, xvi
   and sentimentalism, 29–30, 38–41, **50–51**, 53–54, 66, 86, 89
Mendelssohn, Moses, 124n23
Menke, Christoph, 20–21, 125n23, 126n35, 126n38, 127n54, 128n64, 128n67

Overcoding, **54**, 114

Rancière, Jacques, 90, 115, 135n1, 138n6
Ronell, Avital, **62–63**, 94, 106, 124n20, 128n1, 132n19, 133n25, 135n5
   on resolute simplicity, 68, 71
Rousseau, Jean-Jacques, xiv, 129n13

Index

Schweizer, Hans Rudolph, 127n59, 127n63
Sensation, v, xvii, xx–xxii, **1–26**, 28–29, 31–32, 39, 51, 53–55, 86–87, 89, 107, 112, 113–119, 121n10, 121n13, 124n21, 124n23, 125n24, 126n38, 127n54
Shakespeare, William, xiv

Solms, Friedrich, 20, 125n23, 126n35, 126n42, 127n62, 128n65

Werber, Niels, xv–xvi, 120n3
Wolff, Christian, **12–13**, 18, 20, 125n23, 127n54
    on inferior/superior faculties, 14–15, 126n42

www.ingramcontent.com/pod-product-compliance
Lightning Source LLC
Chambersburg PA
CBHW021143230426
43667CB00005B/239